gH
21.6.05

# Social History in Perspective
General Editor: Jeremy Black

*Social History in Perspective* is a series of in-depth studies of the many topics in social, cultural and religious history for students. They also give the student clear surveys of the subject and present the most recent research in an accessible way.

## PUBLISHED

## FORTHCOMING

*Titles continued overleaf*

Please note that a sister series, *British History in Perspective*, is available which covers all the key topics in British political history.

# EDUCATION IN BRITAIN, 1750–1914

W. B. Stephens
*Honorary Research Fellow*
*University College London*
*and formerly*
*Reader*
*University of Leeds*

First published in Great Britain 1998 by
**MACMILLAN PRESS LTD**
Houndmills, Basingstoke, Hampshire RG21 6XS and London
Companies and representatives throughout the world

A catalogue record for this book is available from the British Library.

ISBN 0–333–60511–X hardcover
ISBN 0–333–60512–8 paperback

First published in the United States of America 1998 by
**ST. MARTIN'S PRESS, INC.,**
Scholarly and Reference Division,
175 Fifth Avenue, New York, N.Y. 10010

ISBN 0–312–21624–6

Library of Congress Cataloging-in-Publication Data
Stephens, W. B.
Education in Britain, 1750–1914 / W.B. Stephens.
p.   cm. — (Social history in perspective)
Includes bibliographical references (p.   ) and index.
ISBN 0–312–21624–6 (cloth)
1. Education—Great Britain—History—18th century.   2. Education–
–Great Britain—History—19th century.   3. Education—Great Britain–
–History—20th century.   I. Title.   II. Series.
LA631.5.S84   1998
370'.941'0903—dc21                                                98–17144
                                                                     CIP

This book is printed on paper suitable for recycling and made from fully managed and sustained forest sources.

10   9   8   7   6   5   4   3   2   1
07   06   05   04   03   02   01   00   99   98

Printed in Hong Kong

*For Tom and James*

# CONTENTS

# LIST OF TABLES

# PREFACE

Much writing on the history of education used to be concerned with 'Acts and Facts' recorded almost in a vacuum and divorced from the general history of the period in which they were set. Fortunately, such an arid and ahistorical approach has now largely been displaced. Modern textbooks on the history of education in Britain, however, do tend to concentrate mainly on the part played by education in national politics and on the development of institutions and administrative structures. Consequently, there is now no shortage of good textbooks dealing in detail with these important aspects of the subject, especially for the nineteenth and early twentieth centuries. For that reason (and because this series is particularly concerned with 'Social Perspectives') I have chosen not to add yet another text treading the same path. Faced with restrictions of space, I have preferred to limit detailed treatment of political and administrative matters (though not to ignore them) and to give more space to aspects of the relationship between education, society and the economy which have concerned social and economic historians in recent years. The literature on these topics is, indeed, now very extensive, a fair proportion of it being in articles and in books not obviously concerned with the history of education. In order, therefore, that this volume may prove a useful introduction to what is now a very large field of study, and so that readers may reasonably easily take further what is surveyed here in outline, I have provided in the Notes exact references to the sources (with page references where appropriate) on which each specific part of the text is based, as well as a Bibliography listing all the secondary sources referred to in the Notes.

Since some confusion arises (especially with overseas readers) over the use of the term 'public' both for Victorian elementary schools and for the prestigious fee-paying boarding schools of the period, I have distinguished the two throughout the text by adopting a capital 'P' for the latter and a lower case 'p' for the former.

This book is not unique in embracing the general history of education in all parts of Great Britain (Scotland, England and Wales), but I am not aware of any recent text that does so. Though the task of covering all three countries has restricted the space which would have been available had I treated only England and Wales or only Scotland, I have felt it important to try to avoid the spatial parochialism which often still seems to attach to this area of historical scholarship.

I am grateful to Donald Withrington for answering some queries on the statistics of Scottish schooling and to my wife for her unfailing support and positive criticism. I must thank, too, the officers of the Macmillan Press for permitting me to exceed somewhat the originally agreed wordage intended for this volume.

W. B. STEPHENS

# 1

## ELEMENTARY EDUCATION TO THE 1860S

### The Diverse Provision of Elementary Instruction

Eighteenth-century Britain was by no means bereft of the means of education. From 1696 rural landowners in Scotland had been legally required to provide a school in each parish and in Scottish towns burgh schools were maintained from municipal funds. Though no statutory obligation to provide schooling existed in England and Wales before 1870, by 1750 schools of some kind were within geographical reach of all but comparatively few children. In England and Wales there was a numerous and diverse array of elementary schools, some private, others connected with parish churches, as well as charity schools, private middle-class schools and endowed grammar schools. In Scotland, particularly in the towns, charity and private schools existed alongside the burgh and parish schools. Most of the Scottish public schools were, in practice, mainly elementary but, unlike the vast majority of elementary schools south of the border, might also provide post-elementary instruction, including mathematics and Latin, and send boys at 15 or younger to the universities.

Throughout Britain large numbers of private day schools were provided by the working classes for the working classes. Dame schools, often run by women for infants, might teach no more than reading or perhaps a little writing. Common day (or 'private venture') schools took pupils up to 10 or so and covered the 3 Rs plus sewing and knitting for girls and perhaps grammar, geography and other subjects for older children. Both in age range and curriculum, however, the distinction between these two types of school was often blurred. They probably multiplied in the eighteenth century and in England and Wales remained an important aspect of working-class culture well into the following century, especially in industrial areas.[1]

Additions to the stock of schools in the eighteenth century included charity and Sunday schools. From the later seventeenth century it had become more common in England for individuals to endow elementary rather than, as previously, classical grammar schools. Although some of these charity schools were set up by Roman Catholics and other non-conformists, most were associated with the Established Church, their foundation being vigorously promoted by an Anglican body, the Society for Promoting Christian Knowledge. So considerable was the multi-plication of these schools in the early eighteenth century that it has been described as a 'movement', though the number of new founda-tions fell in the later part of the century. In addition to endowed charity schools, other charity schools, maintained by subscription, became com-mon. In most places support came from benevolent middle-class donors, but in northern England some subscription schools were main-tained by groups of parents.

Mostly concentrated in towns, charity schools usually provided boys and girls, from age 7 or so, with a free basic instruction in the 3 Rs and religion, plus training for a trade. By the end of the eighteenth century some (often called 'industrial' schools) concentrated on preparing poor children for manual occupations. Others, however, made basic literacy an entry requirement and provided academic instruction at a higher level than did many private or church schools, which children usually ceased to attend by age 8 or earlier. Such charity schools proved attractive to the artisan class and for some provided a means of social advancement.[2]

In Scotland the endowment of distinct charity schools was uncom-mon, bequests for educating poor children in existing schools being preferred. Exceptions, however, existed in the so-called hospitals founded for orphans, mainly in towns, and in schools set up in remote parts of the highlands by the Society in Scotland for Propagating Chris-tian Knowledge (virtually an arm of the Church of Scotland) and sup-ported by the government. Whereas the SPCK in England was essentially a promotional body encouraging the local funding and administering of independent institutions, the SSPCK organized schools and controlled them itself. It raised funds in the lowlands from the public, the Church and burgh officials and used them to pay teachers and maintain schools (provided by the landowners) mainly in the southern and eastern highlands. These 'supplementary' schools were intended to provide education in remote parts of extensive rural parishes where distance prevented attendance at the statutory parish schools. In the eighteenth century many of these schools were itinerant within a locality, though by the early nineteenth they tended to be permanently sited.[3]

Though religion was always taught, the nature of Scottish charity schools varied greatly. Most confined other instruction to reading, writing and perhaps arithmetic, but some offered a broader education embracing also modern subjects, book-keeping, navigation, music and drawing. Others, especially in towns, became middle-class preserves, teaching the classics and preparing some pupils for the universities. Yet others, like those in England, provided vocational training plus the 3 Rs or merely with a modicum of reading and some also offered evening instruction to adults. The SSPCK schools in the highlands were, like the parish schools, antagonistic to Gaelic and sought to teach through the medium of English. This, and the fact that their teachers were often of inferior quality, weakened their impact. Introduction of manual training met local opposition and, except for spinning for girls, had limited success.[4]

The charity-school movement in Wales also had distinctive characteristics but a shorter history than that in England or Scotland. The influence of the SPCK was evident in non-classical schools established in the first quarter of the eighteenth century, but later foundations were associated with an indigenous circulating school movement, planned on a national scale. Welsh peasant society demonstrated little interest in mixed literary and manual instruction and Welsh charity schools, while usually teaching reading and often writing and arithmetic, concentrated particularly on religious instruction. Considerable support was given by the Methodists, then still within the Established Church, and the vernacular was used as a medium of instruction more readily than in Gaelic-speaking parts of Scotland. The circulatory schools catered for adults as well as children and probably had a more widespread influence than the English charity schools. But they were usually financed by subscription rather than endowment and the movement declined in the later eighteenth century, being largely superseded by Sunday schools.[5]

The Sunday-school movement, which emerged in the 1780s as an aspect of the evangelical revival, had a much greater educational impact than the charity schools. In England and Wales, Sunday schools (which might meet for the whole day) were established by both Anglicans and dissenters, but most enthusiastically by the latter. In the early years they catered for adults as well as children, especially in Wales where they were largely nonconformist and often part of the Methodist revival, spawning chapels and taking over the education of the poor after the decline of the circulating schools. Scottish Sabbath schools were established by town councils and magistrates in cooperation with the Church of Scotland, but at first not usually attached to particular congregations. Suspicion (current also in England) that Sunday schools were sympathetic to political radicalism led, during the French wars, to a rift between the evangelicals, the chief supporters of the schools, and the dominant moderate element in the Church and a cooling of the Church's support. Nevertheless, Sabbath schools continued to spread in the lowlands, sponsored by inter-denominational societies, Independents, Methodists and other nonconformists, and the peace of 1815 softened the Church's attitude. Expansion followed, bolstered from 1834 when the evangelicals gained control of the General Assembly and again following the Disruption of 1843 (when the evangelicals broke away from the Church to form the Free Church).[6]

All the early Sunday schools taught reading as well as religion, and though Welsh schools confined themselves almost exclusively to bible study, many English schools and some Scottish ones taught writing and sometimes other secular subjects.[7] The social significance of Sunday schooling was considerable, especially in the early decades of the movement, when industrialization and urbanization created a high demand for child labour while at the same time swamping existing day-school facilities and causing the social disruption of communities. In Welsh-speaking ares, where instruction in the Sunday schools was in the vernacular, they were important for enriching the Welsh language as well as spreading literacy through that medium. In Britain generally their popularity was demonstrated by the voluntary attendance of large numbers of children and had several causes. They provided child workers with some education without loss of earnings and other children with additional instruction. Middle-class supporters saw them as a means of socializing youths and the children of the masses and generally of strengthening the social fabric, while for the religious of all classes they offered additional spiritual advantages. Some (though probably not most) came under working- class control and have been regarded by some historians as part of the labour movement. They certainly became part of working- class culture.[8] By 1851 over 2.4 million pupils attended Sunday schools in England and Wales, 13.4 per cent of the total population, and in Scotland some 300,000, 10.1 per cent.[9]

Sabattarian objections to secular instruction led, especially from the 1820s, to the gradual dropping of writing in English Sunday schools, and after the Disruption of 1843 some Scottish Sabbath schools began to confine entry to those already able to read. The exclusion of secular teaching was, however, sometimes followed by its provision in evening schools, especially in urban districts of England and Scotland.[10]

Though available evidence makes quantification impossible, it is clear that throughout the eighteenth and early nineteenth centuries numbers of working-class men learned to read through their own efforts without attending school and extended the scope of their education through reading either alone or with others as members of chapels or of the many mutual improvement societies and similar groupings of working men which existed over the country. By 1850 the availability of part-time elementary instruction for adults had become common, especially in towns, through a variety of religious and secular evening and Sunday schools and classes – provided by individuals, religious bodies (especially the Quakers and Anglicans), working-class movements, mechanics' institutes and other such bodies. Most attenders at such organizations were of the artisan class, with a preponderance of adolescents. Males greatly outnumbered females, who were usually offered a curriculum restricted to the 3 Rs and domestic subjects. Government grants for evening classes, increasingly available from 1862, were confined to elementary instruction of those age 11 upwards and establishments receiving them were intended to cater for children and adolescents rather than adults.[11]

In the nineteenth century, far-reaching additions to day-school provision were made. In England and Wales a system of public elementary (voluntary) schools under the control of religious bodies emerged – probably the most important educational development of the century – and in Scotland the existing public system was augmented by church schools. From the 1830s these schools attracted state financial aid, leading to an increase in governmental influence and, in England, to some tension between religious bodies and the state. The voluntary school movement in England and Wales was associated particularly with the British and Foreign School Society (established in 1808 as the Royal Lancasterian Society) and the National Society for Promoting the Education of the Poor in the Principles of the Established Church (founded

1811 and known simply as the National Society). The British and National schools were not owned or managed by the societies but were 'in union' with them, receiving advice from them and sometimes funds to add to those raised by clergy and congregations and to the fees they charged parents. The BFSS was a non-denominational body but tended, because the National Society was Anglican, to attract dissenters. To the British and National schools were added voluntary schools established by nonconformist denominations and, from the 1840s, by Roman Catholics. In addition there were many Anglican voluntary schools other than those in association with the National Society.

Although by the mid nineteenth century there were probably nearly as many dissenters as Anglicans in England and Wales, by 1860 Church schools accounted for some 75 per cent of voluntary- school provision against some 10 per cent provided by British schools,[12] though the number of British schools greatly exceeded those set up by any single nonconformist denomination. The remarkable lead achieved by the Church of England is attributable in part to the ready-made administrative structure provided for the National Society by the Church's parochial and diocesan organization. This advantage was augmented by a clergy often better educated than many dissenting ministers and the support of the better-off laity. Fund raising was thus generally easier, and surplus money raised in richer southern parishes was channelled to poorer parishes in the industrial towns, while in rural districts the landed classes (usually Anglican) were able to provide land for school buildings. Some bishops were enthusiastic, encouraging the founding of National schools and establishing diocesan teacher training colleges, while the National Society acted as a unifying body for the numerous local Anglican education societies.

The BFSS, on the other hand, lacked the underpinning of an established territorial administrative structure. Its supporters belonged to different denominations, unevenly distributed geographically. Moreover, they were generally less well off than the Anglicans and where there were concentrations of wealthier and influential dissenters (as in some northern and midland industrial towns) they tended to be less generous in support of day schooling, preferring to sponsor Sunday and evening schools. British schools also failed to attract government aid on the same scale as the Church because the grant system was based on matching local efforts. Thus, over the years 1833–9, 70 per cent of state aid went to National schools. Even in areas like the West Riding and

Lancashire, where nonconformity was strong, Anglican schools generally outnumbered other voluntary schools, though in Wales Church schools were said to be poorly attended with nonconformists preferring private schools.[13]

The receipt by most (though by no means all) voluntary schools of government financial aid brought with it, from 1839, the obligation to submit to government inspection and thus official influence. A public elementary school system was thus created, providing for England and Wales what Scotland had possessed, in theory at least, for more than a century, but also introducing a long period of tension between the Established Church and the state. The sponsors of the voluntary schools had originally seen them primarily as means of promoting religious and social cohesion through a curricular emphasis on reading, scriptural knowledge, Christian duties and morality, with writing and arithmetic (and sewing for girls) added to attract pupils. Government influence (strengthened by inspection and the extension of the grant system), together with the rising expectations of the artisan class, promoted improved and more uniform standards and greater curricular secularization. More emphasis was placed on the 3 Rs, and subjects such as history and geography were included. Government funding helped to replace the monitorial system used in many voluntary schools (whereby a teacher instructed older pupils – monitors – who each passed on the lesson to a number of other pupils),[14] and from 1847 pupil teachers (apprentices) were introduced. Increasingly, too, schools engaged teachers who had passed through the training colleges established by the BFSS and in greater numbers by the Established Church.

A more stringent linkage of government aid to the attainment of individual pupils in secular subjects, introduced in England and Wales in the 1860s and in Scotland in 1873 (under the Revised Code and known as payment on results), has for long been criticized as promoting rote learning, over-emphasizing the 3 Rs and seeking to reduce expenditure on popular education. In fact, however, the Revised Code brought to an end a system under which government was faced with an open-ended, ever-expanding obligation to fund schools over whose standards of instruction it had limited control. Instead government proposed to pay out only to schools which were clearly doing their job of providing a solid basic elementary education. The Code thus represented a 'crash course in literacy' doing much (in England and Wales, at least) to raise standards in the basic subjects, curtail over-emphasis on religious instruction, improve attendance and ensure that all pupils were given proper attention. When standards in the basic subjects had improved, financial aid was gradually extended to achievement in other subjects.[15] Despite such developments, however, the voluntary system had considerable flaws: the provision and quality of elementary education still varied geographically (especially since by no means all voluntary schools were government aided and inspected). Moreover, until schooling became compulsory from the 1870s, levels of attendance differed greatly from place to place and between social and economic groups (topics explored in Chapter 2).

Though the voluntary societies active in England and Wales did not operate north of the border, Scotland also experienced an expansion of elementary schooling. While at the close of the seventeenth century some 80–90 per cent of Scottish parishes had statutory schools, a century later the parochial system was under some strain. In the highlands and islands famine and emigration must have disrupted education, while in the lowlands industrialization and urbanization certainly affected schooling adversely – a topic pursued in Chapter 4. There is evidence, too, that in some other districts the quality of schooling suffered some decline as the high inflation of the 1780s diminished the value of schoolmasters' salaries, making teaching less attractive to the well qualified. An Act of 1803 alleviated the situation somewhat by permitting parishes to raise local taxes, increase teachers' stipends and set up ancillary or 'side' schools.[16] This did not, however, result in parochial schooling being universally available, and the nineteenth century saw various efforts to improve matters. The need was greatest in the poorest urban districts (where burgeoning populations led to shortages of school places) and in some remote rural and insular areas, where it was physically impossible for children in every part of large parishes to reach the parish or side school.

The western highlands and islands, where poverty and illiteracy were widespread among a Catholic Gaelic-speaking population, demonstrated a particular need. From 1838, the central government provided salaries for extra teachers for a few additional schools ('parliamentary schools'), but the main impetus for expanding education in the highlands came in the early decades of the century from religious sources. Evangelically inspired societies, established in various Scottish towns, financed and ran so-called 'Gaelic schools' in the highlands. Often itinerant, these schools offered a limited curriculum intended to teach

Gaelic-speaking children and adults to read, write and speak English, an object supported by the highlanders themselves. To these the Church of Scotland added its own more effective 'assembly schools', open to children of all denominations, including Roman Catholics. More school places for the lowland poor were also created. In the early nineteenth century individual Church congregations or groups of congregations set up in the burghs 'sessional schools', sometimes called 'parochial schools' but differing from the traditional parish schools in concentrating on the 3 Rs and religious instruction and sometimes commercial subjects. Those established to alleviate illiteracy in urban slum districts were appropriately known as 'mission schools'.[17]

From the 1830s, government aid encouraged further expansion. Some Church assembly schools and schools promoted by other denominations were established in lowland parishes and burghs and, after the Disruption of 1843, the Free Church of Scotland set up its own schools, which were especially numerous in rural areas of the highlands and islands and in some lowland urban centres and often placed to complement parish schools by serving different catchment areas. The curriculum of the Free Church schools was similar to that of the parish schools and like those of the Established Church they were open to all denominations, including the Catholic communities of the highlands and islands. Catholic mission schools were set up after 1847, mainly to cater for Irish immigrants in urban districts, and Catholic schools generally became common in Glasgow and the towns of the industrial west. Some Scottish Episcopal Church schools were also established mainly for younger children and, in the cities, of the mission variety. The United Presbyterian Church also set up some schools, but, like the Congregationalists in England, refused state aid. The Church of Scotland did not thus enjoy the same degree of dominance in public popular schooling as did the Church of England south of the border. In 1851 Church of Scotland schools of all kinds catered for some 13 per cent of public-school pupils, parochial and burgh schools 32 per cent, those of other churches 27 per cent (the bulk of them Free Church schools: 21 per cent) and endowed and other public schools 28 per cent.[18]

Large numbers of working-class children were reached by the Scottish public schools, the voluntary schools in England and Wales and by private schools, but, aside from those helped by the Scottish mission schools and a small number of English voluntary schools, the children of the poverty-stricken and debauched (the 'dangerous classes' created by urbanization and industrialization) were largely ignored by or even deliberately excluded from mainstream public schooling. However, middle-class efforts to provide for their education as an antidote to endemic poverty, paganism and crime led to the establishment of other types of school in the nineteenth century. Infant schools sought to cater for the youngest children of the urban poor; ragged, workhouse, industrial and reformatory schools were aimed at slum, destitute and criminal children; while factory, mine and works schools attempted to give child workers some education other than Sunday schooling.

The infant school movement, which was pioneered by Robert Owen at New Lanark in Scotland early in the century and spread to England, was strongest in Glasgow and London, but less significant for its immediate impact on the education of the poor than for its initial pioneering of progressive pedagogical methods associated with Wilderspin, Stow, Pestalozzi and Froebel. These influenced advanced teaching methods in later periods but in practice the schools themselves failed to replace the dame schools in working-class favour and most gradually succumbed to traditional rote-learning and moral and religious instruction, losing any distinctive reason to exist.[19]

The 1830s saw the beginnings of 'ragged' or 'industrial' schools, philanthropic endeavours aimed at saving vagrant and homeless children in urban slum districts from lives of crime. Such schools were founded throughout Britain, mostly in towns of 10,000 population and upwards, but varied in nature. Scottish ragged schools, and some fifteen in England and Wales, were day schools without sectarian affiliation and though they did teach the 3 Rs their emphasis was on industrial training for the potentially delinquent, providing also free meals. Most English ragged schools had a different bias. Those in London were affiliated to the Ragged School Union and met during the day, in the evening or on Sundays, concentrating on the 3 Rs and strongly evangelical religious instruction. In these, humanitarian care for the destitute overshadowed anti-delinquent motives and at least thirty provincial and Welsh schools developed along the same lines. From the 1850s all British ragged schools providing craft training attracted government financial aid and were absorbed into the penal system, supervised by the Home Office, as 'certified' industrial schools. In them convicted and potentially criminal children could be compulsorily detained, and the government also founded new certified industrial schools which operated in addition to reformatory schools.[20]

Under 1834 legislation, local poor-law authorities were permitted to pay for the schooling of pauper children receiving relief 'outdoors' (at home) and obliged to educate workhouse children ('indoor' paupers). Union guardians were usually reluctant to pay school fees for outdoor paupers, but for workhouse children most English and Welsh unions established their own schools for instruction in religion and the 3 Rs. From the 1840s government aid for workhouse teachers' pay became available and some unions cooperated to provide central district schools. In Scotland, however, union children were boarded out and attended local schools and from the 1870s this practice was increasingly adopted in England and Wales, so that by the end of the century most workhouse children had been absorbed into the mainstream of elementary education.[21]

In the later eighteenth and early nineteenth centuries a small minority of philanthropic employers, particularly in mining and manufacturing districts, began to provide their child workers and sometimes other local children with some elementary instruction in factory, mines or works schools, which met for a few hours on weekdays, in the evenings or on Sundays. This kind of part-time education was attractive to some working-class parents for, like the Sunday schools, it allowed children to learn without forgoing earnings. The idea also found increasing official support as a possible alternative to compulsory full-time education which was felt likely to increase taxation and raise labour costs. From the 1830s, legislation, primarily intended to restrict the employment of the very young and protect women and child workers from excessive work hours, began to include effective imposition of educational requirements. Starting by making child employment in textile factories contingent on part-time attendance at school, parliament gradually extended to a variety of other industries what became known as the 'half-time system' (though less time was spent in school than at work). Consequently, increasing numbers of children of age 8 upwards in industrial areas were obliged to attend school for a number of hours a week if they wished to be legally employed in the designated trades. Such attendance could be at any approved school, but some employers preferred to provide their own establishments in order to keep the children under their control and to integrate schooling and work requirements. The Factory Acts did not, however, always result in an increased exposure to schooling and the extension of a half-time system to all children proved impracticable, although vestiges of it survived for older children into the twentieth century.[22]

## Factors in the Development of Popular Schooling

The pattern of popular education outlined above derived from the interaction of a variety of attitudes and policies in a period when the social fabric appeared threatened by the consequences of urbanization, industrialization and population explosion and by revolutionary political ideas. In Scotland belief in popular education predated such developments and there was general agreement that social harmony would best be achieved through continued support for the traditional concept of an integrated national system based on religious unity, embracing all classes and offering a limited opportunity for upward social mobility. Especially in the industrial districts, however, the democratic ideal was in practice increasingly eroded by a division of schooling by social class.[23] In England and Wales there was unquestioning acceptance among the dominant classes that the education of working-class children should be distinct from that of their betters, but no consensus on the kind of schooling which the lower orders should receive. Total opposition to any education for the lower orders, strong in the eighteenth century, had not entirely disappeared even by 1840.[24] By then, however, such a negative position was impracticable since many workers were already literate and a network of working-class dame and common day schools was at their disposal. By the early nineteenth century it was not a matter of whether schooling should be made available to the working classes, but to what extent and in what manner – though opposition to making education compulsory remained strong well into the second half of the century.

Many of the English and Welsh middle classes favoured a clerically controlled education for the lower classes, limited largely to moral and religious instruction with a little reading and (more debatedly) writing. Anything more would make the poor dissatisfied and unfit for their natural occupations and introduce them to undesirable religious and political ideas, threatening the existing social order. A religiously controlled education would encourage acceptance of God-given social divisions and deference to superiors. Such a policy was supported by many who were doubtlessly also motivated by genuine philanthropy and missionary zeal and who sought through schooling to spread Christianity and encourage moral behaviour – convinced that this would save souls and bring the consolation of a blissful hereafter, as well as promoting social harmony. But to many in Britain popular schooling was also a form of insurance against social unrest, taken out by those who benefited most from the political and social status quo. Naturally, such views found strong support in the churches, especially the Church of England – which felt threatened by the spread of utilitarian and socialist influence and the generally secular and independent nature of the working-class private schools. The Sunday and ragged school movements and, in England and Wales, the institution of the voluntary schools represented, in part, a positive reaction against such forces. In Scotland, too, religious influence in education was generally accepted and the increased provision of church schools which could be relied on to inculcate approved religious and social values was intended to counter the popularity of private schools among burgeoning and potentially dangerous urban populations.[25]

Inter-denominational rivalry and internal divisions within churches were also influential in the spread of popular schooling. In Scotland, disquiet in the ranks of the Established Church at the numbers of children attending schools where they were taught by dissenters or those of no particular religious affiliation, and fear of losing influence over the young, led the Church in the 1820s and 1830s to campaign for a strengthened public school system financed by government and supervised by itself. Failure of the state to agree to such a development led the Church to inaugurate its own 'assembly' schools and was a contributory factor in the Disruption of 1843, which (as noted in the preceding section) was followed by the establishment of several hundred Free Church schools. Both the Established Church and the Free Church, as well as the other churches which set up schools in Scotland at this time, regarded schooling, in part at least, as a means of retaining members' loyalty, initiating the young in their traditions and proselytizing the poor.[26]

South of the border, the Church of England saw popular schooling as a means of combating the influence on the working classes of nonconformity and the consequences of Catholic emancipation and Irish immigration. It reacted energetically to the lead taken by dissenters in Sunday schooling and the establishment of British schools (which it feared would spread dissent) by setting up its own Sunday schools, establishing the National Society, diocesan and local boards of education and teacher training colleges, and encouraging parish clergy to promote church schools. Thus in 1814, the Bishop of London proclaimed that 'Every populous village unprovided with a National School must be regarded as a stronghold abandoned to the enemy' (that is the nonconformists),[27] while a midlands vicar described British schools as 'dreadful machines', 'full frought with moral and religious evil to

Church and Country'.[28] In Bristol rival Church and dissenting schools existed side by side, each hopefully 'built to empty [the schools] of other... denominations'.[29]

Though the founders of the English and Welsh voluntary schools valued them mainly as means of strengthening religious belief and morality, various other forces worked to secularize the curricula of those schools. Here the influence of the Benthamites or philosophical radicals, other middle-class radicals and liberal activists and theorists was considerable. The Benthamites were very active in parliament, publicized their views widely and had a strong impact on informed middle-class opinion. Antagonistic to the hegemony of the landed classes and to religious influence in education, they sought the rule of an enlightened middle class supported by an educated upper working class. As well as promoting grammar-school reform, mechanics' institutes, cheap informative literature and untaxed newspapers (treated in other chapters), they campaigned in England and Wales for universal, free and secular state-provided elementary schools for the working classes. Other public figures, too, including some MPs and others prominent in public service in matters of social reform, argued for an end to clerical dominance and for a national school system under central government control to help solve the social problems of the day. Like those who supported a religiously centred education for the workers, these middle-class radicals were united in disapproval of independent proletarian movements including Owenism, Chartism and trades unionism and of working-class private schools, but were more convinced of the social and economic dangers of ignorance of 'useful' knowledge. An enlightened secular curriculum would promote efficiency in the workforce. An introduction to classical economics (including the 'iron law of wages') would convince the workers of the folly of trades unionism and revolutionary socialism and of the identity of their interests with their employers, and perhaps fit them for a minor role in the processes of government.[30]

In Scotland there was less cause for dispute, for the parochial schools, though religiously based, embraced secular subjects. The Scottish Enlightenment was not anti-clerical or secularizing and the Benthamites in Scotland supported the parochial school system. There was general agreement that the inclusion of moral and religious education would strengthen the social order and benefit national unity.[31] In England and Wales, too, many ordinary middle-class folk must have found merit in such an outlook.

Middle-class opinion, whether religious or not, came by the 1830s to believe that properly organized elementary schooling would diminish crime and immorality and promote law and order and acceptance of the existing social and political order, here following Adam Smith's belief that 'An instructed and intelligent people . . . are always more decent and orderly than an ignorant and stupid one.'[32] Thus, Chartist and other popular unrest in the Northumberland and Durham coalfields in the 1830s and 1840s led some employers to establish chapels, libraries and schools and encouraged general support for suitable popular education.[33] Similarly, one Staffordshire coalowner claimed in the 1840s that his provision of a church, a day school and a Sunday school converted an 'ignorant, vicious and depraved' workforce into industrious souls 'respectful and obedient to their superiors' who forcibly resisted Chartist attempts to foment a strike.[34]

Some historians have seen all this as a deliberate, malicious and successful ruling-class conspiracy to use education and religion as vehicles for the control of the thoughts and behaviour of the working classes the better to maintain their own hegemony.[35] The value and validity of such a verdict, however, have been increasingly challenged. In any society, it has been correctly pointed out, 'there is no political or ideological institution which could not in some way be interpreted as an agency of social control'. In all communities public educational policy seeks to have some socializing effect on those being educated, and naturally reflects the norms of the society which provides it. Exclusively applied, the concept of social control (generally as well as with regard to education) provides too simplistic an hypothesis of motivation and change in this period. First, it disguises the plurality of middle-class attitudes already noted, differences between religious groups and the complexity of the interacting factors in the changes which occurred. Secondly, it reduces the role of the recipients to that of putty, passive and powerless in the hands of their superiors, whereas in fact the increasingly congruent attitudes and actions of the great mass of lower middle-class and upper working-class parents, did much to mould the educational system which emerged.[36]

Certainly, throughout Britain, the religious saw education as a means of strengthening the spiritual and moral fibre of the lower classes, and many of the ruling classes felt that education could be used to effect a social reformation, weaning the working classes from socialism and the propensity for crime and disorder. It might also prevent the social chaos threatened by demographic and economic change and repetition of the events in France. These not unworthy motives included a humanitarian and philanthropic wish to help the poor to help themselves and to bring to them the joys of religious faith. Other motivating influences included the view of some employers and governing circles that the national economy needed a better-educated workforce. But, while the provision of factory, works and mines schools by employers may have been intended to support discipline at work (though this is now doubted), it also reflected a paternalistic attitude, which would not find acceptance today but was benevolent, even altruistic, in intent. Though many of these schools left much to be desired, others were, by the standards of the day, excellent.[37]

Again, the view that the overriding aim of the voluntary schools was to inculcate religion and the acceptance of subordination may be over-stressed. The extent to which schools could indoctrinate children was anyway limited by pupils' ages, the length of the school day and parental attitudes. The doctrine of self help and the belief in the possibility of upward social and economic mobility through the thrift, diligence and knowledge acquired at school were widely held – not least by the promoters of the British schools and mechanics' institutes. The Methodists, particularly, supported education as a means of training in community self government.[38]

The success of Sunday schools demonstrates the enthusiasm with which some of the working class quite voluntarily embraced them, and consumer demand also affected the nature of the English and Welsh public elementary schools. Many parents of the artisan class were as religiously steadfast as their social superiors, but in day schooling they sought mainly efficient secular instruction. To prise them from private schools (which did not generally teach religion) and to compete with schools of other denominations, public day schools by the 1830s and 1840s were offering a much broader curriculum than before. The extent of the shift from private to public education, at a time when school attendance was not compulsory (explored in Chapter 2), reflects the success of the public schools in supplying what many working-class parents wanted. Such parents were often willing to put up with a moralizing religious atmosphere so long as the secular teaching was good. They were adept at ensuring that their children discarded values or denominational dogma which they disliked, while taking advantage of whatever else the schools offered.[39] So, in the 1860s, one dissenting father is recorded as sending his son to an Anglican school because he thought its teaching was 'first-rate', claiming 'Do you think if they put anything into the child's head during the day about religion which I did not approve, that I could not shove it out at night?'[40]

Significantly the leaders of the organized labour movement, like the middle-class radicals, did not seek to promote the continuance of the working-class private schools (the so-called 'people's schools'),[41] but campaigned vociferously for compulsory, free, secular state education. Working-class opposition to compulsory schooling when it came 'had little to do with resistance to ruling-class control' but simply represented outrage by poor or indifferent parents at the loss of child wages, or the views of those industrial workers who, themselves uneducated, earned good wages and saw no reason why their children should not do likewise without schooling.[42]

Pressure from central government under the influence of middle-class radicalism also contributed to the gradual secularization of the curriculum of English and Welsh voluntary schools for reasons not explicable simply as the consequence of a policy of social control. Textbooks used by all kinds of voluntary schools demonstrate a shift of focus from religious topics to a range of secular subjects, including grammar, art, science, history, geography and political economy.[43]

In the Scottish parochial schools it was always accepted that older pupils should be able to enjoy an extended curriculum and that schoolmasters should be capable of preparing pupils for the universities. Even in the highlands and islands in 1826 over half the parochial schools were said to teach Latin and book- keeping, and one-third Greek and English grammar, while some 20–25 per cent taught modern languages, mathematics, geography, mensuration, navigation and other subjects. Thus, even though in practice many poorer pupils got little more than religion and the 3 Rs, the opportunity for social advancement through a broader education was there for the children of those who could afford to keep them at school. And while the imposition of English as the medium of instruction in the Gaelic-speaking areas may be seen as a lowland tool to encourage national unity and as an aspect of anglicization, it was welcomed by the highlanders for the economic advantages it bestowed, and promoted by influential Scottish opinion generally as a means of weakening their cultural isolation. Unlike Welsh, the Gaelic language was not strongly associated with national sentiment.[44]

However, the Benthamites lost control of the British and Foreign School Society to the evangelicals, and religious influence was still strong enough in the 1840s for the various churches in Britain to exact from government a say in the appointment and activities of the

inspectors assigned to their schools and to slow the process of secularization.[45] The failure of the middle-class radicals to establish a fully
secular system of public elementary schools for England and Wales
and the eventual compromise of 1870 (discussed in Chapter 5) demonstrate that complete secularization of the public elementary schools
could not have been achieved at that time without splitting the ruling
class and weakening its influence. Nevertheless, far from supporting
elementary education as primarily an agent to render the workers
devout, amenable and obedient (for which bible-based indoctrination
would have sufficed), central government became increasingly unwilling to pay for religious instruction and anxious that its considerable
financial input into public education should show practical returns. This
culminated in the system of payment on results (noted above) introduced by Robert Lowe, the vice-president of the government Committee of Council on Education, an opponent of religious influence in
education. As well as rewarding regular school attendance, grants
were initially tied to proficiency in the basic subjects; later they were
extended to good performance in an increasing number of secular
subjects; they were not awarded for religious instruction.

Indeed an overarching 'social control' explanation exaggerates the
significance of the minority of legislators and administrators who may
have been imbued with such motives. While the traditional Whig interpretation of the development of state education as part of a triumphal
democratic march is no longer tenable, it remains true that many
officials engaged in promoting popular schooling did have an idealistic
vision of education as promoting social harmony and contributing to a
more egalitarian and collective type of government. The content of
government regulations for grant-receiving schools and of the reports
of government inspectors illustrates official interest in promoting a
sound general curriculum and good teaching in all subjects. Condes-
cension is there and the acceptance that working-class education should
differ from that of the middle classes, but no indication that the basis of
policy was the interests of a class other than that of the receivers. The
inspectorate's disapproval of private schooling as supportive of undesirable attitudes stemmed not only from a belief in the better educational
standards of the public schools but also from the feeling that those
schools should act as enlightened substitutes for inadequate parents.[46]

As for the harsh inculcation of subordination, the inspectorate frequently advised against authoritarian methods including physical punishment. There is much evidence, too, not only that working-class

parents often ignored or successfully objected to aspects of school social discipline of which they disapproved, but that the habits and attitudes promoted by the schools were not universally disliked: for 'the respectable working classes wished to be respectable not because some middleclass pundit told them to be so, but because they liked it'.[47]

If the intention of the ruling classes had been to use elementary schooling primarily to increase the power of the churches in society, to create passive workers and force an alien life-style on them and to provide an education of little intrinsic value, through a policy of 'social control', it clearly failed. In fact, the development of public elementary education before the introduction of compulsory schooling embraced the voluntary support of the bulk of the working class, for it provided them with a secular education superior to that of most common day and dame schools (and even to some middle-class schools). It thus contributed positively to the well-being of society generally, a society in which upper working-class and middle-class values had increasingly converged.[48] The failure by mid century of the Owenite, Chartist and other radical working-class attempts to establish proletarian schooling in order to promote their political aims had several causes (not least rejection of those movements by an increasingly prosperous working class), but among them was the preference of the bulk of the working classes for the voluntary schools.[49]

In nineteenth-century Scotland some polarization of working-class and middle-class education did occur, especially in urban areas, as distinctly secondary schools were created and predominantly working-class districts developed. Nevertheless, the enduring Scottish belief that a democratic (or at least meritocratic) educational system promoted social harmony, ensured that divisions between working- and middle-class schooling never became as clear-cut as in England and Wales. The tradition of the 'lad of parts' (according to which universities directly linked to parish schools common to all classes provided the clever working-class boy with opportunity for educational and social advancement) was not a fairy tale. Though most boys who did thus rise came from the middle and skilled working classes, many Scottish schools continued to cater for a range of social classes, and secondary and even higher education remained relatively open and accessible to at least a minority of the lower classes. There were certainly enough ministers, schoolmasters and intellectuals of humble origin to ensure that others should benefit like themselves and to demonstrate that the Scottish system was not 'designed to prepare the poor for a preordained position in life' nor to deny them the opportunity for upward social mobility.[50] Thus, in 1867, one Scottish Liberal MP demanded in parliament an educational system which would provide every clever boy 'even if born in the depths of poverty, an opportunity of pushing his way from one grade of education to another, aided by the State'.[51] In England the relationship between education and social advancement is more complex, but recent research suggests that, despite there being no marked rise in the proportion of jobs requiring literacy and that possession of basic schooling did not guarantee social advancement or higher wages, the chances of attaining these may nevertheless have been enhanced by a schooling embracing, as it did, both literacy and character training.[52]

# 2

---

# SCHOOL ATTENDANCE AND LITERACY: 1750 TO THE LATER NINETEENTH CENTURY

### The Incidence of School Attendance

Measurement of school attendance before it became compulsory from the 1870s is difficult. A plausible assessment, however, suggests a day-school attendance rate for England and Wales *c*.1750 of some 4 per cent of total population, while for Scotland an incomplete survey of some sixty lowland and highland parishes points to percentages varying from almost 8 to nearly 13.[1] Table 1 shows the proportions of the population at day school in the nineteenth century, deduced from contemporary educational surveys. These figures lack the validity of modern statistics, since a 'pupil at school' before the 1870s cannot be taken as a homogeneous unit. Children attended school for periods ranging from weeks to years and then often erratically. Some left at age 4 or 5, others stayed till 10 or over; some might attend for the same number of years as others but at ages at which they may have been more likely to have benefited from instruction. The extent and nature of such variables differed topographically and chronologically, while the curriculum and the quality of tuition also varied considerably. Some pupils, for instance, were taught reading but not writing. Children not recorded as at day school at any particular time included some who had previously attended and others who would attend later. Consequently the

*Table 1*   Children at day school as a percentage of total population, 1818–71

| Year | England | Wales | Scotland |
|------|---------|-------|----------|
| 1818 | 6.6 | 4.8 | 10.9 |
| 1833–4 | 9.3 | 6.8 | 10.0 |
| 1847 | – | 8.0 | – |
| 1851 (a) | 11.9 | 8.7 | – |
| (b) | 9.9 | 7.0 | 10.8 |
| 1864 | – | – | 13.7 |
| 1871 | – | – | 16.4 (c) |

*Notes*: (a) On the rolls; (b) attending on census day; (c) 'scholars' returned in the general census, 1871 (probably exaggerated).

*Sources*: *State of Education in England, Scotland and Wales*, PP 1820, xii; *Abstract of Education Returns*, PP 1835, xli–xliii; Withrington (1988), 178; Anderson (1995), 103, 300; Seaborne (1992), 96; Stephens (1987), 352.

proportion of the child population designated not at school in any particular survey does not equate with the proportion who went completely uneducated – though some nineteenth-century reformers and modern historians have assumed this to be so, thus exaggerating the numbers of the unschooled.[2] Nevertheless, though not exact statistics, the figures in Table 1 probably provide a broadly acceptable impression of national differences in day-school attendance and of change over time which accords with literary evidence. They suggest increasing attendance throughout Britain, with Scotland's considerable lead over England in 1818 being narrowed by mid century, but with Wales continuing to lag well behind.

National figures, however, conceal significant regional differences. In the eighteenth century, schooling was more widely available in the Scottish lowlands than the highlands (though historians may have

*Table 2*   Percentage of the population at day school in the Scottish regions, 1818

| | |
|------|------|
| Central, West | 13.1 |
| Borders | 11.7 |
| Fife, Lothians | 10.4 |
| Highlands | 10.1 |
| North-east | 8.3 |

*Source*: Deduced from Withrington (1988), q.v. for counties included in each region.

exaggerated the dearth there, especially if private schools are taken into account),[3] and regional distinctions persisted in Scotland through much of the nineteenth century. Geographical differences in 1818 are shown in Table 2. Of thirty-three Scottish counties, four had over 12 per cent of the population at school, while only twelve had less than 10 per cent.[4]

School attendance in England in 1818 showed both a general inferiority to Scotland and greater regional diversity. Rates in its forty-two counties ranged from 4.1 to 13.2 per cent of population. Only nine counties had over 9 per cent at school. A block of six of these (Northumberland, Durham, Cumberland, Westmorland and the East and North Ridings) was geographically contiguous with a group of southern Scottish counties and together these formed a large area of relatively high attendance straddling the border. Attendance rates in another twenty-five English counties ranged between 6.1 and 8.8 per cent, roughly similar to that of north-eastern Scotland, the Scottish region with the lowest proportion at school. The counties registering the lowest levels of school attendance in England (4.1 to 6.0), lower than any Scottish county except Nairn, included Somerset, Gloucestershire and Wiltshire in the westcountry, Lancashire and Cheshire in the north and Monmouthshire (then in England). Attendance rates in Welsh counties ranged between 2.9 and 6.8 per cent, with only Pembrokeshire and Flintshire over 6 per cent.[5]

By 1851 (Table 3) remarkable progress had taken place in parts of Scotland: Caithness, Orkney and the north-eastern Scottish counties had joined the borders, the central lowlands and the south-east as the areas of highest attendance. The lowest levels in Scotland were now generally in the west – from Wigtownshire north to Ross and Cromarty, with Dumbartonshire, Renfrewshire, Lanarkshire, Inverness-shire and Ross and Cromarty (and probably Shetland) showing the lowest of all.[6] In England in 1851 a roughly similar hierarchy as in 1818 persisted. The seventeen English counties with the best attendance figures included some in the far north, some along the southern seaboard and a number near and including parts of London. Those with the lowest attendance figures included Lancashire, counties in the midlands and south midlands, and some in the westcountry and along the Welsh border. Of this last group, Gloucestershire, Herefordshire and Monmouthshire, together with Staffordshire, were, however, the only English counties with lower attendance figures than Flintshire, the

*Table 3*     Percentage of county populations at school in 1851
(English and Welsh counties indented)

| | | | |
|---|---|---|---|
| Kinross-shire | 14.1 | Yorkshire, WR | 10.4 |
| Berwickshire | 14.0 | Bute | 10.3 |
| Clackmannanshire | 13.6 | Cambridgeshire | 10.3 |
| Middlesex * | 13.6 | Leicestershire | 10.3 |
| Caithness-shire | 13.2 | Northamptonshire | 10.3 |
| Fifeshire | 13.1 | Argyllshire | 10.2 |
| Kirkcudbrightshire | 13.1 | Cheshire | 10.2 |
| Banffshire | 13.0 | Norfolk | 10.2 |
| Morayshire (Elginshire) | 12.9 | Angus (Forfarshire) | 10.1 |
| Perthshire | 12.9 | Suffolk | 10.1 |
| Westmorland | 12.8 | Somerset | 9.7 |
| Kincardineshire | 12.7 | Buckinghamshire | 9.6 |
| Roxburghshire | 12.7 | Devon | 9.6 |
| Peeblesshire | 12.4 | Dumbartonshire | 9.4 |
| Aberdeensshire | 12.1 | Nairnshire | 9.4 |
| Dumfriesshire | 12.1 | Nottinghamshire | 9.4 |
| Selkirkshire | 11.9 | Worcestershire | 9.3 |
| Hampshire | 11.9 | Bedfordshire | 9.1 |
| Midlothian (Edinburghshire) | 11.8 | Cornwall | 9.1 |
| Surrey* | 11.8 | Ross & Cromarty | 9.1 |
| Huntingdonshire | 11.7 | Shropshire | 9.0 |
| Yorkshire, NR | 11.7 | Lancashire | 8.9 |
| Oxfordshire | 11.6 | Warwickshire | 8.8 |
| Yorkshire, ER | 11.6 | Flintshire | 8.7 |
| Kent* | 11.5 | Inverness-shire | 8.7 |
| Rutland | 11.5 | Lanarkshire | 8.7 |
| Sussex | 11.5 | Renfrewshire | 8.6 |
| Berkshire | 11.4 | Staffordshire | 8.6 |
| Dorset | 11.4 | Caernarvonshire | 8.2 |
| Hertfordshire | 11.4 | Cardiganshire | 8.2 |
| Stirlingshire | 11.3 | Herefordshire | 8.0 |
| Cumberland | 11.2 | Denbighshire | 7.9 |
| East Lothian (Haddingtonshire) | 11.2 | Pembrokeshire | 7.8 |
| Sutherlandshire | 11.2 | Orkney & Shetland | 7.7 |
| Wiltshire | 11.1 | Carmarthenshire | 7.5 |
| Lincolnshire | 10.9 | Gloucestershire | 7.2 |
| Linlithgowshire (West Lothian) | 10.9 | Monmouthshire | 7.1 |
| Durham | 10.8 | Montgomeryshire | 6.4 |
| Wigtownshire | 10.8 | Merionethshire | 6.0 |
| Ayrshire | 10.7 | Radnorshire | 6.0 |
| Derbyshire | 10.5 | Brecon | 5.9 |
| Essex | 10.4 | Anglesey | 5.6 |
| Northumberland | 10.4 | Glamorganshire | 5.3 |

\* Extra-metropolitan. London had 10.8 per cent at school.

*Sources*: *Education Census, England and Wales, 1851*, PP 1852–3, xc; Anderson (1995), 306–7.

county with the best attendance figure in Wales. Attendance in all the Welsh counties was much lower than in the vast majority of

English counties, and about a quarter of the Welsh population lived in Glamorganshire, the county with the lowest proportion of attenders. Only two English counties (Middlesex and Westmorland), however, registered attendance figures as high as those of eastern Scotland and the borders. A dozen or so (mainly in the south and far north) had attendance levels similar to those of the Scottish industrial belt. Fourteen English counties had fewer than 10 per cent of their populations at school compared with six Scottish counties (and probably Shetland).[7]

County figures, however, often disguise considerable local variations. Percentages of population at school in the individual English census districts in 1851 ranged from 5 to 16 per cent (from 7 to 14 per cent within Buckinghamshire, for example). Larger towns, industrial centres and manufacturing and mining districts (especially in the north, midlands and south Wales) had lower proportions than did smaller (particularly southern) towns or market and minor port towns. Similarly in Scotland, attendance was lower in the populous industrial and mining counties of Ayr, Stirling, West Lothian, Selkirk and Angus than in neighbouring rural counties, and proportions of the population at school in some industrial areas in England and Scotland actually fell during the first half of the nineteenth century.[8] Overall improvements in the 1860s did not eradicate local variations (Chapter 4).

## Patterns of Basic Literacy

As a Victorian statistician remarked in 1867, however, 'the great question is, not how many children are at school, but how many children are educated'.[9] Figures of day-school attendance as proportions of population are affected by the age structures of communities and anyway provide only an oblique measure of educational attainment. Not only was the 'pupil' (as noted above) not a homogeneous statistical unit, but some children learnt to read, and perhaps write, by attending only Sunday schools, which before 1850 were often used as substitutes for day schooling, especially in industrial districts and widely in Wales.[10] In the Potteries in the 1840s, for example, nine times as many children attended Sunday as day schools.[11] Again an unknowable, but probably not inconsiderable, number of adults also educated themselves at home or through the many adult and Sunday schools, mutual improvement and other societies and adult institutions which existed, especially in towns, throughout Britain.

Over the past few decades historians have, therefore, supplemented school attendance figures by statistics of those able to sign their names on marriage.[12] These offer the only yardstick of educational standards generally available for spatial and chronological comparison over the whole period from the 1750s to the later nineteenth century. They provide data for equal numbers of men and women, and from 1839 in England and Wales and from 1855 in Scotland a record of every marriage is available – so that from those dates all classes and localities are covered. Several other reasons, too, recommend the use of marriage signatures or marks as a useful, if limited, measure of the distribution of basic literacy. First, the Victorian Registars General of Births, Deaths and Marriages collected these data for the very purpose of measuring the progress of elementary education. 'If a man can write his own name,' argued the Registrar for England and Wales in 1861, 'it may be presumed that he can read it when written by another; still more that he will recognize that and other familiar words when he sees them in print; and it is even probable that he will spell his way through a paragraph in a newspaper.'

A second reason for accepting the value of these signatures for comparative purposes is that the statistics for individual districts do not fluctuate erratically over time. They are remarkably consistent from one year to the next and in relation to those of other districts, and for the changes that did occur there is usually a plausible explanation. Thirdly, throughout much of the nineteenth century and before, there was little point in learning merely to write one's name and nothing else. The possession of such a trick had no pecuniary advantage and illiteracy bore no stigma among the working classes. Making a mark was quite acceptable on the few occasions when attestation was needed. Moreover, if a person did retain the skill of writing until marriage, it indicated a schooling of some length, for marriages on average took place some fifteen years after leaving school, and writing skills barely attained are likely to have been lost by then. Again, throughout Britain, writing was for a long time normally only taught after a certain level in reading had been reached. Indeed, because it was more expensive to keep a child at school long enough to learn to write than to read only, and because for many people reading was a skill more likely to be useful than writing, many more people could read than could sign their names. A variety of evidence suggests that in England in the early nineteenth century over one-third of those able to read could not write. In Scotland the proportions able only to read may have been greater, and both in England and Scotland more women than men were likely to have been in this position.[13] Proportions of spouses signing on marriage thus probably underestimate the numbers of those able to read and perhaps exaggerate somewhat the proportions able to write well. Like statistics of school attendance they are less useful as absolute figures than for comparative purposes – providing a general impression of changes in basic levels of education over time and between one place and another.

Percentages of spouses in England and Wales (taken together) able to sign the marriage register rose from some 50 per cent in 1754 to about 58 per cent in 1840 (grooms from about 60 per cent to 67 per cent; brides from about 40 per cent to 50 per cent). By 1850 the proportion was 61 per cent (69 per cent grooms, 54 per cent brides) and by 1870 76 per cent (80 per cent; 73 per cent), including a level for Wales of 65 per cent. In Scotland marriage signatures were not recorded until 1855, but other evidence suggests that in the lowlands adult male signature-literacy in 1750 stood at about 65 per cent and that of women between 15 and 30 per cent. In the highlands the percentages were lower – perhaps 40–45 per cent for men. By 1855, however, 83 per cent of Scottish spouses signed (grooms 89 per cent, brides 77 per cent). In that year the overall figure for England and Wales was 65 per cent (70 per cent grooms, 59 per cent brides) – embracing 46 per cent for Wales. England with Wales did not reach 83 per cent until 1878, and only in 1900 did the proportion draw level with that of Scotland (97 per cent), suggesting that the educational gap between England and Scotland in the mid nineteenth century was even greater than the figures of school attendance (Table 1) might indicate.[14] Of course, marriage signatures related to a particular age cohort (those in their later 20s) and not to the whole population, in which the proportion who were literate lagged behind the marrying group.

National literacy statistics disguise considerable local variations. In England between 1754 and 1840 market towns and larger commercial and administrative centres tended to have higher (and steadily rising) proportions of literate spouses than did rural areas and industrial towns. The midland and northern industrializing towns and districts had lower proportions of signers than their rural hinterlands, than neighbouring non-industrial centres and than most towns in other areas. Moreover, for reasons explored in Chapter 4, their marriage signature rates often stagnated or declined in this period.

Most non-industrialized rural areas, however, experienced improving levels, though remaining inferior to non-industrial towns.[15]

Scotland lacks similar evidence for this period, but, as noted above, it is possible that a higher proportion of non-writers could read than was so in England. Between the 1750s and the early nineteenth century the lowlands probably became almost universally literate, though, as in England, a decline in proportions of literates may have occurred as migration to industrial areas underprovided with schools took place. Generally, however, urban literacy levels in the later eighteenth century were probably consistently higher than rural ones and highest of all in Edinburgh and Glasgow. The position in the rural north lagged behind. A survey of 1818 suggests that as many as 70 per cent in the north-west highlands and the Hebrides were unable to read, let alone write, and in the rest of the highlands the rate varied from 30 to 40 per cent, suggesting that even if the provision of schooling in the highlands has been underestimated, the level of education reached there was not uniformly high and that the Clearances may have had a disruptive effect. The prejudice against instruction in the vernacular found in the Scottish highlands was absent in the Welsh circulating schools, and in them, in the middle decades of the eighteenth century, some half the Welsh population (adults and children) are said to have learned to read in Welsh.[16]

Similar topographical variations in literacy levels as outlined above persisted after the mid nineteenth century. Urban levels were lowest in England in heavily populated centres (except London) and in the industrial towns generally. Smaller towns, especially those in the south, and market centres, ports, cathedral cities and seats of county government generally had a much better record than larger and industrial centres. In Scotland levels were much lower in Glasgow than in Edinburgh (perhaps reflecting Irish immigration and industrialization in the former and the administrative and social significance of the latter) and town districts generally showed on average somewhat lower levels than mainland rural ones. In rural areas of Britain high levels of signatures were particularly associated with certain zones, including the sparsely populated counties of far northern and north-eastern England, much of Scotland, the relatively prosperous agricultural and seaboard counties of southern England, and counties close to and embracing London (Table 4). The lowest proportions in England were in the northern and midland countries where industry and mining was not confined to urban areas, in agricultural areas (especially in parts of the midlands and the westcountry), where small freeholders, dependent on family labour, farmed often unproductive land, and in rural districts of low-paid farm labourers (especially in Bedfordshire, Buckinghamshire and Northamptonshire) where cottage industry was strongly entrenched.[17]

Table 4 illustrates the persistence of Scottish educational superiority. Only eight Scottish counties in 1855 had lower rates than Westmorland

Table 4    Percentage of marriage signatures by counties, 1855

| Scotland | England | Wales | Grooms | Brides | All |
|---|---|---|---|---|---|
| Selkirkshire | | | 100 | 100 | 100 |
| Berwickshire | | | 99 | 99 | 99 |
| Orkney | | | 98 | 95 | 97 |
| Kinross-shire | | | 100 | 92 | 96 |
| Peeblesshire | | | 97 | 94 | 96 |
| Dumfriesshire | | | 97 | 91 | 95 |
| Kincardineshire | | | 99 | 91 | 95 |
| Aberdeenshire | | | 98 | 89 | 94 |
| Perthshire | | | 97 | 91 | 94 |
| Caithness-shire | | | 96 | 89 | 92 |
| Morayshire | | | 97 | 88 | 92 |
| (Elginshire) | | | | | |
| Banffshire | | | 96 | 88 | 92 |
| Midlothian | | | 94 | 90 | 92 |
| (Edinburghshire) | | | | | |
| Fifeshire | | | 96 | 87 | 92 |
| Roxburghshire | | | 95 | 87 | 91 |
| Kirkcudbrightshire | | | 93 | 87 | 90 |
| Bute | | | 91 | 84 | 87 |
| Linlithgowshire | | | 92 | 82 | 87 |
| (West Lothian) | | | | | |
| Shetland | | | 89 | 83 | 86 |
| Nairnshire | | | 94 | 76 | 85 |
| Clackmannanshire | | | 89 | 71 | 85 |
| Wigtownshire | | | 91 | 79 | 85 |
| Forfarshire (Angus) | | | 91 | 75 | 83 |
| East Lothian | | | 86 | 80 | 83 |
| (Haddingtonshire) | | | | | |
| Stirlingshire | | | 84 | 77 | 81 |
| | Westmorland | | 86 | 76 | 81 |
| Argyllshire | | | 88 | 72 | 80 |
| Lanarkshire | | | 85 | 70 | 78 |
| Ayrshire | | | 83 | 70 | 77 |
| | Cumberland | | 84 | 71 | 77 |
| | Sussex | | 73 | 77 | 75 |
| | Yorkshire, NR | | 79 | 69 | 74 |
| | Middlesex* | | 75 | 73 | 74 |
| | Surrey* | | 72 | 77 | 74 |
| Sutherlandshire | | | 81 | 65 | 73 |

*Table 4*   Contd.

| Scotland | England | Wales | Grooms | Brides | All |
|---|---|---|---|---|---|
| Dumbartonshire | | | 81 | 64 | 72 |
| | Hampshire | | 74 | 71 | 72 |
| Renfrewshire | | | 80 | 63 | 72 |
| | Rutland | | 68 | 77 | 72 |
| | Yorkshire, ER | | 79 | 66 | 72 |
| | Gloucestershire | | 74 | 69 | 71 |
| | Northumberland | | 79 | 62 | 71 |
| | Devon | | 73 | 67 | 70 |
| | Kent* | | 68 | 68 | 68 |
| | Oxfordshire | | 67 | 69 | 68 |
| | Berkshire | | 64 | 70 | 67 |
| | Lincolnshire | | 70 | 64 | 67 |
| | Dorset | | 69 | 64 | 66 |
| | Derbyshire | | 72 | 60 | 66 |
| | Leicestershire | | 72 | 61 | 66 |
| | Somerset | | 67 | 64 | 66 |
| | Warwickshire | | 71 | 62 | 66 |
| Inverness-shire | | | 72 | 54 | 63 |
| | Northamptonshire | | 67 | 60 | 63 |
| | Nottinghamshire | | 70 | 56 | 63 |
| | Wiltshire | | 64 | 62 | 63 |
| | Worcestershire | | 67 | 60 | 63 |
| | Durham | | 72 | 53 | 62 |
| | Herefordshire | | 58 | 67 | 62 |
| | Norfolk | | 59 | 61 | 60 |
| | Yorkshire, WR | | 71 | 49 | 60 |
| | Cheshire | | 68 | 50 | 59 |
| | Buckinghamshire | | 61 | 55 | 58 |
| | Cambridgeshire | | 60 | 57 | 58 |
| | Essex | | 56 | 61 | 58 |
| | Suffolk | | 58 | 59 | 58 |
| | Cornwall | | 64 | 51 | 57 |
| Ross & Cromarty | | | 63 | 51 | 57 |
| | Shropshire | | 61 | 53 | 57 |
| | Huntingdonshire | | 56 | 56 | 56 |
| | Lancashire | | 67 | 41 | 54 |
| | Hertfordshire | | 51 | 54 | 52 |
| | Bedfordshire | | 56 | 47 | 51 |
| | | North Wales counties | 58 | 39 | 48 |
| | Staffordshire | | 56 | 43 | 48 |
| | Monmouthshire | | 52 | 40 | 46 |
| | | South Wales counties | 57 | 35 | 46 |

* Extra-metropolitan. Figures for London were 87: 79: 83.
*Sources*: *Reps, Registrars General of Births, Deaths & Marriages*, PP 1857 (2), xxii; PP 1861, xviii. Separate figures for Welsh counties are not available.

(the English county with the best rates) and, with the exception of Ross and Cromarty and Inverness-shire, the Scottish counties registering the lowest proportions of signing spouses ranked level with the best-performing English counties. Nevertheless, there were still regional variations. The lowest signature rates were in two areas: the highland counties of the north-west (Sutherland, Inverness and Ross and Cromarty), which had absentee landlords and few middle-class residents, and a group of counties in the lowland industrial belt – particularly the counties of Dumbarton, Lanark, Renfrew, Ayr and Stirling, which contained mining and manufacturing villages where the state of schooling was probably the worst in Scotland. The areas with the best literacy rates were the counties of the east and north-east and the border counties of Dumfries, Peebles, Berwick and Selkirk. Separate figures for individual Welsh counties are not available for 1855 but the conflated statistics for north and south Wales and those for Monmouthshire (then in England) were abysmally low (Table 4). Distinct county figures, available in 1871, show that the lowest proportions of signers then were in rural Caernarvon and Brecon and in the mining counties of Glamorgan, Flint and Denbigh. Not quite so low were those in the counties of the rural north and Anglesey. The highest were in the contiguous western counties of Carmarthen, Pembroke, Cardigan and Radnor, but they bettered only three English counties.[18]

## Determinants of Regional Variations in Schooling and Literacy

These regional and local differences in literacy levels reflected a number of variables, including the extent of school attendance and child labour, the quality of schooling and, as the preceding section suggests (and as is further pursued in Chapter 4), the related nature of the local community's economy and occupational structure, as well as the ingredient of gender.

The positive correlation between national levels of day-school attendance and (fifteen or so years later, when most leaving school at about age 10 or so would marry) marriage signatures was not necessarily matched locally: schooling and marriage might occur in different places, while the effectiveness of schooling varied topographically as did the proportions of autodidacts and those educated only in Sunday schools or as adults. An extreme example is Shetland where high male literacy rates co-existed with low school attendance. Nevertheless, there was a broad correspondence between, on the one hand, areas and towns of good day-school attendance and subsequent high literacy rates, and on the other of areas and places where proportions of children at school and of later marriage signature rates were lower. Thus, in two cases out of three, the proportion of illiterate spouses in the mid 1860s was greatest in those English towns where day-school attendance had been lowest in 1851.[19]

Provision of public schooling in different localities of England and Wales was particularly related to the strength on the ground of the Established Church and the attitude of its clergy. The Church's educational impact was affected by the level of interest and energy displayed by individual bishops and parish priests, by the amount of financial assistance forthcoming from better-off parishioners and by the opinions of individual clergy on the type of education they felt suitable for the lower classes. Despite some channelling of funds from richer to poorer parishes, Church school provision was weakest in industrial districts and towns, where dissent was also often strong (as, for instance, in Wales, Monmouthshire, Lancashire and Yorkshire), and where the lower reaches of the labouring clases were often indifferent to religion. It was weak, too, in those rural areas where resident gentry (the class on which the Church depended for financial support) were absent. In areas of absentee landlords, tenant farmers were left as the leading laymen and they displayed little interest in helping to provide education for labourers' children. Indeed they often put pressure on their workers to put their children to work on the land rather than to send them to school. In the late 1860s, for example, Nottinghamshire farmers were said to 'practically coerce parents . . . to send [their children] at seven years of age into the fields . . . where they work from dawn to dusk'. Church effort was also affected adversely in some areas (like the Fens), by a lack of resident clergy, while in others bishops or clergy lacked enthusiasm for working-class schooling or had a restricted view of what it should comprise. A few incumbents felt that Sunday schools should suffice, while a not-inconsiderable number favoured day schools limited to the teaching of religion with a smattering of the 3 Rs, and rejected the state aid which would have brought with it inspection and the obligation to provide a broader curriculum.[20] Other Church schools were unable to quality for government assistance because poverty prevented them from meeting the necessary requirements. This and the low levels of education provided in many unaided Church of England schools is pursued in Chapter 5.

Also crucial in determining both levels of schooling and literacy (especially in England and Wales) was a community's social and occupational structure. By the eighteenth century, landed and professional classes, and by the nineteenth century, the middle classes generally, were on the whole signature-literate, with male traders and craftsmen next most likely to be able to sign, and with factory workers, urban and rural labourers, fishermen and miners (in that order) most likely to include higher proportions of illiterates. Unskilled labourers tended to be most often illiterate, though levels for farm labourers varied geographically. Consequentally, the higher the proportion of working-class men in a community the lower was likely to be its marriage-signature rate, which also varied according to the relative proportions of particular occupational groups. While the English and Welsh working classes were virtually all able to sign on marriage by 1914, some occupational groups achieved that position more quickly than others. Traditional handicraftsmen could mostly all sign by the mid to late 1890s, but male metal and textile workers took a decade longer to reach that position and miners and skilled labourers two decades, while unskilled labourers did not do so until 1914.[21] Changes in literacy rates in different places were sometimes the result of in and out migration of different occupational groups.

Market towns, ports and administrative centres (especially London), and cathedral cities tended to have well-established school facilities, concentrations of the professional and middle classes and ready employment for the literate of all ranks. They attracted literate immigrants and encouraged artisans to school their young. Consequently they had relatively high school attendance and literacy levels. The growing factory towns, on the other hand, contained much higher proportions of working-class people, offered plenty of unskilled and semi-skilled employment for the illiterate and poorly schooled and much opportunity for child labour. Floods of illiterate immigrants, including especially miners and Irish labourers, altered the social and occupational composition of industrializing districts throughout Britain and depressed their literacy levels. Traditional craftsmen (especially the handloom weavers both in England and Scotland) were pauperized by factory competition, and often had to give up schooling their children and send them to work.

At the same time, burgeoning populations might swamp existing school facilities.[22] The very poor literacy rates in mining areas and the

populous manufacturing districts which grew up in the rural hinterlands of factory towns, reflected the lack of traditional urban facilities
(including schooling), the paucity of middle-class residents and thus (in
England and Wales) the financial weakness in those parts of the Church.
Such areas were dominated by comparatively prosperous miners,
metalworkers and potters (groups with the lowest proportions of literates). These, both skilled and unskilled, felt little or no need of elementary education for their young, who, from an early age, could easily earn
a good living without it (a topic pursued further in Chapter 5). The
same apparent irrelevance of schooling probably accounts for the high
illiteracy rates of Cornish and Scottish fishing communities and of areas
of domestic industry in the English midlands and south. Cottage industry districts, moreover, were often characterized by absentee landlords
and populations of low-paid agricultural labourers as well as female and
child home workers. Here poverty, rather than prosperity, encouraged
large-scale child labour beginning at ages younger than in the factory
districts, and tenant farmers, as noted above, discouraged the education
of labourers' children, fearing loss of cheap labour.[23] 'If I were scholar,'
said a Lincolnshire farm labourer in the 1860s, 'I shouldn't be here, and
that's the reason why the farmers hold against this 'ere scholarship'.[24]
Literacy levels in such areas were further depressed by the migration of
schooled youngsters to London and other towns offering greater
opportunities for the educated. In rural Devon in the 1860s, for
instance, it was remarked that 'the best young men, i.e. those who are
best educated, go away to the police, railways, etc.'[25]

Again in rural areas of poor soil, where smallholders dependent on
family labour dominated, education similarly suffered. Indeed, since it
was the better-off middle class who traditionally sponsored schooling for
the working classes, where they were absent or few in number the
provision of schooling and encouragement to use it suffered. In the
Scottish highlands and western isles, particularly among fishing and
crofting communities, absentee landlordism, poverty and remoteness,
combined with antagonism to the Established Church by a Gaelic-
speaking Catholic population, created a drag on the extension of schooling. Thus, as late as 1880, when the national marriage-signature rate
was 89 per cent, the proportion of literate spouses in 'insular rural'
districts of Scotland was only 70 per cent and in Ross and Cromarty 63
per cent. Similarly in Wales and Monmouthshire educational progress
suffered from the difficulties Welsh speakers experienced in schools
using English as the medium of instruction, from the absence of

resident gentry, the weakness of the Church of England and the opposition of dissenters to its influence. This was compounded by widespread poverty and the expansion of coal mining.[26]

In strong contrast were the rural Scottish lowlands and borders and some prosperous English farming districts (especially in the counties of the far north) where resident landowners were prone to treat their labourers better and to support village schools. Comfortably off independent yeomen, who dominated some such areas, and also many of the rural labourers in those parts looked favourably on education as a good in itself. Thus, in the 1830s it was said of one Angus parish that there a man who could not read was regarded as a curiosity, and a Northumberland vicar claimed 'I scarcely know an instance in which the children of an agricultural labourer have not been sent to school, for the most part at his own expense.' Similarly in the 1860s it was reported that in one rural village in Northumberland 'public opinion would send any man earning wages...to the position of a brute who did not send his child to school'.[27]

## Aspects of Female Literacy and Schooling

Gender also played a part in changing educational levels.[28] In the eighteenth century it is probable that in every kind of community in Britain far more men than women could read and write. In England, the excess of grooms' signatures over those of brides fell only slightly between 1754 and 1840: from about 20 percentage points to some 17. Evidence for Scotland is weaker, but it has been suggested that in the lowlands in the 1750s there was a male literacy lead (in adults generally, not just the marriage cohort) of between 35 and 50 percentage points. The Victorian period, however, saw an increasing convergence. By 1855 bridal signatures in Scotland as a whole were only 12 points behind those of grooms: a remarkable advance. In England and Wales by then brides lagged behind by 11 points, by 1870 by 7 and by 1885 only 2 points. By 1895 both partners signed in almost all marriages in Britain. This, of course, represents literacy levels of men and women in their later 20s; attainment of near-universal basic literacy in the population at large naturally took longer.

Female literacy rates and their relationship to those of men, however, varied over different types of community. In Scotland, in the period

1640–1770, proportions of literate women in towns were considerably higher than in rural areas. In England, in the period of the Industrial Revolution, both male and female rates in northern manufacturing towns were lower than in other urban centres and often seem to have declined or stagnated: any narrowing of the gender gap in literacy levels derived from a greater decline in male than female rates rather than from female improvement. In English rural areas and non-industrial towns in this period, however, improvements in overall literacy levels often embraced greater rises in the proportions of brides than of grooms signing.

A more definitive picture of gender difference can be provided for the Victorian period, when complete marriage-signature statistics become available. These illustrate particularly the superior position of Scottish women over women in the rest of Britain. Not until 1875 did the level of bridal signatures in England and Wales reach the level achieved in Scotland in 1855. But throughout Britain topographical variations in the relative literacy rates of men and women persisted. By 1855 (Table 4), except in Selkirkshire and Berwickshire, where virtually all spouses signed, fewer brides than grooms signed their names in every Scottish country, though the gap varied from 3 to 18 percentage points. In general females lagged furthest behind males in parts of the highlands and in the industrialized and urbanized counties of the lowlands (and especially in Glasgow), and approximated to male levels most nearly in Orkney and in some lowland and border counties. Evidence for the 1860s shows that generally the gender gap in literacy rates was narrower in rural mainland districts than in the towns (Edinburgh being a notable exception) or the islands. The relative improvement of women, however, took time, though by 1880 Orkney had joined Selkirkshire and Berwickshire with as many brides as grooms signing, and in Kinross-shire more brides than grooms signed. Nevertheless, in the highland north-west female inferiority remained considerable: in Ross and Cromarty brides lagged behind grooms by over 28 percentage points, in Inverness- shire by nearly 19, in Nairnshire by 16 and in Shetland by 13. In the industrial counties of Renfrewshire and Lanarkshire there was still a lag of 12 percentage points.[29]

While Scottish literacy levels tended to show the same topographical pattern for both sexes, with brides scoring well where grooms scored well, and less well where grooms scored less well, this was not the case in England. There, areas existed in which high or low literacy levels in one sex were not mirrored in the other, and others in which the levels of one sex fell or stagnated while those of the other improved. Nevertheless, whereas in the early 1840s bridal literacy lagged behind that of grooms in all forty-two counties, by 1855 (Table 4) there were ten counties (concentrated in the south-east and East Anglia) in which the percentage of literate brides was equal to or greater than that of literate grooms. From then on relative female improvement spread northwards and westwards, so that by 1865 there were nineteen such counties, by 1870 twenty-one. By 1885 more brides than grooms signed the registers in twenty-six counties – a majority. By then male superiority persisted in two areas – the counties of the far north (together with the East and North Ridings), where male literacy levels had always been not only high but well in advance of female, and in the industrial counties of the north and midlands together with Monmouthshire, where they shared low levels with men. In Wales women lagged behind for longer: even in 1871 only one county (Carmarthen) registered more signatures for brides than grooms, the gap being greatest in remote rural western counties (Anglesey, Caernarvon, Cardigan, Brecon and Pembroke) and the mining county of Glamorgan.[30]

The geographical pattern of female literacy is harder to explain than that for men. Occupational data are not as readily available and it is thus difficult to link types of female employment with marriage-signature evidence. Nevertheless the correlation (in both England and Scotland) of low bridal literacy rates with areas of widespread female employment in factories, workshops and in cottage industry,[31] suggests that women in such occupations were more often illiterate than was general. On the other hand, female literacy levels in many communities appear to reflect male occupational structures.

Research into this topic is lacking for Scotland, but for England it has been shown that the likelihood of a bride being literate often bore some relation to her father's occupation, perhaps reflecting differing attitudes towards the schooling of boys and girls. The daughters and wives of miners in particular were less likely to be literate than miners – themselves a highly illiterate group. Thus in mining districts female literacy lagged far behind male: as late as 1871, for instance, there was a gap of 13 percentage points in both County Durham and Glamorganshire.[32] More surprising is the poor performance of daughters of skilled artisans relative to that of their brothers, and the fact that they continued to lag behind until the last decades of the nineteenth century. The daughters of unskilled agricultural labourers, however, often tended to have better rates than their brothers. Consequently in many places the overall level of female literacy related to the male occupational structure without necessarily corresponding to the male literacy level.[33]

A small or closing gap between proportions of boys and girls at school sometimes indicated progress in female education, sometimes not. In Scotland in 1833–4, girls' attendance in the highlands and north-east was only 50 per cent of boys' (when the national proportion was 70 per cent). An increase in the ratio in those rural areas to 70 per cent by 1851 (nationally 79 per cent) coincided with a general regional rise in school attendance. But an increase in the proportion of girls at school in the industrial lowlands to over 80 per cent of that of boys by 1851 was combined with an overall decline in school attendance generally. Here greater parity merely reflected a demand for boys in the mines and the fact that both boys and girls were leaving school for work at an early age.[34]

In England a smaller proportion of girls than boys aged 5–14 attended school in every county in 1851. Although there is some evidence that in purely agricultural areas girls tended to stay longer at school than boys, in areas of heavy female industrial employment, like the textile factory districts and where cottage industry flourished, girls attended school more irregularly than boys and left at an earlier age. Thus, in fifty-seven of the sixty-four census districts of the West Riding in 1851 a higher proportion of boys than girls was at school, and even in the late 1860s only 17 per cent of girls over 10 were still at school in Birmingham compared with 21 per cent of boys. According to a school inspector in the 1840s, in the midlands cottage industry districts it was 'impossible in most places to keep up a girls' school'. In such areas low wages for farm labourers necessitated child, particularly female, labour from an early age and parents preferred to send their daughters to small 'schools' where they were taught to make lace, plait and so on, rather than to read and write. At that time there were no National schools for girls in such centres of domestic industry as Luton, Dunstable or Leighton Buzzard, and in the surrounding villages attempts to start girls' schools were rarely made.[35]

Another ingredient of gender difference in literacy rates was the differing experience of schooling of the sexes. In some places standards of instruction in boys' schools were superior to those in girls'. Earlier leaving by girls in some cases meant that they did not reach the stage when writing instruction began, and anyway the curriculum for girls was less directed towards writing and often paid more attention to sewing. Even in the early 1850s, while some 87 per cent of both boys and girls in England and Scotland were learning to read, 61–2 per cent of boys were learning to write against 56 per cent of girls in England and 52 per cent in Scotland. In parts of the highlands and islands, schools, especially the Gaelic society schools, tended to restrict tuition in writing for girls or to neglect it altogether. In addition, far fewer women than men attended adult schools or societies, and those who did spent more time learning domestic skills than academic subjects.[36] All of this incidentally supports the likelihood (suggested above) that women's ability to read probably lagged much less behind men's than their ability to write.

The remarkable relative improvement in female literacy rates in the Victorian period is attributable to changes in the education of girls and in female employment. By the 1860s in Scotland, outside the industrial areas, girls were being taught to write more often than previously, and, on the eve of the introduction of compulsory education, they were staying at school almost as long as boys and in some places longer. In England improvement may well have stemmed from an increased use of public elementary schools in which girls were more likely to be taught writing than in the working-class private schools, especially after the introduction of the Revised Code in the 1860s.

From the mid century the growth in middle-class demand for domestic servants may also have been a factor in this development – since employers preferred girls who had been to the voluntary or charity schools where, though they were taught to read and write, they were also (more significantly for employers) instructed in the virtues of obedience, cleanliness and morality and in the essentials of Christianity, and had not been coarsened by early employment in the factory or on the land. This encouraged working-class parents to send their daughters to such schools at a time when demand for young girls in some other kinds of work was falling. Certainly there is a positive correlation at county level in England and Wales between varying proportions of women employed in domestic service and proportions of bridal signatures. Counties with low proportions of middle-class households (as in the sparsely populated rural communities of Wales) tended to have fewer domestic servants and lower levels of female literacy.[37]

# 3

## SECONDARY AND HIGHER EDUCATION TO THE 1860s

### The Evolution of Secondary Schooling

Before the mid nineteenth century the concept of elementary and secondary schooling as sequential stages of education was undeveloped. In England and Wales it was usual to distinguish rather between 'middle-class' schooling (for the better-off) and 'elementary' schooling (for the working classes). In Scotland the tradition was for common schools not distinguished by level of instruction. Historians, however, have customarily used the term 'secondary' to refer to schooling of children from age 10 or so, as well as to the education of the middle and upper classes generally, and that convention is followed here.

Popular rhetoric in Scotland supported the ideal of a national system embracing education from the elementary level onwards. It was commonly held that all social classes should mix in the schools, that there should be no distinction in the kind of schooling enjoyed by rich and poor and that it should be possible for talented boys (though not girls) of all classes to proceed to university. Only in the largest towns did burgh schools provide a mainly secondary education; otherwise both parochial and burgh schools might teach at both primary and post-primary levels and send boys to university, while a good deal of university tuition overlapped what was taught to senior school pupils. This traditional pattern was suited particularly to a rural society, enjoying a common, religiously based, culture in which social differences were relatively small and where poor communications and sparse populations made a common local school acceptable. Industrialization and urbanization, however, brought greater social differentiation with, on the one hand, a mass of artisans and labourers with limited educational ambitions, and, on the other, a growing middle class desirous – for professional and social reasons – of specifically secondary and higher education for their off-spring separate from the schooling of the bulk of the working classes. Meritocratic elements of the traditional ideal were sustained into the twentieth century, but by the later eighteenth the pure democratic ideal of the past (though still generally acclaimed) had become a myth – not false, but an increasingly romanticized version of a more complex reality.[1]

In eighteenth-century Scotland there was a growth in academies offering (in contrast to the more traditional fare of the grammar or burgh schools) commercial, technical and other modern subjects. These were commonest in the cities and, though most were private establish-ments, some were established by town councils. From the early nine-teenth century middle-class pressure for the establishment of distinctly secondary schools grew. Only a handful of boarding schools on English lines were created in Scotland, for the Scottish aristocracy patronized English Public schools.[2] The bulk of the Scottish middle class, including professional parents, however, preferred local day schools. Reform thus often took the form of the amalgamation of burgh schools and acad-emies into loosely structured federal institutions (often called academies or high schools) under lightly exercised municipal control. These pro-vided considerable choice of courses from a broad classical, modern and commercial curriculum, and even embraced the use of private teachers. Lack of a standard curriculum and extensive parental choice contrasted strongly with English secondary schools.

Though they contained some working-class pupils, these schools were essentially middle-class. In Glasgow and Edinburgh proprietary acad-emies and private schools competed with the public high schools and a social hierarchy based on levels of fees emerged, but in most smaller towns the public academy served the whole of the middle class. At the same time schools which were purely elementary and predominantly working-class developed in the cities. The democratic ideal nevertheless survived, particularly in the rural parochial schools, and throughout the nineteenth century the drive for distinctly secondary (and thus middle-class-dominated) schools competed with loyalty to the traditional con-cept of the common school. In the later 1860s the Argyll Commission's report on secondary education found it lacking in quantity in the cities and in quality in other towns. Even in the burgh schools the vast majority of pupils went straight to commercial jobs and studied subjects related to these; only a minority studied the classics or mathematics. Out of eighty-two public schools supposedly teaching at secondary level only five were strictly 'secondary' – the rest presented 'a confusion of Infant, Primary, and Elementary Schools combined in one'. The commissioners thus supported middle-class demands for more specialized secondary and university education leading to formal qualifications which would give access to British career opportunities. The need for this was enhanced by the government's gradual imposition on Scotland of the Revised Code, putting pressure on parochial schools from the 1860s to concentrate on elementary education.[3]

Traditionally, secondary education in England and Wales in this period has been discussed by historians mainly in terms of the grammar and Public schools. Only recently has the enormous significance of middle-class private schooling, especially in urban areas, been acknowledged. Not until the latter half of the century did the slow reform of the grammar schools and the expansion of the Public schools (discussed below) result in a relative decline in private schooling and even then it remained significant. Before the mid nineteenth century a multitude of private schools of great variety dominated secondary schooling, and this is explored later in this section.[4]

The eighteenth-century grammar schools have been depicted by some as suffering decline in status and enrolments consequent on forsaking the classics for elementary tuition. Others have seen their decay to stem from statutes tying them to the classics and preventing adoption of the modern curriculum sought by the middle classes. Subsequent changes undertaken by the schools have been portrayed, on the one hand, as successful adjustment to combat financial difficulties and meet modern requirements, and on the other as a usurpation by the middle classes of free secondary education intended for the poor. Class interest was certainly significant in the changes which occurred, but such interpretations oversimplify complex developments.[5]

Already by the eighteenth century a handful of grammar schools had emerged as preserves of the aristocracy and the landed gentry. Offering a strictly classical education, these were boarding establishments recruiting fee-paying pupils nationally rather than locally. By the early nineteenth century these 'great' (or Public) schools included Eton, Harrow, Winchester, Charterhouse, Rugby, Westminster and Shrewsbury. By then, however, contrary to popular myth, the grammar schools as a whole were not confined to the teaching of the classics; nor was all tuition free. The statutes of those founded in the sixteenth and particularly the seventeenth and eighteenth centuries often permitted or required subjects additional to the classics to be taught. Curricular and other innovations were, moreover, often adopted by older foundations quite legally in the eighteenth and nineteenth centuries – particularly by masters and governors, but also by episcopal visitors, by permission of the Court of Chancery, or by private Act of parliament. Most commonly 'English' and commercial subjects or the 3 Rs were introduced – most of the Welsh grammar schools, for instance, were teaching modern subjects by the 1860s alongside the classics. The right to take fee-paying pupils was also often secured and was endorsed by a legal judgment of 1805 which laid down that subjects other than the classics might be taught to fee-payers so long as they were not supported from endowments for the classics. Even this restriction was diluted by an Act of 1840 which permitted a commercial curriculum to be supported by the endowment when a school's financial stability could not otherwise be maintained. Often, however, curricular changes were introduced over the years with debatable legality and without any formal permission being sought.[6]

The picture of universal decay of the grammar schools has been based partly on a rigid view of the desirability of an exclusively classical curriculum and partly on a debatable interpretation of the levels of enrolments compared with those in earlier times. Nevertheless, most grammar schools, founded to serve small towns or villages where a minority of boys of mixed social backgrounds could without difficulty share the same schoolroom, hardly met the needs of an increasingly socially stratified, urban, industrial population. By the early nineteenth century many were anachronisms. The Schools Inquiry (or Taunton) Commission, which reported on the grammar schools in the mid 1860s, found that of the 791 schools investigated, 50 were in abeyance and 340 had become in practice elementary schools. Since these latter were usually in rural places, where sons of farm labourers created no call for classical or indeed any secondary education, it might be argued that they had adapted themselves to changed circumstances rather than that they had simply decayed. Often, however, the instruction they provided was inferior to that of the public elementary schools.[7]

The remaining grammar schools exhibited little homogeneity. The view that declining middle-class support derived from their adherence to the classics is simplistic. Of the 791 noted above, 218 were classical

and 183 had a mixed curriculum.[8] Those which successfully maintained
a mixed classical and modern curriculum included a large group of
mainly urban schools with endowments substantial enough to fund the
legal processes necessary to secure permission to broaden their curricula, bring in fee-payers and thus cater for the professional and better-
off urban middle classes. At the same time, a smaller number of grammar schools succeeded in attracting well-off fee-paying parents precisely
because they offered the same kind of residential classical education as
the Public schools – whose ranks some joined as the century progressed.
The most highly educated teachers were virtually all classicists and
knowledge of classics was an attribute of élite status. As the nineteenth
century progressed, opportunities – in the professions and in the
armed, civil and colonial services – for boys with such an education
increased.[9]

Yet despite the successful changes made by some grammar schools, in
general they did not provide the secondary education demanded by the
middling ranks of the greatly expanded and increasingly affluent middle classes. In many parts of England, and especially in Wales, there
were insufficient of them, there was a mismatch between their location
and concentrations of likely pupils, and many were ill-housed. Trustees
and entrenched masters were often unwilling to initiate changes to
render their schools more acceptable, or lacked the financial means to
effect legal reform. There was widespread incompetence in administration and teaching, with masters legally difficult to remove, however old
or otherwise unsuitable. Indiscriminate free schooling for foundationers, moreover, created a social mix unpopular with the better-off
parents whose fee-paying capacity was essential to the financial viability
of any school seeking to give a good secondary education to more than a
handful of pupils.[10] Virtually none catered for girls.[11]

The discontent of better-off parents and of radical politicians with this
situation led to a strengthening of alternative forms of secondary schooling and of demands for grammar-school reform. In the eighteenth
century, as in Scotland, pressure for technical, scientific and commercial
education, together with modern languages and geography and history,
resulted in the spread of private institutions (often called academies)
providing such tuition (sometimes with the classics) and this development is discussed in Chapter 4. In the early nineteenth century the
Benthamites and others pressed for a modern non-classical education
for the middle classes and reform of the grammar schools to increase
opportunities for it – but with limited success. The better-off middle-

class parents began increasingly to favour the social cachet of a classical curriculum. Free of restrictive statutes private schools proved more flexible than the grammar schools. They were more open to innovation, offered greater curricular breadth and were thus more successful in meeting the aspirations of the bulk of middle-class parents. By the early nineteenth century not only were there more private schools for the middle classes than grammar schools, but they probably catered in aggregate for many more pupils. Moreover, as demand for secondary education increased, it was met largely by the proliferation of such private schools, which continued to dominate boys' secondary schooling until the mid nineteenth century.[12]

Private schools varied in size, quality, curricula and cost according to the social class of parents, vieing with the Public schools at one end of the scale and merging into the common day schools at the other. Since the grammar schools normally took only boys, private schools and governesses accounted for virtually all the education of middle-class girls. Yet while some girls' schools provided a liberal education (embracing modern languages, literature, grammar, history and geography, and sometimes even arithmetic and science), most tended to concentrate on decorative 'accomplishments' rather than academic instruction.[13]

John Roach has identified four overlapping categories of middle-class private schools. First, there were those owned and run by individuals entirely for private profit. These varied greatly in the curriculum offered and the social strata catered for, some providing a sound education, many an indifferent one. Those in towns sometimes took both boys and girls but most for older children were single-sex establishments. Secondly (and increasingly as the century progressed), boys' schools of a corporate nature were founded by groups of proprietors as joint-stock enterprises. Able to employ larger staffs they could provide a broader curriculum than schools run by individuals. Many of these establishments were day schools, found particularly in places without an effective grammar school. Most had a short life, but some which were boarding schools succeeded in establishing themselves as Public schools for the affluent. To these boys' schools may be added a few élite 'ladies' colleges', such as Queen's College, London and Cheltenham College for Young Ladies, which pioneered a more intellectual curriculum than the general run of female seminaries. Though affecting directly only a tiny minority of middle-class girls, they turned out some who became competent governesses and teachers in private schools. A third group comprised other corporate institutions for boys established by religious bodies, mainly Anglican but also nonconformist and Roman Catholic. These generally offered both classics and modern subjects and many eventually entered the ranks of the Public schools.[14]

Lastly there was a disparate group of corporate schools often known as middle-class schools. Of these, schools founded by Nathaniel Woodard and other schools known as 'county' schools were boarding establishments, usually Anglican in outlook, which provided a curriculum graded according to the social level of the parents, but mainly aimed at farmers' sons. A few of these (including, for example, Framlingham and West Buckland) eventually became Public schools. Others, catering mainly for the lower middle classes and, like many other private schools, offering a basically commercial education, included those established by groups of Anglicans and by the Established Church in association with its teacher training colleges, and in a few places secondary schools set up by mechanics' institutes.

A major development in the middle decades of the nineteenth century was the reform and expansion of what was becoming known as Public-school education. In the early nineteenth century the original seven 'great' (Public) schools (noted above) were not particularly prosperous. They were attacked for failure to teach modern subjects and science, but also for inefficient, often corrupt, financial and administrative practices, for poor discipline and moral tone and for unsavoury physical conditions. The landed classes whom they served were largely indifferent to these defects, but the advent of evangelically minded upper middle-class parents, enriched from business and professional activities, influenced change. Between the 1830s and 1860s, under ambitious and able heads, like Arnold of Rugby, the 'great' schools somewhat improved their administration, discipline and staff–pupil ratios, ameliorated living conditions and raised their moral and religious tone. In some cases they broadened their curriculum, especially to include mathematics, but the classics, dear to the aristocracy, gentry and schoolmasters, remained dominant, and were now accepted by the upper middle classes as the hallmark of an élite education.[15]

These achievements were publicized by the largely favourable report in 1864 of the Royal Commission (the Clarendon Commission) set up to investigate the seven 'great' boarding and two prestigious London day schools (St Paul's and Merchant Taylors'). While the Commission criticized the financial regimen of the schools as corrupt and the quality of their teaching and academic achievement as mediocre, it found such drawbacks to be far outweighed by the character-training provided. The prefectorial and house systems, the emphasis placed on organized games and the highly moral and religious ethos of the reformed schools were producing men of outstanding quality, well qualified to become leaders in British political and social life and to administer, protect and expand the Empire. The Commission suggested some broadening of the curriculum but was happy that classics should remain dominant.[16]

The subsequent Public Schools Act (1868) imposed sounder financial and administrative structures on the 'great' schools and abolished foundation places in the interest of internal social homogeneity, but made only very modest curricular changes to ensure some teaching of French, mathematics and science. It also incidentally endowed the seven schools with a distinct legal identity which they had not previously possessed, thus endorsing their claim to be an élite group and ensuring their position at the apex of a developing social hierarchy of secondary schools.[17] That these reforms also resulted, as has been suggested, in the 'separation of the public schools from those of all other classes ...[and] created an...entirely segregated system of education for the governing classes'[18] is only partly correct. In many ways (as will be discussed in Chapter 6) they became a model for English and Welsh secondary education generally as it expanded in the later nineteenth and the twentieth centuries.

Already by the 1860s the seven Clarendon boarding schools had become a minority among establishments recognized as Public schools. Over the previous three decades they had, as already noted, been joined by some leading grammar schools, some of the proprietary, denominational and middle-class schools and by a few outstanding private schools – all offering expensive residential schooling and a curriculum basically classical and humane (though with a somewhat broader curriculum than the seven) and mostly Anglican. Thus, in response to the demands of professional men, other affluent parents and the clergy for such an education, not a tiny isolated clique but a 'vast network of upper-class schools' was created.[19]

The significance of this development lies in the part which these schools played in the growing fusion of the landed and the new opulent upper middle classes into a larger, broader-based and more professional governing and social élite than had previously existed, thus avoiding class conflict. It ensured that the aristocracy and gentry were not worse educated than the professional and entrepreneurial classes and shared a common type of schooling based on the not unworthy ideal of the

Christian gentleman. The landed classes assimilated the competitive values and religious propensities of the middle classes and, as elaborated on in Chapter 6, were thus enabled, helped by background and connections not shared by the newcomers, to retain much of their social and political dominance down to the Great War as well as to gain entrance to the higher professions.[20]

The success of the Public boarding schools and the general expansion of private middle-class schools further damaged the grammar schools, many of which were left with pupils who sought only elementary or commercial education. This fuelled renewed demands that grammar-school endowments be used to expand effective secondary day schooling. In 1868 the Taunton Commission recommended the grading of grammar schools according to the social needs of the communities in which they were set. First grade schools would, like the Public schools, provide a mainly classical education to age 18 for children of the landed classes, the higher professions and wealthy industrialists as a preparation for the universities; second grade schools would serve lesser professional and businessmen's children to age 16 with a modern curriculum including Latin, mathematics and science, English literature and economics; and for the offspring of the lower middle and upper working classes, to age 14, third grade schools would teach history, geography, elementary mathematics and Latin or a foreign language. Free foundation places, the commission recommended, should be replaced by competitive bursaries.

Recognizing the particular needs of the lower middle classes for post-elementary schooling, the commissioners envisaged that most reformed grammar schools would be of the third grade. They recommended that endowments might be amalgamated to provide more viable institutions and that some endowments should be used to provide girls' secondary schools. This last was timely, for opportunities for female clerical and other workers were growing (civil service recruitment of women began in 1869), while other factors (discussed in Chapter 6) made it likely that more middle-class women than previously might have to earn their own keep.[21] The Endowed Schools Act of 1869 embraced these recommendations and established a central authority of three Endowed Schools Commissioners to prepare 'schemes' for the reform of existing endowments. The effect of this development is explored in Chapter 6.

Changes in the Public and grammar schools, both before and after the legislation of the late 1860s, particularly the swamping and marginalizing of foundationers by fee-paying day and boarding pupils and the eventual abolition of traditional free places, have been seen as marking a significant deprivation of working-class rights and an undesirable sub-version of endowments for the poor in the interests of the better-off.[22] But this is simplistic. Certainly the principle, upheld in the legislation, that costs of secondary education should generally be borne by parents or, if free, be through exhibitions based on merit, reflected Benthamite concern for the reform of outdated institutions and Victorian emphasis on competition and examinations. The abolition of foundation places in the seven Public schools, however, was of marginal significance since by 1861 of 2,293 pupils they accounted for only 342, many of whose education was not entirely free and who mostly came from compar-atively well-off families.[23]

As for the grammar schools, the term 'free' school' did not necessarily denote absence of all charges. Practice varied considerably. Usually only a handful of foundation pupils received free tuition, and they, like other pupils, were normally charged for subjects other than classics and per-haps also entrance fees. Thus the grammar school at Widnes in Che-shire was free to local children 'for instruction in English, reading and classics; but for teaching writing and arithmetic, mathematics and geo-metry the master [charged] 10s to £1 11s. 6d.'.[24] In some schools, more-over, despite the wording of the statutes, charges had always been levied on all pupils. In Lancashire some schools taught both classics and elementary subjects free, others charged for classics and not the 3 Rs, while some charged fees for elementary tuition.[25] Moreover, in some schools which, though founded for the classics, had become elementary schools, fees were commonly charged. Thus, by the early nineteenth century the amount of free education in the grammar schools was very limited and often confined legally (if not in fact) to tuition in the classics.

Again, the definition of 'poor', in school statutes, is frequently unclear. Though opposition to the abolition of free places was certainly invoked in the name of the poor, in reality such places were usually taken up not by the poor (if that meant the labouring class) but by children of the lower middle classes – tradesmen, shopkeepers, master craftsmen, clerical workers and the like, who valued the grammar schools for their social superiority over the public elementary schools. Their sons had been enjoying in the grammar schools an education, sometimes free, often of a higher elementary or commercial kind, away from labourers' children. They would have preferred the grammar schools to have moved further in this direction – hence their opposition to wealthier boarders and fee-payers and to a first grade curriculum.[26]

Moreover, if revision of curricular and charitable provisions from the later eighteenth century often appears to have overturned founders' intentions of providing poor local boys with a classical education, this does not necessarily indicate sinister motives. By the early nineteenth century such a combination was anachronistic: there was virtually no demand for a classical or mixed classical and modern curriculum from labouring parents, and free places for the classics went unfilled at a time when schools often needed greater fee income to function efficiently. Oftentimes choice had to be made as to which of the founders' intentions was to be upheld – a post-elementary curriculum or free tuition for the poor. If the latter, the schools would all have become elementary and often disappeared. Since many elementary charity schools for the poor had been founded in the eighteenth century, and in the early nineteenth century a whole system of public elementary schools for the working classes established (and, moreover, given government financial assistance), it was not unreasonable for the Court of Chancery to tend to uphold the basic classical curriculum while permitting fee-paying pupils to be taken. Nor was it unreasonable that later the Taunton commissioners took the view that the grammar schools should provide a truly secondary education and that free places for a handful were an anachronism unless awarded to children manifestly able to benefit from such an education. Here they were more solicitous for the talented working-class child than those opposing the abolition of the foundation places.

Pertinently, had the grammar schools remained free, teaching at a much lower academic level than did the Public schools, 'there would have been a wider and deeper division in English society' than in fact occurred.[27] Hand-wringing for confiscated rights of the poor not only ignores the reality of the situation but disguises the really significant educational deprivation that occurred – that of the lower middle classes, and this topic is pursued in Chapter 6.

## Higher Education

The traditional picture of eighteenth-century Oxford and Cambridge (henceforth where appropriate referred to as Oxbridge) as commu-

nities of largely frivolous upper-class students and well-paid idle teachers, dilatorily following a narrow classical curriculum, is somewhat
exaggerated. There was some conscientious teaching and learning, a
thriving cultural life outside the official curriculum and some attention
was given to science and particularly mathematics. Nevertheless, the
English universities were backwaters in national life, characterized by
dull and mechanical teaching, an absence of intellectual zeal and Anglican domination.[28] Their stagnation contrasted strongly with the state of
the essentially liberal and secular Scottish universities (in Glasgow,
Edinburgh, St Andrews and Aberdeen) which, unlike most European
universities, were flourishing, their student numbers almost trebling
during the eighteenth century.

Despite weaknesses stemming from an antiquated official curriculum
and regulations restrictive of change, poorly paid professors and admission of many very young students, Scottish universities in the eighteenth
century were the keystone of the Scottish Enlightenment. At its zenith in
the years 1750–80, this urban intellectual movement was manifested in
remarkable levels of attainment in philosophy, history, literature, economics, social theory and, especially, in medicine. From this last sprang
interest, within and outwith the universities, in other sciences and in the
application of science to agriculture, transportation and manufacturing
(a topic explored in Chapter 4). Unlike Oxbridge, Scottish universities
were national institutions, partly funded by the state, with students
more socially mixed, no religious barriers to admission and a profes-
soriate committed to promoting good teaching. Their interests linked
them to the professions and to the intellectual life of the Scottish
nation and of Europe generally. They were influential, too, in the
intellectual and economic development of Britain as a whole and served
as models and sources of staffing for the English and Welsh Dissenting
and other private academies, establishments more fully discussed in the
next chapter.[29]

By the early nineteenth century, like most European universities, the
Scottish universities combined provision of general liberal education
with training for the professions (law, medicine and the Church).
Oxbridge, however, still offered a narrow specialized curriculum, largely confined to the classics (and, at Cambridge, mathematics), to sons
of the landed classes and the Anglican clergy. Preparation for the professions was absent except in so far as the classical curriculum was
considered appropriate for holy orders and Public and grammar-school
teaching. Fellowships and student bursaries were usually tied to classics

and mathematics, encouraging the replication of a narrow curriculum in the schools. Expensive, with graduation open only to Anglicans, staffed wholly by clergy of the Established Church and with teaching often mediocre, Oxbridge continued to be largely irrelevant to the educational requirements of the entrepreneurial classes (which included many nonconformists) and indeed to the cultural and economic needs of the country at large. Even for the classes represented in the student body, the education purveyed was by no means essential for membership of the ruling élite, nor for a clerical career.[30]

In contrast, the more flexible Scottish universities not only provided professional training but were situated in large towns, had no residential requirements and charged fees which were consequently low. There were, too, numerous bursaries for the less well-off – who could enter directly from the parish schools. The Scottish universities catered for more students (per head of population) than any other country and had a much broader social intake than Oxbridge, which, at this time, contained no working-class and few middle-class students. Two-thirds of Cambridge students, 1800–49, were sons of landowners or clergy and over 90 per cent of Oxford students, 1752–1886, came from gentry, clerical and military backgrounds. Subsequent careers were in the same narrow mould. But one-third of Glasgow students in 1830 were working-class and by the 1860s nearly a quarter of Scottish university students were from the working classes as against about one-third from professional families.[31]

Nevertheless, as the Industrial Revolution brought greater fusion of English and Scottish economic and intellectual life and enlarged British opportunities for Scots, and as political and religious division affected the Scottish universities and professions, the Scottish Enlightenment faded, and by 1830 was over.[32] The popular nature of the Scottish universities and their continuing overlap with school education, moreover, made the development of specialist higher education more difficult. In the 1860s some 15 per cent of Scottish university students came direct from parish schools and the student body included a large number of adolescents aged 12 to 16 or so, many of whom still did not take degrees. There were many part-time students and much of the teaching was outdated, perfunctory and at an elementary level.[33] So, it has been suggested, though somewhat simplistically, had the ancient English universities been abolished in 1850 the impact on national life would have been infinitesimal, and if the Scottish universities had suffered the same fate they would have been missed chiefly as secondary schools.[34]

Some significant developments in British higher education, however, did occur before 1870. First, there were modest changes in the Scottish universities. Stricter examination and degree regulations were adopted and attempts were made to extend the numbers specializing in science (though with limited success). The introduction of an entrance examination was confined to medical students in this period but became general later in the century as more widely available secondary schooling reduced the need for relatively low-level instruction in the universities. At all events, by the 1860s, few students entered younger than age 15.[35]

Secondly, creation of a sound examination structure at Oxbridge in the late eighteenth and early nineteenth centuries encouraged higher academic standards, though resulting in even greater concentration on classics at Oxford and mathematics at Cambridge, and some decline in science teaching at Oxford. As in Scotland, proposals for university reform created great controversy. Internal pressure from liberal dons for modern subjects and stronger university control over colleges to promote funding of engineering and science, was supported externally by Utilitarians and others. In 1848 Cambridge established new degrees in natural science and moral science (embracing history and law) and in 1850 Oxford set up schools of law, modern history and science. But further change was limited by strong internal opposition from conservatives antagonistic to research and to the introduction of new subjects, who defended concentration on classics and the financial dominance of individual colleges.

It required legislation to effect more substantial reform. Acts of 1854 and 1856 made Oxbridge government more democratic, enabled nonconformists to graduate (though not until 1871 to become Fellows), opened to competition bursaries previously confined to certain families or localities, further reformed the examination structure to improve academic standards and made administrative changes to facilitate the financing of scientific and modern studies. The ground was thus prepared for significant change, though it came slowly, and the effective transformation of Oxbridge, and any substantial increase in numbers reading science, took place mainly after 1870. Nevertheless, success in competitive bursaries required expensive schooling, serving to exclude the few less well-off students who had previously gained entry.[36]

A third development was the foundation of other institutions of higher education and professional training in England. In the provinces, Durham University (established 1832) and Owens College,

Manchester (1851), however, had only limited success. They were insufficiently differenced from secondary schools to achieve much prestige and, though their curricula included such subjects as science, modern languages and economics, their general degree schemes attracted few takers. They imitated the intellectual attitudes and aspirations of Oxbridge and failed to meet the needs of local industry sufficiently to attract the entrepreneurial classes. Durham did teach engineering and science but was predominantly a theological training college.[37] In addition, the expansion of public elementary schooling led from the second quarter of the nineteenth century to the foundation of institutions of modest intellectual standing for the training of teachers. In Scotland all the main colleges of this kind between 1845 and 1905 were in the hands of the churches. South of the border the British and Foreign School Society established a few excellent institutions (the best known being that at Borough Road, London), but the Anglican Church controlled most colleges. By 1840 there were six diocesan colleges, by 1861 twenty, plus three run by the National Society (including St Mark's, Chelsea).[38]

Much more significant in the development of British higher education was the foundation in London of University College (1828), a secular Benthamite institution, and of its Anglican rival, King's College (1831). These sought not to ape Oxbridge but to offer an alternative, providing a broad curriculum and professional training. University College, where there was influence from Scotland and from Jefferson's University of Virginia, offered to a broad spectrum of the middle classes a spread of traditional subjects plus the natural and social sciences and training for careers in medicine, architecture, the law and engineering. King's, too, embraced a similarly broad curriculum and preparation for the professions, including engineering, medicine and the Church. These rival institutions were brought together under the umbrella of the University of London, founded in 1836 as an examining body. By 1851 over eighty colleges in Britain and the Empire were affiliated to the University and from 1858 its degree examinations were opened to individual external students. London also became the model for the later provincial university colleges, an important ingredient of which were the local medical schools (founded in the 1820s and 1830s), which became affiliated to the University.[39]

London was associated, too, with the development of higher education for women. They were admitted to lectures at King's and University College from the start, but the absence of good girls' secondary schooling and contemporary concepts of decorum limited the practice.

Consequently the teaching staff of those colleges extended their assistance to two female institutions – Queen's College, Harley Street (Anglican in nature and originally founded, 1848, to train governesses) and Bedford College, London (1849), a non-denominational establishment. In this period, however, both these institutions were essentially academic secondary schools.[40]

Despite these developments, a structure of higher education suited to a growing industrial urban economy was still lacking in Britain in the 1860s. In particular, there was insufficient provision for professional training (except in medicine) and for women generally. Moreover, in England, increases in the numbers of university graduates failed to match population growth: graduations in 1855–65 were approximately one-third of those in the early eighteenth century – though, it has been suggested, the country may thus have avoided the troubles the continent suffered in 1848 partly at the hands of graduates for whom there was no employment.[41] Significant expansion of university education had to wait until later in the century, and this is considered in Chapter 6.

# 4

---

# EDUCATION, SCIENCE AND INDUSTRIALIZATION, 1750s–1850s

## Elementary Education, Skill and Industrial Expansion

Social scientists have suggested that for a national economy to achieve self-sustaining industrial growth, some 30–40 per cent of its population need to be literate, and that the British Industrial Revolution exemplifies this: literacy rates in both England and Scotland had crossed that threshold by 1750.[1] Such a vaguely defined concept is, however, of dubious value when applied to British economic expansion in this period. It is not evident why, even if applicable to twentieth-century economies (which is uncertain), it should pertain to eighteenth- and early nineteenth-century conditions. Evidence for measuring economic growth rates in that period is often less than adequate and the chronology of industrialization contentious, and while signature evidence is useful for spatial and chronological comparison of levels of elementary education, it is rudimentary as an absolute measure (Chapter 2). Moreover, by the mid eighteenth century most nations in north-west Europe had literacy levels as good as or better than Britain's without experiencing an industrial revolution.[2]

This does not, of course, rule out the spread of elementary education as a factor in economic growth, and the relationship between the two is a matter of current debate. Those historians supporting a positive connection stress that the Industrial Revolution embraced commercial, financial and transportation revolutions, and increased the proportion of jobs for which literacy was necessary or useful. Without literate managers, supervisors and technicians in manufacturing and suitably educated human capital for engineering, transport, commerce and financial services, economic growth could not have been sustained.[3] The advantages for employers of a pool of talent on which to draw, combined with workers' ambitions for advancement, it is argued, stimulated the creation of a larger body of literate workers than was actually required at any particular time and oiled the wheels of expansion. Thus, improvements in general levels of education went hand in hand with industrialization. Decline in the proportions of literates in the early years of the Industrial Revolution (noted in Chapter 2) was not caused by industrialization as such but by a temporary inability of school facilities to cope with population increase and redistribution. That decline was halted as the economy grew and school places, not least in industrial towns, expanded. By the 1850s literacy levels were above those of the 1740s and their improvement from about 1800 coincided with the full effects of large-scale factory production.[4]

On the other hand there is supportive evidence for a more pessimistic scenario. Even some of the leaders of the Industrial Revolution, such as James Brindley, Joseph Locke, James Nasmyth and Joseph Whitworth, though skilled craftsmen, were virtually uneducated, and there is every reason to suppose that the British Industrial Revolution was achieved with a workforce extensively and increasingly illiterate. The vast bulk of jobs in all types of manufacturing and in mining and transport did not require literacy, and educational backwardness was particularly associated with those in occupations in expanding industries.[5] Moreover, the need for literacy in supervisory and managerial jobs has probably been exaggerated. Some mine managers, for instance, were completely illiterate and owners of small mines often barely schooled. Similarly many successful mine contractors and agents, controlling hundreds of men, could not read or write and were unable to understand a plan. Even in the 1860s and 1870s many textile masters and foremen were quite unlettered.[6]

Existing school facilities, like other services in expanding industrializing towns and districts in Britain, suffered dislocation at the same time as opportunities for child labour multiplied in a great variety of occupations. Sunday, evening and factory schools provided part-time education where previously day schooling had been more common. As has been illustrated in Chapter 2, surveys of the distribution of schooling and the regional incidence of literacy show a strong tendency for industrial centres and areas of mining and domestic industry to have higher proportions of illiterates and lower proportions of population at day school and to rely more on Sunday schools than was so in non-industrial towns and districts.[7] Even in Scotland, where the national levels of school attendance and literacy were high, illiteracy among factory children in Glasgow and other Scottish industrial towns was as extensive as in the English cotton districts.[8]

Moreover, the rise in literacy levels for England and Wales (measured by marriage signatures) between the 1750s and 1840 was very modest – only 8 percentage points. This suggests that continuing industrialization occurred without further substantial overall advances in basic educational standards.[9] Indeed, between the 1750s and the 1830s, literacy levels in most industrial and mining areas in northern and midland England experienced periods of either stagnation or actual deterioration. For instance, signature rates in the Lancashire–Cheshire cotton belt were lower in the 1830s than in the 1750s.[10] At Ashton-under-Lyne they fell from 56 per cent in the 1750s to 32 per cent in 1791–1800 and to 10 per cent in the 1830s, moving a contemporary to observe that 'if writing...is to be considered a criterion of the education of a people, verily the inhabitants of this town are in a pitiable condition: and what makes the matter worse...[is] that we are in a state of rapid retrogression'. It was a retrogression which may also have taken place in parts of Scotland. In Paisley almost the whole population was allegedly literate in 1807; by 1820 three thousand children and many adults in that town were illiterate.[11]

Significantly, the proportions of illiterates among male textile workers, potters, metal workers and miners – the four leading trades associated with the Industrial Revolution – were considerably greater than among men in traditional crafts, but those, too, were affected. Among both skilled craftsmen and those in expanding factory, workshop and transportation occupations, proportions of illiterates rose over the period from the 1750s to the early decades of the nineteenth century.[12] Falling literacy levels in a community reflected both influxes of illiterates and, as noted in Chapter 2, a generational decline as traditional craftsmen suffered from factory competition and were obliged to put their children to work rather than, as previously, to school.

Demand for child labour increased into the 1850s. The putting out of some processes by the factories to workers outside the jurisdiction of the Factory Acts accounted for some of this, and the expansion of labour-intensive domestic industry was also significant. In the traditional hosiery, lace, straw-plait and gloving industries of the rural midlands, East Anglia and the south-west, levels of child employment in the mid nineteenth century sometimes exceeded those in the northern factory counties. This was reflected in poor school attendance figures and abysmally low literacy levels: over the period 1839–45, Bedfordshire and Hertfordshire, with no factories but extensive cottage industry, had higher proportions of illiterate spouses than Lancashire with its concentration of cotton mills.[13] Child labour was encouraged on the one hand by parental poverty and on the other by the relatively high child wages available in times of prosperity. In industrial areas of all kinds the opportunity cost of education was thus raised and demand for schooling negatively affected, the more so since much schooling failed to produce a level of education of practical use in the workplace.[14]

Not only did most jobs in the expanding economy not require literacy, but recent research suggests that there was no marked rise in proportions of the English workforce engaged in occupations in which literacy was an advantage or a necessity: commerce, the professions and the running of large-scale agriculture. It has been estimated that, as late as 1841, only 4.9 per cent of men and 2.2 per cent of women in England and Wales were in jobs strictly requiring literacy, proportions probably no higher than in the eighteenth century. Half the men in employment and one-quarter of the women were in jobs where literacy was unlikely to have been of use.[15] The intermediate category – those in jobs where literacy, if not essential, may have been useful – undoubtedly included very many who were illiterate or made no use of reading and writing.[16] Even relatively advanced economies could operate with few literates: as late as 1901 clerks formed only 4 per cent of the English workforce.[17] The conclusion must be that, while the contribution to economic growth of the spread of basic literacy in the general population must have been positive, it was not a central causal factor in the British Industrial Revolution.[18]

Elementary schooling, however, probably did contribute to economic development in indirect ways, particularly in creating a society more receptive of change and in breaking down the isolation of hitherto backward and conservative communities. It is likely to have facilitated the spread of information on new techniques and processes, the availability of commodities, market outlets and employment opportunities. Geographical and occupational mobility was thus enhanced and the allocation of human resources optimized.[19] Again, the ordered atmosphere of the schoolroom and the habits and attitudes of mind instilled by schoolteachers may have played a significant part in facilitating the transition from the unsupervised work environment of the independent handicraftsman and cottage industry to the disciplined regularity of time-driven cooperative labour on the shop floor and from the seasonal and occupational variety of farm life to the monotony of machine production.

Many employers attested that schooled employees were more reliable, more amenable to reason, and more disciplined in working practices and personal behaviour than the uneducated.[20] 'Generally speaking,' a report on Monmouthshire in 1846 declared, 'the most intelligent workmen are found by the masters to be the best disposed and most easily guided . . . Good schools will bring to the employers who support them their own reward.'[21] Most public elementary schools of all kinds, and especially those run by mine and factory owners,[22] were indeed characterized by rigid organization and teaching methods biased towards rote learning and repetition, and backed by rewards and punishments. It is not surprising that the rules for a Yorkshire Sunday school in 1815 were said to 'resemble nothing so much as Ambrose Crowley's regulations for the operation and management of his iron works'.[23] The training given in punctuality, cleanliness, regularity, diligence, moral integrity and obedience were of greater value to many employers than ability to read and write. Indeed, one eighteenth-century Scottish schoolmaster accepted that his task was in part 'to reconcile the lowest classes . . . to the fatigues of constant labour and . . . servile employment . . . when young'.[24] At a more general level this training helped to minimize crime, and political and social unrest, so helping to create a beneficial environment for business activity.[25]

The contribution to economic development of skills learned outside the schoolroom also deserves consideration. A Royal Commission in the 1860s did indeed distinguish between practical skill and schooling: many illiterate or semi-literate men were highly skilled and well paid, possessing a body of knowledge learnt at work.[26] The part played in industrial expansion by such skills is, however, controversial.[27] Some historians, following contemporary critics such as Ure and Engels, argue that machine production replaced skilled craftsmen by semi-skilled or unskilled factory hands supervised by a comparatively few skilled foremen. Thus initial industrialization adversely affected the possession of both literacy and practical skills, at the cost of much human misery but without detracting from the progress of the Industrial Revolution.[28] Other scholars, however, while admitting that factory competition destroyed some handicraft skills, follow Adam Smith in stressing that the division of labour which characterized the new production methods led to the development of surprisingly high levels of skill in workpeople. This was so much the case, it is argued, that it can no longer be alleged that British factories by 1830 operated with a largely unskilled (as opposed to illiterate) labour force. Moreover, industrialization created a host of new labour-intensive practical skills, as hand and steam technologies, representing concurrent phases of capitalist growth, fed on each other's activities. The Industrial Revolution destroyed the need for some skills and increased the need for others. At all events, many working-class parents recognized that putting their children to work at ages when they could most readily acquire occupational skills was economically more beneficial to them than a smattering of letters. Early introduction to labour was regarded as a form of apprenticeship for a lifelong occupation – a kind of education more useful than the ABC. In many cases it must also have been of greater benefit to their employers and thus to the economy of the time.[29] That greater significance attached to skills learned through experience or apprenticeship than in formal education is exemplified at a higher level by the contribution to new technologies made by some leading engineers of the day – such as Joseph Clement, Joseph Locke, George Stephenson, James Nasmyth and Joseph Whitworth – and this is discussed in the next section.[30]

## Science, Technology and Innovation

If the contribution of the spread of reading and writing in the mass of the population to industrial expansion is doubtful, the role played by more specialized knowledge appears, on the face of it, stronger – but this again is a matter of controversy. Certainly by 1700 England was regarded as a leading scientific nation. The eighteenth century brought the Scottish Enlightenment, in which science became an integral part of public culture, and in Britain generally a growing and widespread interest in science and its economic potential found institutional expression. The Royal Society, founded in 1660 to promote the application of technology to industry, was concerned in the eighteenth century with the economic potential of steam power. Likewise the Society for the Encouragement of Arts, Manufactures and Commerce (later the Royal Society of Arts), founded in 1754 specifically to encourage technical innovation in agriculture and industry, and the Royal Institution (founded 1799) sought to disseminate knowledge of science, conduct experiments and act as clearing houses for innovatory ideas on technology and the practical application of science.[31]

Outside London, similar institutions emerged in the Scottish cities and English provincial towns, most of them professing interest in the application of science to practical purposes. A member of a Manchester society, for instance, commended 'the happy art... of connecting together liberal science and commercial industry'.[32] The Lunar Society of Birmingham, which has been described as 'an informal technological research organisation', was especially interested in steam, transport improvements, metallurgy and scientific instruments.[33] The more serious of these societies had members who were also Fellows of the Royal Society, had links with the Society of Arts or were sometimes members, too, of other provincial societies. Indeed, these voluntary organizations formed a national network, linked by personal connections, correspondence, visits and so on. They acted as agents for the dissemination of scientific and technical information and were used by scientists to publicize their researches. Particularly strong in the manufacturing towns, their membership included local industrialists as well as scientists: prominent manufacturers, such as Matthew Boulton, James Watt and Josiah Wedgwood, and the scientists Joseph Priestley, Erasmus Darwin and James Keir were members of the Lunar Society.[34] Most societies built up libraries and disseminated knowledge of science by means of discussions, demonstrations, experiments and lectures, some open to the public.[35]

In addition, in the provinces, inns were sometimes venues for gatherings to discuss scientific matters, and London coffee houses 'rivalled the Royal Society as locus for scientific discussion' and experimentation, some spawning scientific associations. Societies of a more popular kind than the Lunar Society and its like also grew up, some sponsoring public lecture courses, and by 1850 there were over one thousand associations for promoting technical and scientific knowledge in Britain with a membership of at least 200,000.[36] In Scotland, teachers in the universities, institutions central to the Enlightenment and to the cultural life of the cities, were active (particularly in Edinburgh, Glasgow and Aberdeen) in philosophical societies, and did much to promote popular interest in science. The Royal Society of Edinburgh had a particular interest in geology and attracted landowners interested in mining. Anderson's Institution, founded in Glasgow in 1796 to promote links between science and local industry, provided adult artisans with scientific instruction, and was followed by the Edinburgh School of Arts (1821) where James Nasmyth taught mathematics and chemistry. From the 1820s mechanics' institutes, aimed at disseminating science to skilled artisans, spread from Scotland throughout Britain, numbering over seven hundred by 1851, with concentrations in industrial areas.[37]

General interest in science and technology was also stimulated from the latter half of the eighteenth century by itinerant lecturers who sought to demonstrate, often with the aid of apparatus, how the principles of science might be applied to practical matters. Some of these men were purely popularizers, others also inventors, skilled instrument makers and clockmakers, interested in mechanical devices. They included, too, men of greater distinction: Fellows of the Royal Society, masters of academies and engineers. One, George Birkbeck, was professor of natural philosophy at Anderson's Institution and associated with the foundation in London of University College and the London Mechanics' Institute. Another, Adam Walker, who travelled widely in Scotland, Ireland and the north of England, lecturing on mechanics, chemistry, electricity, magnetism, hydrostatics and so on, was an inventor and engineering consultant.[38]

Clearly stimulated by the expansion of trade and industry, the proliferation of scientific and technical publications from the eighteenth century provides another indication of the widespread interest in science and its application. To textbooks, technical journals and serious monographs were added encyclopedias and dictionaries of arts and sciences. Bookshops grew in number and subscription libraries and book clubs included scientific and technical works at a time when accessible public libraries were few.[39]

The developments in formal education which contributed to the growth of a technological and scientific culture took place largely outside traditional institutions. In England, science was taught informally at Oxbridge to interested students, the universities had links with the Royal Society, there were chairs in pure science, mathematics and (at Cambridge) in engineering, and alumni included scientists and engineers. But science never became an integral part of degree courses in this period and interest flagged considerably in the early nineteenth century, with science chairs being filled by classicists and theologians.[40] Similarly, the English and Welsh grammar and Public schools provided little science teaching and the Scottish burgh schools neglected it almost completely into the 1860s.[41]

As at Oxbridge, however, mathematics was taught in these schools and some of them taught modern languages, accountancy and technical subjects, such as mensuration and navigation. More significantly, the eighteenth century saw the emergence in England and Wales of institutions, known as academies, straddling what today would be regarded as secondary and tertiary education. These, together with some other private schools, provided a broader education than the grammar schools, adding to classics and modern subjects, commercial and technical subjects such as surveying, mechanics, hydraulics, machine drawing, mensuration, hydrostatics, optics and architecture. Some specialized in mathematics or (for future sailors) navigation and astronomy, and many academies also taught pure science. Among these were the so-called Dissenting academies, established to train nonconformist clergy and, since Oxford and Cambridge excluded non-Anglicans, to provide advanced education for lay dissenters.[42] These establishments could boast of some outstanding teachers, among them men with strong interests in science and technology. Joseph Priestley, for example, taught chemistry and physics at the Warrington academy and Abraham Rees, of the Hackney academy, produced an encyclopedia of science and technology, while the academy at Hoxton, London, had three FRSs on its staff.[43] The curricula of these institutions were attractive to middle-class parents generally, and the Dissenting academies were attended by Anglican as well as nonconformist youths, particularly those seeking careers in engineering, industry and commerce.

In eighteenth-century Scottish burghs, too, specialized education on such subjects as accountancy and navigation became increasingly available.[44] More significantly the Scottish universities had much stronger interests in science than Oxford and Cambridge. Indeed, Thomas Jefferson in 1789 attested that in science 'no place in the world can pretend to competition with Edinburgh'.[45] Natural science was firmly established at Aberdeen in the 1750s while Glasgow and Edinburgh universities were major centres for medicine from which developed the study of chemistry, geology and other sciences. The Enlightenment was characterized by an interest in the application of science to fisheries, agriculture, transportation and industry, and the Scottish universities, in stark contrast with Oxbridge, forged links with manufacturing industry. Public lectures were aimed especially at those engaged in industry and at Glasgow attracted local industrialists. Over the century beginning in 1740 some 40 per cent of Glasgow undergraduates came from industrial and commercial backgrounds (some from England) and many alumni had successful careers in commerce and industry. In Aberdeen courses were developed which were more modern and utilitarian than in other British universities and at Glasgow Joseph Black (whose connection with James Watt is well known) developed a special interest in steam and the application of science to industry.[46]

That this ferment of interest in science and its practical application coincided with the upsurge of technological innovation associated with British industrialization, has led some historians to argue that advances in scientific knowledge must have been 'related somehow, to the... industrial revolution'.[47] Certainly from the mid eighteenth century there was a remarkable upsurge of industrial innovation. The proliferation of patents, however dubious as an absolute measure of innovative activity, was too extensive to be denied as some evidence of that,[48] and, as every schoolboy used to know, manufacturing output in key sectors was greatly enhanced by new machines and by steam power. But the part played by science in the Industrial Revolution remains highly controversial. It is, in fact, difficult to establish with certainty either that economic circumstances stimulated science-based innovation or that technological improvements were driven by a growth in scientific knowledge.[49]

It is true that some contemporaries believed that industrial advance was the fruit of applied science.[50] Credence is given to such a view by the enthusiasm with which scientists, tutors in the Dissenting academies and the Scottish universities, itinerant lecturers and scientific societies all sought to investigate and debate how science might be harnessed to the needs of industry. It is supported, too, by the plentiful evidence of personal intercourse between industrialists, inventors and men of science, and by the interest taken by leading manufacturers and engineers in the findings of pure scientists.[51]

Much of the case made by historians for a primary role for science in the Industrial Revolution rests on the accumulation of evidence of this kind. It is, however, at best largely inferential: existence of intent and interest are not enough to establish a direct link. Many branches of science in this period were underdeveloped and characterized by 'prevailing amateurism'.[52] Consequently attempts to apply science for industrial purposes were largely misdirected, and there are strong reasons for doubting that scientific theory made any major impact on technical advance or industrial development before the mid nineteenth century.[53]

The Royal Society's interest in practical science withered in the eighteenth century, its record comparing unfavourably with its French equivalent, the Académie des Sciences. Neither it nor the Society of Arts can claim any part in the great inventions of the Industrial Revolution, nor indeed in any technical innovation really significant to industry or agriculture. The part played by the Dissenting academies has also been exaggerated. Many were never equipped to teach science effectively and where the academies did advance scientific knowledge it was mostly in astronomy, electricity, natural history and physiology – areas with no bearing on the technology of the day. By 1800, regarded as seats of radicalism, they were out of favour. Many had ceased to exist, while the remainder survived mainly as theological colleges. Similarly in the first half of the nineteenth century, as the Scottish Enlightenment waned, there was a decline in the quality of instruction in science and mathematics in the Scottish universities. As for the philosophical societies, the Lunar Society was moribund by 1800 and soon disappeared, while physical science ceased to be central to the interests of local philosophical societies generally and, as the mid nineteenth century approached, of establishments like the mechanics' institutes. The undoubted stimulus to higher education in science, engineering and medicine engendered by University College and King's College, London from about 1830, came too late to affect the Industrial Revolution.[54]

Another reason for doubting the significance of interest in and knowledge of pure science as a significant causal ingredient of the British Industrial Revolution lies in the fact that Britain was not unique in this respect. Scientific knowledge was not easily restricted by national frontiers and many European nations shared Britain's knowledge and interest in science. Yet they failed to industrialize as quickly or as effectively. France, in particular, matched or surpassed Britain in progress in pure science, possessing scientists of high calibre interested in the industrial application of science. Moreover, France had scientific societies and institutions where businesmen and scientists mixed, and there was government support for scientific research and a state-promoted system of technical schools and advanced technological institutions. This official interest was not matched in Britain, where government support for science was directed mainly at botanical and geological reseach. France could boast, too, of a wide diffusion of scientific knowledge, an advanced chemical industry and as significant a record as Britain in invention and of scientific discovery of potential industrial utility.[55] Yet 'no correlation [is discernible there]...between the areas of the greatest progress in industry and in science', except perhaps with chemistry, though even that is doubtful.[56]

Many historians now consider that technical advances in the important sections of the economy owed little if anything to scientific theory
and that for the period before 1850 technological improvement was
almost entirely the achievement of technicians and craftsmen.[57] It is well
known that the early textile inventions and steam power were the fruit
of empiricism, and the view that Watt's separate condenser was influenced by the formulation of the concept of latent and specific heat by
Joseph Black at Glasgow University is no longer accepted.[58] Again, the
expansion of the chemical industry and the application of chemicals in
the textile industry probably owe less in this period to chemical theory
than was once thought. The use of chlorine in bleaching and the
production of synthetic soda for the cotton industry were both the result
of empirical investigation, and, anyway, sources of natural soda were
plentiful.[59] Similarly, glass production benefited from the application of
steam power and from other technical innovations rather than from
chemical theory, and most of the fruitful innovations in the pottery
industry were based on trial and error. Though Josiah Wedgwood
used scientific terminology, his work on colours and glazes was essentially empirical. Indeed, neither the work of Lavoisier, the initiator of
the chemical revolution, nor that of Dalton on atomic theory, which did
so much to make chemistry a true science, were of any direct or
immediate industrial utility.[60]

It is doubtful, too, whether before the mid nineteenth century the
expansion of agriculture, necessary to feed the burgeoning industrial
population, owed anything to chemistry, while scientific knowledge
played little part in the transport revolution or in developments in the
iron and steel industry. Mining of the day had only limited links with
geological research, which was inspired more by biblical controversies
over the age of the earth than the potentialities of coal production, and
the absence of a precision engineering industry prevented advances in
the theory of ballistics being utilized in gun founding.[61]

Technological advance then owed more to skilled craftmanship and
innovative empiricism than directly to pure science. Britain's technicians
might lack theory but were skilled and willing to experiment. Thus
a visiting German physicist in 1780 found English mechanics lacking in any scientific knowledge yet able to construct machines 'so
excellently'.[62] Britain had had no very obvious advantages over France
in scientific knowledge or economic resources, but, unlike scientific
knowledge, technical skill on a large scale was not readily exportable.
It is likely that the widespread superior skill of Britain's craftsmen and

entrepreneurs was an important reason for Britain being first to industrialize – at a time when British manufacturers were spared the negative influence of the French social, bureaucratic and political system and a disruptive revolution.[63] France lacked a body of technicians of the calibre available in Britain and lagged behind in relevant inventive activity. Its industries developed more slowly and even then did so by acquiring technologies developed elsewhere, mostly in Britain, and with the help of foreign technicians, again often from Britain.[64]

The significance of advances in scientific knowledge in Britain in the eighteenth and early nineteenth centuries lay not in their impact on initial industrialization, but in the basis they provided for later developments. In the later nineteenth century, when new industries needed the direct input of scientific knowledge, science did begin to contribute directly to economic activity. But if pure science had little or no direct impact on industrial expansion in the period before 1850, the culture it engendered did have an indirect influence. The scientific outlook in this period proved more important than scientific knowledge, encouraging the easy diffusion of ideas, attitudes and techniques. In promoting the spread of an attitude which rejected the conservatism of custom and embraced enquiry, it stimulated innovation. Curiosity about the material world and realization of the potential of innovation thus helped to create economic growth.[65]

Again, though the successful empirical innovations of the day were not based on the application of scientific theory, neither were they normally the accidental fruits of uninformed tinkerings. Rather they were achievements of highly skilled craftsmen and mechanics using the scientific method of rational analysis of problems, observation and experimentation. This was not research based on scientific theory but it was technological research influenced by scientific practice. From science was learned, too, the need for precise measurement, the value of quantitative data in providing generalizable principles and the utilization of scientific devices like the hydrometer and thermometer.[66]

Historians who have awarded scientific knowledge a significant role in the Industrial Revolution have done so largely by blurring the distinction between applied science and technology. Though it is debatable not only whether technology was a necessary ingredient of the Industrial Revolution but also whether it was sufficient in itself to induce other necessary factors, certainly the impact on the economy of technical training and knowledge is likely to have been much greater than that of education in pure science.[67] It is in this sphere, directly relevant to machinery in manufacturing, mining and transportation, that the Dissenting and other academies and the itinerant lecturers, with their emphasis on technical subjects and mechanical devices, were most important. Again, as Adam Smith stressed in 1776, mathematics, too, was valuable in many industrial trades, and was especially important in the techniques of engineering, industrial design, mining, surveying, navigation and instrument-making. It was taught extensively in England and Wales in the academies, middle-class private schools and modernizing grammar schools and in Scotland in the academies, larger burgh schools and universities.[68] Some of the great engineers and inventors (Samuel Crompton and John Rennie, for instance) had a formal education in mathematics and, though unnecessary for the bulk of operatives, mathematics was an essential basis for subjects like machine drawing, geometry and mechanics which were valuable to the numerous millwrights, wheelwrights, mechanics, clockmakers and the like, whose cumulative innovations contributed greatly to mechanical breakthroughs in industry, mining and transportation.[69] Moreover, since the Industrial Revolution embraced a commercial and entrepreneurial revolution, mathematics and allied subjects such as accountancy were significant for managers and other leaders in trade and finance, as well as those in manufacturing.

### Social and Religious Aspects of Scientific and Entrepreneurial Culture

In recent years some historians have sought to interpret the spread of scientific culture in the eighteenth and nineteenth centuries as inspired by social and political motives rather than economic ones, while others have linked religious attitudes to child-rearing with economic growth. Thus some scholars have depicted science in this period as primarily a consumer good, providing a fashionable focus for intellectual and social intercourse attractive to progressive elements in divers walks of life and for various reasons.[70] The national and provincial philosophical societies were meeting places, it is pointed out, not only for industrialists and scientists but for the better-off intelligentsia generally. The Royal Society had far more 'gentlemen' members than serious scientists and the membership list of the Society of Arts reads 'like a cross-section of mid-eighteenth century society', embracing dukes, admirals, bishops and judges as well as actors, booksellers, clockmakers and industrialists. The membership of the Edinburgh Philosophical Society was dominated by professional men and wealthy landowners rather than merchants or industrialists, and evinced no interest in manufacturing.[71] A disinterested concern for the advancement of scientific knowledge generally was exhibited also in the foundation between 1768 and 1830 of the Linnean, Zoological, Astronomical, Geological and Geographical societies, the activities of none of which were directly pertinent to the economy. Many provincial scientific societies were likewise concerned primarily with aspects of science which had no industrial relevance.[72] Numerous society members were, moreover, as or more attracted by literary, theological and historical matters as science. William Roscoe of the Lunar Society, for instance, was primarily interested in the Italian renaissance.[73] Similarly, the itinerant lecturers included those who catered for literary tastes or presented science as a form of spectacular entertainment.[74]

Philosophical societies and other cultural associations and adult education institutions were favoured in many industrial and other towns by an emerging élite of manufacturers, traders, professional men and other middle-class citizens of progressive outlook as a means of attaining social respectability, prestige and local influence. They provided access for socially marginal groups to polite society and entry to the local élite, as well as to an entertaining intellectual life, otherwise lacking in often grimy industrial environments. Moreover, science was not an essential focus: in industrial Leeds attempts to set up scientific societies had little success, partly because the same social objectives were achieved through activities relating to art, music and literature.

Again, for many in the nineteenth century, interest in science and technology was fashionably modern. It represented not just material change but progress – a vehicle for a new socio-economic order challenging the conservatism of existing establishments and attracting those of a radical political or religious disposition. The Lunar Society was adversely affected by popular reaction against a perceived leftish political tendency within its ranks, and members of philosophical societies were certainly active in seeking parliamentary reform and the abolition of the Test Acts, and often belonged to the class opposing the repression of the American colonists and initially sympathetic to French revolutionary ideas. The decline of popular provincial scientific culture by 1850, it is suggested, derived not only from political reaction to radical views but also, particularly from the 1840s, from changing social needs. Interest in

purely scientific and technical subjects in voluntary societies and institutions waned as erstwhile marginal groups became absorbed into the
local élites and more broadly based means of intellectual activity and
entertainment emerged.[75]

Such theories have been particularly applied to the development of
mechanics' institutes, and they may well help to explain the shift which
occurred from the 1840s in some of those establishments – from provision of science for artisans to the supply of general cultural activity for
the middle classes. But they do not provide an adequate blueprint for
the development of mechanics' institutes generally nor for the part
played by science in them. Indeed study of the social, educational and
economic significance of the complex mechanics' institute movement
has been hampered by over-generalization. They were institutions
which (though sharing a common nomenclature) in fact differed considerably in nature and experience from place to place. Though part of
a national movement, each institute was an independent organization,
the creation of its local community. Some were neither founded nor run
by marginal men, but by established community leaders,[76] while diversification from a science base did not always represent deference to
changing bourgeois tastes or middle-class take-overs. Often elementary
subjects were introduced specifically for working men (and occasionally
women), and broadening curricula reflected the demand of working-
class as well as middle-class members. After mid century, erosion of the
centrality of science stemmed also from development by the government of more formal arrangements for technical and scientific instruction (described in Chapter 7).

Other theories assign a sinister role to science in the mechanics'
institutes. Some modern writers have accepted as generally applicable
the allegation of Engels in 1844 that by then the workers had recognized
the mechanics' institutes to be agents of middle-class domination purveying science and economics geared to bourgeois interests, and
rejected them in favour of socialist institutions.[77] There is certainly
evidence of instances of secessions of socialists to set up proletarian
establishments and of the popularity of some of these,[78] but this picture
fails to stand up to examination as a generalization of the development
of mechanics' institutes as a whole.

Though some institutes were always middle-class establishments and
most did not attract many labourers, membership in many always
included high proportions of the artisan and lower middle classes,
between whom social distinctions were blurred. Some institutes, like

that at Glasgow, were actually controlled by members from these groups, some even by Chartists. Not a few attracted and retained substantial numbers of artisans, many of whom supported radical political views, including Chartism and Owenism. The Church of England certainly initially regarded the institutes as radical establishments, and though this usually reflected its opposition to Benthamism, some historians have seen them as seedgrounds for socialism, Chartism and the cooperative movement.[79] In fact, the distinction between orthodox and 'socialist' institutions has probably been overdrawn. The general ethos, curriculum and activities of both were very similar and in some cases individuals can be found as promoters of and teachers in both kinds of institution. Moreover (*pace* Engels and apostles), it was the Chartist and socialist institutes which tended to disappear after the mid century as their parent ideologies fell out of favour with the working classes, while around 1850 there was an expansion of the mechanics' institutes. A goodly number of these continued to provide for the educational and cultural needs of the working and lower middle classes into the late nineteenth century and beyond, some developing into modern institutions of further and higher education.[80]

Dubious as a generalization, too, is the thesis that the mechanics' institutes were predominantly inaugurated for purposes of social control, choosing pure science as a curricular focus not for its practical value to the economy or to the members but because it was value-free, promoted acceptance of unchangeable laws and did not encourage politically undesirable speculation.[81] Certainly an element of social control was sometimes present, but there is little evidence that it was usually a dominant or sinister motive. Much middle-class support of the institutes derived from a desire to civilize the workers and to wean them from what were seen as potentially self-destructive socialist views through introducing them to classical economic theory. But the institutes also sought to promote social progress and, through education, to make working men potential participators in the political process. Promoters often saw the institutes, too, as providing workers with a means of upward social mobility and as promoting cultural egalitarianism. Politics and religion were usually proscribed in the institutes as much to prevent friction between middle-class members as to exclude socialist dogma or religious dissent.

There is, moreover, little evidence that pure science was chosen because it was politically safe rather than because of its economic value to industry or the individual institute member. In fact, the concept that science was value free and did not lead to speculation about society is dubious. The institutes often gave an important place to the study of natural history, which fostered an interest in evolution and through that helped spread interest in social Darwinism and social reform. Science in the nineteenth century, as indicated above, symbolized not only a belief in material, but also in social, progress. Civic pride – probably a far greater impetus to the development of the mechanics' institutes than social control – was bolstered by the existence of institutes which promoted science, since they seemed to demonstrate that the local community was in the van of progress.[82]

Oversimplified, too, is the view, derived initially from the premature verdict of contemporary critics around 1850, that by then the mechanics' institutes had failed: they had not achieved their basic objective (to bring science to the artisan class) and had become middle-class recreational clubs.[83] Often, it is true, institutes, faced with working men insufficiently well grounded in the 3 Rs to understand serious science, found it necessary to provide elementary instruction and science at a simple level. Paucity of experienced science instructors and general interest in non-scientific subjects led to a broadening of their curricula. Financial considerations dictated the need to attract members by providing social events, popular lectures and so on. Libraries and newsrooms were developed to meet a growing thirst for news and general reading matter (see Chapter 8) and, in places where grammar-school education was deficient, some provided a scientifically biased part-time secondary schooling for lower middle-class youths. This diversification admittedly marked a shift from original objectives but was 'failure' only in a technical sense, since willingness to adapt to market needs ensured that the institutes performed a broader, eminently worthwhile, educational function.

During the second half of the nineteenth century some did become largely middle-class cultural societies while some, especially in Scotland, disappeared or became largely ineffective. But others continued to offer lectures and classes in science (as well as other subjects) and remained an integral and significant part of provincial scientific society.[84] The verdict of some historians that the mechanics' institutes were the 'main agents of technical education throughout the greater part of the nineteenth century'[85] is exaggerated, especially for the later part of the century, but certainly they played a not unimportant role in that field. Some indeed from the 1850s became significant centres for science classes in collaboration with the Department of Science and Art, and some developed into or spawned technical institutions under the local authorities which became increasingly responsible for the provision of technical education.[86]

The possible relationship between economic behaviour and religious outlook, supported in Max Weber's linkage of capitalism with protestantism and R. H. Tawney's emphasis on the positive influence of the puritan ethic on business activity, has also been explored in connection with the Industrial Revolution. The apparent explosion in the number of potential entrepreneurs in British society, which made the Industrial Revolution possible, has been linked to a seemingly disproportionate number of English nonconformists and Scottish presbyterians found among industrial leaders and innovators.[87] This phenomenon, it is argued, stemmed from a combination of legal restrictions on dissenters and their life style, education and religious upbringing.[88] Exclusion of non-Anglicans from Oxbridge, it has been argued, led to the development of the Dissenting academies, with their curricular emphasis on subjects suitable for business and industrial careers. Future economic leaders (including Matthew Boulton, Benjamin Gott and John Wilkinson) attended these establishments, while others joined Scottish students in universities where again an education more attuned to business and industry than at Oxbridge was available. English dissenters and Scottish presbyterians were consequently peculiarly fitted to contribute to economic growth. Of a sample of some 500 technologists and engineers born in Britain, 1700–1850, almost 20 per cent were educated in Scotland.[89]

Again, exclusion of dissenters from parliament and from public office is said to have channelled their energies into industry and commerce, while the ethos of English and Welsh dissent and of Scottish presbyterianism favoured success in business. The practice of thrift, the avoidance of conspicuous consumption and the economic cohesion of an excluded minority facilitated capital accumulation, while adherence to the biblical parable of the talents ensured that money was put to good use. Abhorrence of idleness and entertainment, and the belief that business success indicated God's approval, encouraged pursuit of that goal. Some social scientists, moreover, suggest that the child-rearing practices of dissenting parents tended to produce individuals particularly endowed with entrepreneurial characteristics. They claim that quantification of the level of entrepreneurial zeal in society demonstrates a discernible connection between the Methodist revival, a consequent upsurge in numbers of individuals fired with a desire for material success, and the

Industrial Revolution. D. C. McClelland thus argues that Methodist child-rearing practice (midway between authoritarianism and laxity), with its insistence that children should develop constant personal communion with God and seek Christian perfection in this life, promoted self-reliance and a strong desire for achievement – the very characteristics of the successful entrepreneur.[90]

It is not difficult to accept that the Scottish universities and the Dissenting and other academies, probably conferred business skills on many who attended them, enhancing their chances of success. Other aspects of the thesis outlined above, however, are certainly flawed. The theology of dissent was not always supportive of capitalist endeavour, and often it is likely that the capitalist spirit influenced religious views rather than vice versa.[91] 'Driving ambition and innovational creativity [were] common to the English middle ranks, whatever their... religion',[92] and many enterprising businessmen were Anglicans. Moreover, though members of the old dissenting sects formed a small minority of the population at large, they accounted for a much greater proportion of the middle social ranks from which businessmen were drawn. Again, the extent to which, in practice, dissenters were excluded from public life is debatable: the law could be by-passed and some nonconformists did become mayors, sheriffs, town councillors and MPs, while others were able to enjoy considerable social prestige and local influence without holding public office. Moreover, since the established Church of Scotland was presbyterian, the argument of exclusion has no validity for lowland Scots.[93]

The emphasis on Methodism is particularly suspect and the relationship between firm but relaxed child rearing and the creation of enterprising character fits uneasily with the facts. First, the Methodist revival took place too late to affect in childhood all but a few of the new industrialists. Secondly, the dissenters among the inventors and entrepreneurs of the period were almost exclusively from older sects than the Methodists (who tended also to come from lower down the social scale). Thirdly, the Methodist child-rearing practices of the time were, as exemplified by the teaching of John Wesley (who advocated the breaking of the child's will by repeated whipping), extremely harsh, and unlikely, according to McClelland's premises, to engender enterprise. There is some evidence that the educational practices of Quakers, Unitarians and Congregationalists, who produced many more industrial leaders than the Methodists, did conform more to the methods alleged to promote the entrepreneurial character. But this was not so of Scottish presbyterianism. Though the Church of Scotland after 1740 tended to look more favourably than previously on the pursuit of wealth, Scottish school and home discipline remained notably authoritarian. Yet Scottish-educated men undoubtedly contributed disproportionately to the British Industrial Revolution, and Scottish economic growth in this period was not merely an English import.[94]

All in all, the balance of evidence would suggest that neither the formal literary skills provided by elementary schooling, nor the theoretical scientific knowledge disseminated at a higher level were as significant in the flowering of the British economy in the period of the Industrial Revolution as sometimes suggested. On the other hand, formal schooling and the pursuit of scientific information are both likely to have contributed to economic enterprise indirectly, through influencing the way men thought and behaved, and by assisting (through technical instruction) the exploitation of the practical skills learned elsewhere. Particular kinds of religious attitudes towards the upbringing of children, however, seem unlikely to have been significant in the spread of successful entrepreneurship.

# 5

---

# ELEMENTARY EDUCATION FROM THE 1860S TO 1914

## Compulsory Schooling and State Involvement

Before the mid nineteenth century British governments were suspicious of bureaucratic centralization and state intervention, and felt it unnecessary to emulate the mass system of state schooling adopted by some European countries for the purpose of strengthening centralized government, promoting national unity, encouraging economic development and buttressing ruling élites. In Britain the ruling classes felt little need for a supportive bureaucracy, while national unity and economic prosperity were achieved with a minimum of state interference. It is true that, in Scotland, belief in the national educational system inaugurated in the seventeenth century persisted, with tradition giving the Church (in lieu of a Scottish state) an intimate role in schooling and with the universities regarded as state institutions. But England was the dominant partner and preferred to regard secondary schools and universities as independent institutions and to leave elementary schooling to voluntary effort with limited and indirect state support.[1]

Yet between 1870 and 1902 elementary education became both free and compulsory, state elementary and secondary schools were established and central government control over education increased greatly. The reasons for this change are complex. Support for the schooling of the masses as a means of promoting social order was not new, but, especially from the 1850s, crime, endemic poverty and social unrest appeared to be spiralling, especially in urban areas, spawning fear of social disintegration. To this were added the threat of commercial competition from countries apparently benefiting economically from state education and the belief that Prussia's military victories were built on the advantages bestowed by its system of compulsory elementary schooling.

By the 1860s a sufficiently high proportion of working- class children in Britain were at school for imposition of compulsory attendance to be considered a practical feasibility.[2] Expansion within the existing framework, however, posed problems. In Scotland the traditional system was unable to cope with the needs of urban populations: the Disruption of 1843 had weakened the Church of Scotland's educational influence and by 1850 its funds for schooling were near exhaustion. The Free Church, too, found its schools a financial drain. By the 1860s many Scots saw a system under lay control (but providing Christian values) as essential to cope with the problems of the day.[3] In England and Wales, too, the churches and other voluntary bodies which ran the public elementary schools had difficulty in maintaining their existing schools (though the Established Church was reluctant to relinquish its domination of public elementary education). The distribution of schools in England and Wales, moreover, reflected the local strengths of Anglicanism and dissent, the energy or otherwise of individual clergy and the relative affluence of neighbourhoods – rather than demographic needs. This resulted in over-provision in some areas while poorer districts were often inadequately served.[4] This situation was compounded by the system of government grants which were related to the level of funds raised locally, regular attendance, levels of scholarly attainment and the employment of qualified teachers. Consequently good subsidized schooling was least often available in poor districts (particularly in sparsely peopled rural areas, as in Wales and the Scottish highlands, and in urban slums) where middle-class support was absent, attendance irregular and certificated teachers too expensive (a state of affairs elaborated on below).

Many English and Welsh nonconformists, moreover, realized that they could not seriously match the Church of England's input into voluntary schooling and even those dissenters previously opposed to state interference began to join middle- and working-class radicals in calling for a system of rate-supported public schools, secular or unsectarian. The National Education League (founded 1869) and the Welsh Educational Alliance (1870) spearheaded such demands in opposition to the National Education Union, which sought to expand voluntary schooling and to oppose compulsion.[5]

The government, however, was reluctant to assume full financial responsibility for a wholly state system. At the same time, the Church of England was unwilling to withdraw from the scene even though recognizing its inability to assume the education of the bulk of the nation – a situation leading some churchmen, like the Bishop of Oxford in the late 1860s, to oppose the introduction of compulsory schooling.[6] The gulf between the entrenched body of opinion favouring continued religious control of elementary schooling and voices demanding a secular or non-sectarian public system, with compulsory attendance, ensured that in England and Wales change was achieved only by compromise. The Education Act of 1870 sought to supplement rather than supplant or annex the voluntary schools. It provided that, wherever there were insufficient places in efficient voluntary schools, extra schools, controlled by locally elected school boards and funded by local rates, should be established. Boards could compel attendance and by 1873 some 40 per cent of the population lived in school-board districts where attendance was obligatory. Compulsion became permissible in other districts from 1876 and universal to age 10 in 1880. The desirable corollary of free places for the poor followed, and by 1891 public elementary schooling both in the board and voluntary schools was free.

This dual system, with public schooling controlled partly by democratically elected local bodies and partly by voluntary religious organizations, was an untidy compromise. But it did represent another step towards secularization and state control. This had been presaged by state grants and government inspection of aided schools from the 1830s and, from the 1860s, the linkage – through the Revised Code – of state aid to pupils' attainment in secular subjects. To allay nonconformist fears that board schools might promote Anglicanism, the 1870 Act permitted those schools to provide only undenominational religious instruction or none.

Change was effected more easily in Scotland, where an Act of 1803 had already increased lay influence in the running of the parochial schools. The Education Act of 1872 may be seen as a manifestation of anglicization, but had much indigenous support. By 1871 the Church of Scotland, fearing disestablishment, was amenable to making concessions to smooth the way for legislation. The Free Church, too, came round to the view that only a national system embracing religious instruction would ensure the continuance of a Christian society. Under the Act, existing parochial and burgh schools were taken over by popularly elected school boards supported by local rates. Within a few years, virtually all state-aided church schools (except Roman Catholic and Episcopalian ones) and even some private schools were also transferred voluntarily to the boards. The acceptance of the principle of permissive sectarian teaching (rejected in England) avoided the religious difficulties experienced south of the border and a virtually unified system was created. Conditions peculiar to Scotland were reflected in other ways, too. The Act introduced compulsory attendance immediately, with a more satisfactory system than existed in England and Wales for parochial assistance for the poor (free schooling came, as in England, in 1891), and Scottish boards, unlike English and Welsh ones, were permitted to support some post-elementary schooling.[7]

Historians have placed various interpretations on these changes. Traditionally, the legislation of the 1870s has been seen as a direct reponse to the enfranchisement of urban artisans in 1867 (1868 in Scotland), primarily aimed at ensuring that the new voters were well enough educated to exercise their franchise in a rational way.[8] Such an explanation is, however, unsatisfactory. The artisan class was schooling its children long before 1867 and posed no serious political threat. Elementary education was not considered a significant or urgent issue in the 1868 election, and before considering the elementary sector the new government gave legislative priority to the Public and grammar schools in the Public Schools Act (1868) and the Endowed Schools Act (1869). In fact, other factors were more important in promoting change than was extension of the franchise. The Acts of 1870 and 1872 followed pressure for public educational systems exerted from early in the century – manifested from the 1850s in a succession of unsuccessful Bills proposing such reform both for Scotland and for England and Wales. In Scotland the reports in the 1860s of the Education Commission (Scotland) (the Argyll Commission) further stimulated demands for change. In England and Wales the National Education League of 1869 had been preceded by over two decades by the campaigns of the National Public School Association for a free, secular, rate-supported and locally controlled national system of elementary education. By the 1860s support for a more comprehensive system was widespread, though possible legislation remained controversial and thus difficult for governments to tackle.

The Acts of the 1870s became feasible when, for the first time for decades, a government emerged with a sufficiently large parliamentary

majority to carry legislation opposed even by some of its own supporters. The educational significance of parliamentary reform in 1867–8 lay
in the enfranchisement not of ill-educated potential trouble-makers but
of men who were often Liberals and nonconformists and who, like many
middle-class radicals and dissenters, disliked the Anglican domination of
voluntary schooling.[9]

Educational historians have traditionally tended to regard the advent
of compulsory state-funded and state-controlled public schooling as a
development benevolently contrived and part and parcel of the democratization of society, bringing benefits to all. In recent decades, however, historians of different outlooks have cast doubt both on the
motives of those who supported and engineered change and on
whether it was necessary or desirable.

Historians of the left have tended to regard compulsory education in
state-controlled schools as an intensification of the use of schooling as a
tool of social control (discussed in Chapter 1).[10] Not only did it bring
under public supervision those children of the submerged classes
unreached by the reformatory, industrial and workhouse schools and
other children with insufficient schooling, but, as it became free, it
sought to entice children away from working-class private schools.
These schools, so derided by the reforming middle classes (as well as,
traditionally, by many historians) as educationally deficient and morally
bereft, were, it is now claimed, often reasonably good. They were,
moreover, 'the people's schools' where working-class teachers provided
the sort of education approved of by working-class parents, without the
imposition of middle-class morality or the inculcation of subordination
to social superiors found in the public schools.[11] Their extinction served
to strengthen middle-class hegemony.

Neo-laissez-faire historians, too, have regretted the disappearance of
these private schools – but as free enterprise stifled by an unwarranted
extension of state bureaucracy. They suggest that, left alone, private
schooling could well have coped with working-class needs. The defi-
ciences of such schools were exaggerated by politicians and by an
Education Department whose officials and inspectors had a vested
interest in public schooling and lobbied for its extension. Moreover,
the quality of private schools would undoubtedly have improved as
longer periods of schooling followed the rise of working-class incomes
and the decline of employment for the youngest children. Rate-supported board schools destroyed the free market in schooling, competing
unfairly with existing schools and becoming 'cancer cells in the hitherto

growing structure of private education'. Promoters of the 1870 Act, it is argued, exaggerated the shortfall in school places, the numbers of children completely unreached by schools, and the inability of existing private and voluntary schools to make good any deficiencies as did exist.

Again, the argument goes, since school attendance had risen steadily from 1800, there is every reason to suppose that it would have continued to rise without state interference. The Royal Commission on Popular Education (the Newcastle Commission) reported in 1861 that by the late 1850s children in England and Wales attended school on average for 5.7 years, with few escaping schooling altogether. Similarly, proportions of marriage signatures rose steadily over the century and by the mid 1880s (before the legislation of the 1870s could have affected those then marrying), 88 per cent of spouses in England and Wales and 92 per cent in Scotland signed the registers. Why, it is argued, should it be supposed that this upward trend would not have continued without the introduction of board schools?[12]

Though containing some truth, such views ignore the fact that a free market in schooling disappeared not in the 1870s but in the 1830s with state aid to voluntary schools, and that, anyway, many private schools (especially in England and Wales) were mainly day-care centres for infants. They also fail to appreciate that private schools in Scotland, 'never established themselves as the leading sector, or impressed the public by their efficiency',[13] and that in England and Wales working-class attendance at private schools was in decline long before 1870. In the early nineteenth century, small, intimate neighbourhood schools run by members of their own class often seemed more attractive to parents than the larger, more harshly disciplined voluntary schools. Private schools deferred to parental wishes over regularity of attendance, dress and appearance, provided basic reading (and writing if required) and avoided religious indoctrination and the inculcation of social subordination.[14] But, whereas the nature of private schooling tended to remain unchanged, the quality of publicly funded schooling clearly improved over the century. Increasingly, government-inspected voluntary schools possessed trained teachers, books, other equipment and purpose-built accommodation and worked to well-constructed syllabi, less and less dominated by religious instruction. Such clear advantages overcame other objections, including enforced socialization, especially as employers began to favour the products of such schools, and upper working-class parents in particular were won over in growing numbers.[15]

Attendance at private schools in England and Wales fell from some 70–80 per cent of day-school pupils in the mid eighteenth century to about 40 per cent in 1833 and 33 per cent in 1851 (in Wales alone from 58 per cent in 1833 to 26 per cent in 1851). In Scotland attendance at private schools fell from about 50 per cent in 1818 to some 25 per cent in 1851 and perhaps 15 per cent in 1870.[16] Since these figures include middle-class children, actual proportions of working-class children at private schools must have been even lower. The claim that Scottish educational superiority by 1870 derived not from the parochial schools but from 'more widespread and more rapidly growing private schools' catering for far more pupils than public schools,[17] is based on a mis-taken categorization of schools. It was the publicly funded church schools, which were not private schools, which increased their intakes.[18]

Nevertheless, the educational state of the British working class taken as a whole was by no means as satisfactory in 1870 as claimed by some revisionist historians. It seems unlikely that the situation could have been improved greatly without compulsory attendance and state inter-vention to provide enough satisfactory schools. True, the estimates of W. E. Forster (the promoter of the 1870 Act) of the numbers of unschooled or poorly schooled children in England and Wales in 1870 have been fairly criticized as exaggerating the length of schooling reasonable at the time, overestimating the numbers who went entirely unschooled and ignoring good private schools.[19] But the Newcastle Commission's suggestion that the usual length of school attendance was 5.7 years is highly dubious. In many parts of England and Wales, and even Scotland, many workers' children were attending only for three years at most.[20]

Again, the quality of education in many schools was low. While some private schools may have done good work, in general they were unsat-isfactory and certainly appear to have been less effective in teaching reading and writing than the grant-aided public schools.[21] While private school teachers in Scotland were sometimes as well qualified as those in the public schools, this was by no means always so. In Glasgow, where private schools served mainly the poorest of the working class (especially the Irish) they were grossly inefficient, and in industrial towns in Scotland generally they were widely condemned as being so.[22] In England and Wales in 1851 some seven hundred private-school teachers could not sign the census forms, being unable to write even their own names.[23]

Moreover, despite the invaluable contribution of voluntary schooling generally, many voluntary schools in England and Wales were far from satisfactory. While progress in the grant-aided schools was indisputable, the parlous state of many unaided voluntary schools has been insufficiently remarked by historians. These schools tended to lag far behind inspected schools in standards of tuition, accommodation and teachers' qualifications. The quality of Scottish parochial schools on the eve of the 1872 Act was also by no means always adequate, and in the Western Isles only 15 per cent of schools received grants and few teachers were well qualified. Only half the parishes of England and Wales, according to W. E. Forster in introducing the 1870 Act, had government-aided schools.[24] Statistics compiled by the Church of England, moreover, indicated that 58 per cent of Anglican day schools in 1866–7 (accounting for 57 per cent of pupils in such schools) were not in receipt of annual treasury grants.[25]

The reasons for this situation were several. First, the grant system, as noted above, was weighted against poor parishes. Schools had to meet certain requirements of staffing and accommodation to become eligible for parliamentary grants, which anyway could not exceed what was raised locally through fees, subscriptions or church funds. Consequently it was difficult for schools in very poor rural areas (especially those without a resident gentry), or in highly industrialized or otherwise deprived urban districts with few middle-class inhabitants, to obtain aid.[26] Parishes with limited resources were forced to run their schools cheaply with uncertificated teachers and poor equipment – but this debarred them from obtaining grants and a bad situation was compounded. As one Devon clergyman complained in the late 1860s: 'Under the present system of granting aid rich localities who are able to pay certificated masters get all, the poorer who are not able get none. Torquay... [gets] several hundreds a year, while the poorer parishes in the neighbourhood get none.'[27] In Scotland there were examples of government funding being given to two schools run by different churches in the same neighbourhood where one school would have been sufficient, while poor areas were left without any funding. Again the fact that government aid was intended to support only schooling for the poorer classes created further difficulties for Scottish schools where there was a greater social mix than in England and Wales.[28]

Secondly, some schools in England and Wales went unaided because they did not seek official assistance. This happened in some rural areas where clergy were too thin on the ground to give time, in addition to their other duties, to making parish schools efficient. More often it occurred where bishops or parish priests lacked sufficient energy and enthusiasm for popular education, or where they had a conservative view of what Church schooling should offer. Some considered Sunday schools quite sufficient for the lower orders and, indeed, in Lancashire some clergy diverted funds intended for day schools to Sunday schooling. Other incumbents felt that day schools concentrating on religion and a smattering of reading and writing would suffice, and were antagonistic to providing more or to submitting to government inspection to obtain funding. Consequently, some unaided schools were indistinguishable from dame schools and inferior to the better private schools. In one Nottinghamshire Church school, it is recorded, 'a common labourer (whose respectability was his single qualification) [was] promoted by the clergyman to the office of schoolmaster'.[29]

Gaps in reasonable school provision become more obvious when local rather than national data are considered. Though in 1869 numbers of places in voluntary schools in England and Wales exceeded average attendance by 50 per cent, this concealed a mismatch between location and population.[30] In Bradford, for example, schools in some districts were half-filled, while elsewhere in the town others were overcrowded. Local deficiencies of places in efficient schools are illustrated by the spate of voluntary-school building after the 1870 Act (undertaken to avoid board schools being imposed), and by the fact that, nevertheless, by 1891 school boards had had to be imposed in areas inhabited by 17 per cent of the English population and 36 per cent of the Welsh.[31]

Similarly, claims that the high national marriage-signature rate achieved by 1860–70 indicates a satisfactory level of education ignore the continued existence of local variations. The 77 per cent of spouses who signed in 1871 in England and Wales embraced some Welsh counties with only 50–60 per cent, Bedfordshire with 68, Monmouthshire with 62 and Staffordshire with 60. In Scotland a national 84 per cent average for the 1860s included within it Inverness-shire with 59 per cent and Ross and Cromarty with 57. Moreover, within the boundaries of many counties there were considerable local differences, some representing particularly black spots: Staffordshire's poor 60 per cent overall (1871) included Dudley with only 41 per cent, and Lancashire's 82 per cent embraced 52 per cent in Wigan. Such examples could be multiplied. Even in 1885, when marriage signatures reflected the state of schooling in England and Wales on the eve of the 1870 Act, over 16 per cent of spouses were illiterate in five English counties (4 points below the national rate) and in Monmouthshire, Staffordshire and north and south Wales some 20 per cent. For Scotland a national literacy rate for 1887 of over 90 per cent included 30 per cent illiterate spouses in Ross and Cromarty, 23 per cent in rural insular districts, 18 per cent in Inverness-shire and 14 per cent in Sutherlandshire. As in earlier decades, these concentrations of considerable backwardness were primarily in remote and poor rural areas, mining districts, centres of domestic and factory industry and urban slums. As late as 1880, the literacy rate in industrialized Glasgow was 15 percentage points below that of Edinburgh and 7 points below the Scottish national rate.[32] In the industrial West Riding in the 1860s education was said (perhaps with a degree of hyperbole) to be as backward as in Siberia and to contain many untaught children 'as though they belonged to Fiji rather than England'.[33]

Regional variations still existed, too, in the relative educational standards of men and women. Thus in highland Scotland in 1887, 42 per cent of brides in Ross and Cromarty, 23 per cent in Inverness-shire and 18 per cent in Sutherlandshire were unable to sign their names, compared with, respectively, 18, 14 and 11 per cent of grooms. In England and Wales in 1885, when overall male and female signature rates were only 2 percentage points apart, female rates were 4 to 8 points lower than male in seven manufacturing and mining countries, and in nine agricultural counties male rates lagged behind female by a similar range. At the level of census districts within counties even greater differences existed between the sexes in some areas.[34]

As in the past (see Chapter 2), gender differences often reflected different attitudes towards schooling for boys and girls, and the sorts of employment open to each sex. Indeed, as in earlier periods, general levels of education were usually related to occupational structure. Poor school attendance rates and illiteracy continued to be associated with concentrations of labourers and those engaged in mining and certain kinds of manufacturing industry. The attitudes of certain groups to schooling continued to be affected by social and occupational factors. Though by the later 1860s a high proportion of working-class parents willingly schooled their children, there remained concentrations of those who were most unlikely ever to see that their offspring obtained an adequate education – unless compelled to do so. At the very bottom of the social pile the children of the residuum, generally uncatered for by the public schools and mostly untouched by the industrial and reformatory institutions, often lived in a state of near savagery, completely untutored. In certain parts of Britain, high proportions of the children of illiterate Irish immigrants went unschooled through parental apathy and their priests' reluctance to condone attendance at non-Catholic schools.[35]

Other relatively poor parents (in urban slums, factory districts, areas of crofts and small family farms or of underpaid agricultural labour and cottage industry) still felt unable to forgo their children's work or wages. In areas of domestic industry, 'gloving', 'lace' or other small 'schools', teaching craft rather than academic skills, continued sometimes to be preferred and the quality of schooling generally was poor.[36] Of Somerset children engaged in glove making, it was said in 1869 that 'they grow up in a state of deplorable ignorance, very few [can] write even their own names...Sunday schools do a little for the best of them, but the roughest will not attend' even those.[37]

Other parents (especially in some English mining and manufacturing districts) were well able to afford schooling, but were indifferent to it or saw no need of more than a hasty acquisition of the rudiments, since good wages could be earned by the illiterate. Of the Dudley (Staffs.) district, the Newcastle Commission commented that 'To the mass of parents...the advantages of education...cannot be very apparent, while its attendant disadvantages are manifest....They see the most prosperous [of their neighbours] who have attained this prosperity without any other education than that of the nail shop, the pit or the forge...they see no greater if any equal prosperity attending the people who read and keep books, shopkeepers, lecturers, ministers of religion. Learning is rather thought a drawback.'[38] Such parents would even reject free tuition and in some localities school places often went unoccupied.[39] Many working-class parents, moreover, whether able to afford schooling or not, resented any restriction on their right to do what they liked with their children.[40] It was, for example, Monmouthshire parents rather than coalowners who, when legislation restricted child labour in the mines, conspired to continue sending girls and under-age boys to work underground illegally.[41]

All this suggests that the achievement of universal schooling of a reasonable standard required not only the provision of extra schools but the imposition of compulsory attendance. Indeed, by the 1860s, this view was accepted by much middle-class opinion.[42] It had become obvious that extension of the half-time system, which, as outlined in Chapter 1, was once thought a possible alternative to compulsory full-time schooling, was not the answer. It could not easily be imposed on domestic industry, nor on family farms or the multifarious workshop trades of the English midlands, which collectively still employed thousands of children from age 7 upwards. Moreover, in those trades on which half-time schooling had been imposed, commensurate increases in school attendance had not always followed. Rather than send children to school, parents often shifted them to unregulated occupations, or kept them at home in idleness or to undertake household chores, mind infants or to undertake casual work.

The need for schooling clearly did not loom large in the minds of some parents. In 1851, 40 to 50 per cent of boys aged 5 and 6 in England and Wales and about one-third of those aged 7 to 11 (together with much higher proportions of girls in those age groups) were neither at school nor returned in the census as employed. Forty per cent of 12-year-old girls were at home, double the proportion at school.[43] In 1871, of 10-year-olds in England and Wales, 36 per cent of girls and 27 per cent of boys were neither at work nor at school, and about that time over 30,000 Glasgow children were not on the roll of any school.[44] The 'large class' of degraded children whom Mary Carpenter, the social reformer, observed in 1861 swarming the streets of Warrington 'utterly untaught and uncultified' was not unique to that Lancashire town. In industrial towns throughout Britain in the 1850s and 1860s there were allegedly thousands of children who passed the day idling about the streets. In Birmingham there were said to be over 50,000 such children, and in 1868 in that city, of some 45,000 working-class children aged 3–15, 48 per cent were at home, 38 per cent at school and only 14 per cent at work. Many of them could neither read nor write. In some areas, such as the West Riding in the 1850s, increasing proportions of children were leaving school before the age of 10.[45] A sample of Birmingham working-class streets reveals that a decline in the proportions of 6–10-year-olds at work between 1861 and 1871 was not accompanied by greater school attendance but by dramatically higher proportions 'at home' and a reduction in proportions at school (Table 5).

At the same time child labour was not dying out. In the transportation industry, surface work at mines, the metal industries and textile manufacturing, it was actually expanding: numbers of child workers in textile factories rose from 29,000 in 1838 to 80,000 in 1868. Technical changes sometimes permitted sub-division of tasks which increased the employment of children. This was reflected in a rise in child wages between the 1840s and 1860s in the pottery, lace, hosiery, glass-making and metal trades, encouraging a preference for work over school. In rural districts greater production of root crops created more jobs suitable for children. In 1861, when over 40,000 children under 12 were in outdoor

*Table 5*   Children in some working-class streets in Birmingham, 1861–71

| Ages | At work (%) | | At school (%) | | At home (%) | |
| --- | --- | --- | --- | --- | --- | --- |
| | Boys | Girls | Boys | Girls | Boys | Girls |
| 5–8 | | | | | | |
| 1861 | 0 | 0 | 42 | 39 | 58 | 61 |
| 1871 | 0 | 0 | 38 | 39 | 62 | 61 |
| 7–8 | | | | | | |
| 1861 | 2 | 0 | 56 | 42 | 42 | 48 |
| 1871 | 0 | 0 | 35 | 38 | 65 | 61 |
| 9–10 | | | | | | |
| 1861 | 21 | 22 | 36 | 31 | 43 | 47 |
| 1871 | 6 | 2 | 37 | 33 | 57 | 65 |

*Source*: Derived from Heward (1992), 140–1, 144–5.

agricultural employment, it was reported that children in some farming areas were leaving school at increasingly lower ages. From the 1870s the agricultural depression caused men to be replaced on the land by women and children who could be paid less. In some areas male unemployment and falling farm wages also encouraged existing domestic industries, already heavy users of child labour, to expand to help family budgets. Even after the 1870 Education Act, but before compulsory schooling, boys in East Anglia were at work full-time on the land by age 7 or 8.[46]

Although the 1871 census shows fewer than 1 per cent of children aged 5–9 as in employment in England and Wales, this figure disguises local concentrations of child workers. In Bedfordshire, a centre of domestic industry, for instance, 11 per cent of girls and 5 per cent of boys in that age range were at work, and these county figures embraced even higher proportions in certain census districts. Similarly, of 10–14-year-olds, 32 per cent of boys and 21 per cent of girls nationally were in work, but again much higher proportions are recorded in certain regions: over 40 per cent for boys in seven counties and over 28 per cent of girls in the same number of counties. In Scotland, the Argyll Commission reckoned that 'little more than one-third' of school-age children were at school in the mid 1860s and the census of 1871 shows that a quarter or more of children aged 5–13 in four rural counties and four industrial counties were not then attending school (though this may be somewhat exaggerated). Older children did not account for all these: the figures include, for instance, over 10 per cent of 9-year-old boys in Dumbartonshire and, in Glasgow and seven other industrial towns, and in Airdrie, 20 per cent of 9-year-old girls. Higher proportions in certain parts of towns were to be found: in Bridgeton, a textile manufacturing district of Glasgow, 23 per cent of 9-year-old girls were not attending school. Not surprisingly, among factory employees in Bridgeton, where over 90 per cent of men could write, only 58 per cent of women could do so.[47]

## School Boards and Local Education Authorities

The evidence outlined above gives overwhelming support to the view that the legislation of the 1870s and the imposition of compulsory education were necessary to achieve, within a reasonable period, universal school attendance and the reduction of gross educational inequalities between classes, communities and sexes. The contrary suggestion that upward trends in school attendance and literacy rates would have continued and rendered this unnecessary is doubtful.[48] National marriage-signature rates may not have markedly accelerated from the mid 1880s (when children affected by the 1870s legislation began to marry), but examination of data by location and occupation shows that school boards and compulsory schooling were followed by disproportionate improvements in literacy levels in places with high proportions of people in occupations traditionally associated with low educational standards. Between 1841 and 1871 signatures in Staffordshire, for instance, rose by only 11 percentage points, but between 1884 and 1895 they increased by 16 points. The proportions of labourers and miners able on marriage to sign their names surged from about 70 per cent in 1884–9 to 99 per cent by 1904–9.[49] Recent research suggests that compulsory schooling and legal restrictions on child labour may account for up to 15 percentage points of the rise in English national literacy levels from 1840 to 1900, while improvements in the provision of subsidized schooling over the period may have been responsible for between 4 and 25 points. Since these are national estimates the impact of officially funded schooling and compulsory attendance would certainly have been greater in places where educational backwardness had initially been most extensive.[50]

In Scotland the compulsory schooling introduced in 1872 resulted in increased attendance: the proportions of 8–10-year-olds at school rose from 90–2 per cent of boys and 88–9 per cent of girls in 1871 to 96–7 per cent of both sexes in 1891, and by 1901 all but 2–3 per cent of children aged 7–11 were at school. In England and Wales, under the school board system, which continued until 1902, places in efficient public schools increased, often being provided where none had existed before. Attendance rates for working-class children rose from 68 per cent in 1871 to 82 per cent by 1896.[51] At Reading, for instance, compulsion brought an immediate 20 per cent increase in school attendance, and in two Welsh rural parishes attendance at inspected schools rose by about 50 per cent in the eight years after 1870.[52] Resistance to compulsion was overcome partly by the abolition of school fees, but also by legal enforcement of attendance – though not without resentment at the loss of parental rights and, among the poorest families, financial hardship. The development of rate-funded board schools, often in new buildings, adversely affected both the private and the voluntary schools. Indeed private working-class schools virtually disappeared, especially after the introduction of free public schooling, while the numbers of children in the board schools rose more rapidly than those in the voluntary schools. Between 1890 and 1900 enrolments in voluntary schools in England and Wales increased from 2.3 to 2.5 million and those in board schools from 1.5 to 2.2 million.[53]

From the start, however, the compromise of 1870 manifested considerable weaknesses. Though some National and a larger proportion of British schools, especially in Wales, were given over to school boards, antagonism towards non-sectarian education remained strong among Anglicans and Roman Catholics, while dissenters resented the continued existence of Anglican and Catholic schools.[54] Attempts to prevent the establishment of school boards had resulted in a spate of new Church schools after 1870, but this momentum proved impossible to maintain. The voluntary schools, especially (but not only) in rural areas, lacked the financial advantages of the board schools – particularly access to local rates. Consequently Anglican and Roman Catholic schools were generally less well equipped and housed than many board schools, had fewer well-qualified teachers and, though government grants rose on the abolition of school fees and eased the situation, they still found it difficult to meet the curricular requirements imposed by the Education Department. By 1900 many voluntary schools were in a very unsatisfactory state, unable to compete with rate-supported board schools, yet having to charge higher fees to keep going while still providing an inferior secular education.[55]

The school board system itself also brought a great deal of conflict and attendant difficulties.[56] Between supporters of the voluntary schools (mainly Anglicans, Catholics, Conservatives and all those seeking avoidance of compulsory school rates) and those nonconformists, Liberals and secularists who wanted to promote the board schools, there was often damaging rivalry. Local opposition was sometimes so strong that (as happened at Chester) it led to delay in or avoidance of the establishment of boards – even when circumstances indicated that they were legally required. Elections for urban boards were frequently dominated by politics and sectarianism, and were contested for motives not primarily educational. In particular they were used by trades unionists and other working-class radicals to promote their participation in local affairs and extend their general influence. In their support of board schools, working-class leaders did not, however, always speak for the rank and file. Large numbers of the lower working class resented the school boards' power to override the parental right to control children's lives by imposing compulsory schooling. The strength of such feeling was illustrated at Luton in the early 1870s when the number of illiterate workmen casting their votes (in a local opinion poll) against the institution of a school board exceeded the total of people voting for one, and a board was temporarily avoided. In rural Wales the enthusiasm with which school boards were elected reflected political antagonism to English landowners as well as nonconformist dislike of the Established Church. In Liverpool, school board politics became part of the struggle between Orangemen and Roman Catholics. More generally, as is well illustrated in Birmingham, religious and political controversy often absorbed prodigious amounts of school boards' time and money. In particular, differences over religious matters, especially over religious instruction in the board schools, caused much acrimony.

Sometimes, as happened in Manchester, Salford, Sheffield and Leeds in the 1870s, clerical and other opponents of board schools gained control of school boards. In such cases parsimony often ruled, the development of board school education suffered and policies were tailored to suit the interests of local voluntary schools rather than the board's own schools. In particular, boards dominated by friends of the denominational schools used their legal right to pay the fees of indigent children at those schools rather than at the board schools, thus diverting rate money to the voluntary sector. On the other hand, boards controlled by secularists showed harmful antagonism to existing voluntary schools and sought to prevent the institution of new denominational schools. More generally, the system of triennial elections ensured that boards were always mindful of the unpopularity of rate rises, with the result that some boards found themselves without adequate resources.

A particular weakness of the dual system lay in the impetus it gave to centrifugal local influences. National provision had been achieved without creating an integrated system, and the quality of education consequently varied very considerably not only between voluntary and board schools but between the schools of some boards and others. Central government also found it difficult to administer efficiently a system in which each of the 20,000 voluntary schools and the 2,500 or so school boards in England and Wales had direct access to the Education Department.[57] The boards varied in size from rural one-or two-school boards to city boards controlling many schools: the London School Board, for instance, was responsible for over 1,400 schools with some 13,500 teachers. In rural districts where Anglican influence was strong, but sufficient school places so lacking that boards had to be compulsorily imposed, the boards consisted largely of local farmers and Anglican laymen and clergy, antipathetic to the education of those they regarded as future agricultural labourers. In such districts rates were kept low, exemptions were granted liberally to children wishing to leave school early for employment on the land and educational efficiency was not pursued with any great enthusiasm.

On the other hand, some of the powerful city boards, like those of London and Birmingham, pursued active and progressive policies and numbered influential personalities among their elected members – T. H. Huxley, for instance, served on the London School Board. They employed outstanding architects in the large-scale building of schools and made progressive curricular innovations. Some inaugurated special schools for the handicapped, truant schools, residential schools, industrial schools and post-elementary schooling in the shape of 'higher grade schools', while medical and welfare services were pioneered by some boards.[58]

The fusion from 1900 of the Education Department and the Science and Art Department into a Board of Education (which also assumed the Charity Commission's educational work) and the Education Act of 1902 were intended to remedy the defects of the dual system and to establish more effective central control of both elementary and secondary education. The multifarious school boards were replaced by some 300 local education authorities (committees of local government councils) which were given the task of administering public elementary schooling. The

education authorities of county borough councils and the county councils were also enabled to promote secondary education, taking over the
higher grade schools and the functions of the technical instruction
committees.[59] The Act reflected the waning political influence of the
Church of England, though that body was still strong enough to ensure
that the voluntary schools survived. The financial difficulties of the
Church schools were alleviated by the extension of rate aid to them,
and by the requirement that the local education authorities should
maintain their buildings and pay their teachers. These were controversial measures, resented by nonconformists and Liberals, especially in
Wales. None the less, they greatly increased secular control, creating a
more unified public system which reduced differences in the secular
education provided in the council (formerly board) schools and the non-
provided schools (as the voluntary schools became) – though religious
controversy was not stifled.[60]

   Central administrative power over Scottish education was strengthened when the Scotch Education Department (established in 1885 and
based in London) took over the educational work of the Science and Art
Department in 1898–9, but the school board era in Scotland lasted to
1918 and had a different impact than in England and Wales. The share
of private schools in working-class education before the 1872 Act was
already much smaller than in England, so that their virtual disappearance after the imposition in 1872 of compulsory attendance (at schools
recognized as efficient) and the abolition of fees in public schools did not
mark so great a change as in some parts of England. Scotland, moreover, was spared the damaging results of religious division institutional-
ized in a dual system. Instead the school boards quickly achieved a near
monopoly of public elementary education as the Established Church
and the Free Church transferred most of their schools voluntarily to
them. By 1891 only some 10 per cent of public schools were still run by
religious denominations, over half of those by the Roman Catholics.[61]

   The impact of legislation on post-elementary education in Scotland
marked another departure from English and Welsh experience. On the
one hand the restriction of the use of grant and rate income to elementary education marked a break in the traditional role of Scottish public
schooling, for the parish schools – though somewhat more often in
theory than practice – had been able to teach to secondary level and
prepare their pupils for the universities. On the other hand, the 1872
Act gave Scottish school boards (unlike those south of the border) the
right to provide some sort of post-elementary schooling if they wished

(though not to fund it from the public purse). In general the 1872 Act did much to diminish existing inequalities between the highlands and lowlands, between urban and rural districts and between the better-off and poorer workers.[62]

Nevertheless, the Scottish school board system, though lasting for a generation longer than that south of the border, exhibited some of the same weaknesses evident in England and Wales. The Scotch Education Department had to deal with nearly one thousand boards, covering topographical areas and populations which varied greatly: in 1905, for example, Lanarkshire (including Glasgow) had fifty boards for 1,315,000 inhabitants, while Perthshire had seventy-nine for 124,000. The boards also differed considerably in efficiency and in the zeal and effectiveness with which they enforced attendance, and were often affected by internal disputes between those who wished to restrict expenditure and those willing to spend more liberally. Some (though by no means all) rural and small town boards, especially where dominated by tradesmen and farmers, were parsimonious, antagonistic to providing schooling above the elementary level and sympathetic to tailoring school attendance to meet the needs of agriculture and other seasonal industries. On the other hand, city boards, which often numbered among their members prominent local figures, like university professors, philanthropic industrialists and eminent clergy, were more positive in their approach. They built substantial school buildings and pursued active and progressive policies, especially in the provision of post-elementary education (a topic pursued in Chapter 6), evening classes and welfare services. By 1890 many city board schools had special facilities for gymnastics, arts and crafts and domestic science. By 1900 the school boards of Edinburgh, Dumfries, Kirkcaldy and Govan had arrangements for medical inspection, and in Glasgow needy children were supplied with meals and clothing. As in England, however, as public education became more complex, and its use as a medium for social reform and welfare provision developed, its control by so disparate and numerous an array of authorities, each pursuing its own policy, increasingly came to be seen as inappropriate.[63]

Nevertheless, despite the distinctive nature of Scottish education, by the first decades of the twentieth century a pattern of mass education had emerged which was in many respects similar to that prevailing in the rest of Britain. An undifferentiated arrangement, in which parish schools, burgh schools and universities had overlapping functions, had been largely replaced by a sequential system in which elementary, secondary and higher education were linked formally and performed distinct functions. In particular, the elementary education provided by the Scottish board schools, especially those in the towns, was much the same as that offered by public elementary schools in England and Wales, and the Act of 1872 was followed by strong efforts to impose English as the medium of instruction in Gaelic-speaking areas.[64]

By 1914 elementary education in Britain had been both compulsory and free for a generation, and public systems of elementary and secondary schooling, controlled largely by local and central government, established throughout England, Scotland and Wales. The former influence of the churches over schooling had practically disappeared in Scotland and was greatly diminished in England and Wales, and popular schooling had become predominantly a matter of secular instruction. Despite the continuance of some working-class resistance to compulsory attendance, the vast majority of children received a basic education – which had certainly not been the case in 1870.

While progress had been considerable, however, both the quality of education provided in the pre-war public elementary schools and the general levels of education in the population at large must not be exaggerated. Though by 1914 practically all young people were able to sign their names on marriage, about 10 per cent of the population of Edwardian England were still completely illiterate and many of the middle-aged and elderly, especially unskilled workers, had a limited grasp of reading and writing. Moreover, for many not in clerical posts and the like, what was learned at school frequently played no significant part in the world of work (though, as shown in Chapter 8, it often did in the world of leisure). Despite lip-service paid to schooling as a means of providing a more skilled workforce, industrial employers in practice frequently paid little heed to school achievements, seeking other, more traditional, qualities in recruiting workers. Promotion at work often depended more on practical skills and personal reliability than on standards of elementary education.[65]

Nevertheless, the duty of the state to provide basic schooling for all had been acknowledged, and a public elementary system better than existed in 1870 and capable of being improved and extended had been created. The early twentieth-century beginnings of continuation and junior technical schools (as detailed in Chapter 6) evidenced a groping towards what might have later developed into an acceptable provision of post-elementary education for less academic children (see p. 105). In addition, especially after the Boer War highlighted a supposed danger

of national 'physical deterioration' (stemming from poverty, slum housing, malnutrition and disease), the elementary schools became the focus
of public efforts to improve the general welfare of children. This
included the provision of meals, medical facilities and physical exercise
– and represents an important aspect of child and school life, on which,
however, lack of space prevents elaboration here.[66]

# 6

---

# SECONDARY AND HIGHER EDUCATION FROM THE 1860S TO 1914

This period is noteworthy for some convergence in the nature and organization of secondary schooling north and south of the border, yet the Scottish experience remained sufficiently distinctive for it to be treated here separately.

### Developments in Secondary Schooling in England and Wales

In England and Wales significant changes in secondary schooling down to 1914 included the restructuring of the grammar schools, the extension of secondary schooling to girls and the advent of state secondary education. In the decades following the Endowed Schools Act (1869) (detailed in Chapter 3), many grammar schools improved their administration and teaching, increased their pupil intake and effected a modest broadening of their curricula. By 1900, moreover, some eighty girls' grammar schools were created. Yet the process of grammar school reform was cumbersome and clashes of interest between the Endowed Schools' Commissioners, headmasters, governors, parents and local communities were often very time consuming. Even when (as required) a revised scheme for each endowment was submitted by the commissioners to the Education Department it had also to go to the Privy Council and to both houses of parliament, all of which delayed progress

– in some cases for years. Moreover, political disagreements over the role of the commissioners led to their abolition in 1874 and responsibility for their work passed to the Charity Commissioners whose cautious approach tended to slow progress up even more.[1]

Consequently, the extent of reform achieved varied, and provision of secondary schooling through the grammar schools remained educationally, socially and geographically patchy. The anticipated flowering of the grammar schools into a national secondary-school system did not happen. In particular, the educational needs of the (often nonconformist) lower middle classes were not met. While the upper and wealthiest middle classes benefited from the growth of the Public schools, the somewhat less affluent middle classes from corporate private schools and some of the reformed grammar schools and the working classes from state-aided elementary schooling, the lower middle classes were often left without subsidized schooling suited to their needs and socially acceptable to them. They were the main losers in the abolition of free places (consequent on the 1869 Act), their ability to pay full fees being overestimated by the Taunton commissioners. Moreover, the new competitive scholarships were mainly restricted to pupils from the largely Anglican public elementary schools. From the 1880s some board schools in the larger cities did become dominated by lower middle-class pupils,[2] but for some time after 1870 many respectable parents in that class were often wary of sending their children to local board schools where they would sit alongside the poor, the uncouth and the unwashed.

Lower middle-class and nonconformist attempts to secure the abolition of Anglican influence in the governing bodies and headships of grammar schools (a special grievance in Wales), to retain commercial or elementary instruction in them and to secure the creation of the third grade schools recommended by the Taunton commissioners, generally failed in face of the opposition of the wealthier middle classes. These, often supported by entrenched heads and governors and the Established Church, sought first grade schools, able to prepare boys for the professions, (or at least second grade ones) and upheld the retention of Anglican influence – all partly to discourage lower middle-class attendance and reinforce social exclusiveness. In some places pressure for a first grade school was motivated, too, by civic pride. Anglican privileges were usually upheld and fewer third grade schools were created than envisaged by the Taunton commissioners. Even so, by the 1890s many grammar schools were underfunded and poorly staffed and housed. Consequent delays in provision of science teaching led some parents to prefer the new higher grade schools and technical colleges (discussed later), while some first grade schools lost pupils to the Public and private schools.[3] By the 1890s it seemed clear that state intervention would be required to ensure a soundly financed secondary system.

Some private schools, in this period, embraced innovation more readily than the grammar schools, attracting well-qualified staff and entering boys for public examinations. Particularly successful were the larger proprietary schools (especially those with denominational connections), girls' schools (see below) and the Public schools. From the 1860s, too, the raising of the age of entry to the Public schools and the institution of entrance examinations to them (following recommendations of the Clarendon Commission, for which see Chapter 3) inaugurated an increase in the number of those private schools which became known as preparatory schools. These took boys up to age 13 and prepared them for entry to the Public schools. But, though middle-class private schooling of all kinds remained significant down to 1914, overall, private schools (particularly the smaller ones) experienced a relative decline. This stemmed partly from failure to combine to support their own cause, but mainly from financial difficulties and competition from public elementary schools (which gradually became more acceptable to the humbler middle classes), public secondary and technical education and the Public schools.[4]

Though few new Public schools were founded after the 1860s, the existing schools were given a focus by the Headmasters' Conference (established in 1869 to resist state interference) and emerged as a coherent body of (by 1900) about one hundred schools. According to E. C. Mack, the social and political amalgam they served – the landed, professional and wealthier commercial families – was motivated by a 'combination of direct self-interest, class snobbery, and that satisfaction of their social and economic needs which they believed the public schools gave'. Historians have criticized them for complacency in defending a stereotyped status quo, in particular for failing to embrace significant curricular change and for philistine arrogance stemming from wealth and connections.[5] But scholarship was not, in fact, absent in them, and standards improved from the third quarter of the nineteenth century consequent on the institution of external public examinations (particularly the Oxford and Cambridge 'Locals') and of competitive examinations for the Indian and home civil services and for army commissions.

Again, the social exclusiveness of the Public schools in this period can be exaggerated. Though (as is explored further in Chapter 7) only a tiny proportion of middle-class boys attended them, the actual numbers of those who did so probably doubled between 1860 and 1914. The agricultural depression of the later nineteenth century weakened the ability of some landowners to pay expensive school fees and the expanding numbers of Public schools began to recruit from a wider spectrum of the upper middle classes. Though there was some complaint that the schools were thus becoming 'schools for the sons of plutocrats rather than of aristocrats', not all the newcomers were very wealthy. Most were sons of professional men, bankers and others engaged in financial and commercial occupations, together with offspring of some who derived their income indirectly from industry as shareholders (rather than actually being engaged in manufacturing).

The significance of the Public schools in this period, moreover, lies less in their intellectual achievements than in their political and social impact. The broadening of their social intake led to a shared experience and commonly held attitudes in pupils originally from different backgrounds. This helped to broaden the outlook of the landed classes, reduce their exclusiveness and thus preserve their influence in a new ruling élite – an élite moulded to some extent by Public-school education. At the same time the schools provided opportunities for upward social mobility for a wide range of the better-off middle classes. The extra-curricular ingredients of Public-school education, praised by the Clarendon Commission (and described in Chapter 3), engendered high levels of initiative and self reliance and ideals of loyalty, honesty, courage, patriotism and public service. They produced leading statesmen and remarkably good soldiers, pioneers of Empire and civil and colonial servants, promoted a stable political structure and bound the Empire together.[6] The myth of Public schools as baneful influences on the economy is discussed in Chapter 7, and their positive influence on the grammar and public secondary schools is treated below.

Until 1902 England had no centrally organized and financed system of state secondary schooling and British governments felt less obliged than leading European countries to provide one. The traditional view was that secondary education should not be vocational nor an extension of elementary schooling, but middle-class, and thus not to be publicly funded or controlled. In the later nineteenth century, however, the perceived needs of the economy, combined with demands for an extended schooling for the artisan and lower middle classes, resulted in a change. First, from the later 1870s, some larger school boards developed (for older pupils from elementary schools) 'higher grade' schools – effectively lower secondary schools with a scientific and technical bias. By the mid 1890s there were some sixty of these schools in England, the largest and most successful in the northern industrial cities such as Bradford, Sheffield and Manchester. Secondly, the Department of Science and Art provided grants for these and for grammar schools and other institutions whose pupils were successful in its scientific and technical examinations. Thirdly, from 1889, government-established county and county borough technical instruction committees, with substantial funds from local rates and excise money, provided further grants to establishments teaching scientific and technical subjects, inaugurated scholarships and supported some new technical schools and institutes.[7]

By the mid 1890s a system of publicly financed, locally controlled secondary education was emerging piecemeal, with an intake of mainly lower middle- and artisan-class children from public elementary schools. But it was a system lacking in homogeneity and geographically patchy, with responsibilities divided untidily between school boards and technical instruction committees.[8] An Act of 1889, however, inaugurated in Wales (where there was a dearth of proprietary and grammar schools) a system of intermediate schools controlled by county education committees and financed from local rates and government grants: by 1902 almost one hundred such schools had been created.[9] Then, in 1895, the Royal (Bryce) Commission on Secondary Education recommended the institution of a public secondary-school system for England and Wales. When a legal judgment of 1899 deemed the higher grade schools to be secondary schools (and thus improperly supported by school board rates) a crisis was precipitated. Consequently, the 1902 Education Act, drawing on the experience of the technical instruction committees and the Welsh intermediate schools, inaugurated a secondary system administered by local government. New schools were created and most existing grammar and higher grade schools absorbed into this state system.

Controversy surrounds the way the new secondary system was subsequently developed. Many historians have tended to blame Public school influence in the Board of Education (the central authority for education from 1899) and its permanent secretary (1903–11), R. L. Morant, for imposing on the new secondary system the traditional literary curriculum of the grammar and Public schools – in preference to developing in them the technical and vocational bias of the higher grade schools. Thus the economy, it is argued, was denied suitably trained manpower and the working classes the practical education they needed. A middle-class stamp was imposed on public secondary schooling and the cultural gulf between middle-class and working-class education was thus widened. Moreover, this supposedly baneful course was perpetuated well into the twentieth century.[10]

Such strictures oversimplify the facts and ignore the implications of the alternative – a policy which would have channelled all intellectually endowed working- and lower middle-class children into secondary schools greatly differenced curricularly from those of the governing classes. There was, in fact, considerable support at the time for the view 'that extending opportunity to the working class meant a right to share in liberal education of the highest form'.[11] Government policy reflected not a desire to create a middle-class preserve but the view of many contemporary educationists, politicians, clergy, parents and even technologists that a lop-sided technical curriculum, hived off from the schooling of the élite, should be avoided.[12]

Ensuring that public secondary education should be academic, and that broad-based education should precede specialization, did not, anyway, equate with a neglect of technical or scientific instruction. As argued in the next chapter, it is unlikely that the British economy was harmed by a deficiency in this area. Moreover, the curricular distinction between the new secondary schools and the higher grade and Welsh intermediate schools should not be exaggerated. The scientific syllabi of the latter had been both academic and practical, and their curriculum often included literary subjects.[13] At the same time the academic bias of the secondary schools was modern and general rather than overly literary or classical. While avoiding vocational training it embraced serious study of mathematics and science as an integral part of general education in a way not inconsistent with the real interests of sound scientific education. The inclusion of Latin increased opportunities for upward social mobility.

Certainly, the cultural gap between the secondary education of the minority and the elementary schooling of the mass of the population was not abolished by the advent of public secondary schooling. There was, too, a social divide between, on the one hand, the new local authority secondary schools and former third grade schools and, on the other, the old first and second grade grammar schools. Though Morant genuinely sought a system which would open the universities and the professions to intelligent children of all classes, he did not conceive of a single system of secondary schools nor of making working-class entry to secondary education easy. The chances of children of labouring parents obtaining a secondary schooling were not immediately greatly enhanced. The new secondary schools charged fees, and access to them remained dependent for the most part on parental income. Scholarships were competitive and tended to be won by children of the lower middle classes, now willing to use respectable elementary schools to prepare their children for secondary entry. However, following the Liberal victory at the polls in 1906, the new government instituted a considerable expansion of free secondary-school places. Up to one-quarter of school intakes were to be allotted (free of fees) to elementary-school pupils who passed a qualifying examination. This marked a considerable shift towards acceptance of secondary schooling as sequential to elementary, and strengthened the expectation that it should be extended further down the social spectrum. This was so even though at times it seems that working-class aspirations for secondary education fell short of the chances offered. Valuable scholarships sometimes went unfilled, uptake being limited by cultural inhibitions and by the opportunity cost of lost child earnings.[14]

Nevertheless, state secondary schooling had been established with a sound academic liberal curriculum and worthy corporate ideals. By 1911 over 82,000 former elementary-school pupils were at secondary school (some 60 per cent of the intake); and about one-third of these were receiving free education. Over the three decades from 1890 some 10–13 per cent of English and Welsh 11-year-olds were in secondary school, some 16–20 per cent of whom came from lower middle-class or artisan backgrounds, In 1913, 20 per cent of grammar-school boys were working-class, and the assumption that a distinctly vocational and technical secondary system for the nation's most talented lower middle- and working-class children would have been as successful or preferable is doubtful. It would have been regarded as intellectually inferior and probably failed to accord with parental ambitions. Indeed, when a small minority of state secondary schools experimented with vocational courses, parental response was antagonistic.[15]

The chosen path avoided a deeper division of English and Welsh secondary education along class lines than in fact occurred. The distinction between Public schools, the leading grammar schools and the developing state secondary schools and lesser grammar schools was social rather than academic – instead of both. Such convergence was further enhanced by the movement of Public-school alumni and staff into the inspectorate and teacher training and into the grammar and newer secondary schools, often as heads, and by the emulation by many secondary schools of the organization and ethos of the Public schools. Public-school influence was manifested in the state schools in the status of their heads, the professional standing of their staff and in their promotion of character training and the corporate spirit through athletics and the prefectorial and house systems.[16] As with the Public schools, the quality of education in grammar and other secondary schools (including private middle-class schools) benefited, too, from the spread of public examinations. From the 1870s, particularly, increasing numbers of able boys in secondary schools of all kinds were thus enabled to obtain educational qualifications giving access to worthwhile careers, and to compete for university scholarships and for entry into public service and the professions.[17] Though the middle classes were the immediate beneficiaries, and real equality of opportunity for working-class children was extremely limited before 1914, a system potentially capable of becoming more democratic was created and a Public-school monopoly of élite liberal secondary education avoided.

Moreover, the 'educational deprivation' of the majority of less intellectual working-class children must not be exaggerated. Certainly many children received only a basic elementary schooling and there were many dead-end jobs. Yet outside the school system a successful structure of formal and informal technical and vocational training was established (details of which are explored in Chapter 7), much of it part-time and thus suited to the needs of those whose future lay as artisans in industry and whose wages were needed by their families. In addition there were some schools for children from age 12 attached to technical colleges and from the 1880s to the London polytechnics, and the early twentieth century saw moves to extend such facilities. Though progress before 1914 was very limited, from 1905 the government encouraged the development by local education authorities of central and junior technical schools and continuation schools to provide for children over the compulsory school-leaving age (12 until 1918). By 1914 some 60 per cent of children were remaining at school until age 14 or older. Failure to develop such types of schooling and any subsequent dearth of skilled labour belongs not to the period covered by this volume but to the interwar years and beyond.[18]

### Developments in Secondary Schooling in Scotland

The development of Scottish secondary education in this period reflected continued and deepening disagreement over whether there should be a clear-cut distinction between elementary and secondary schools, as in England. Reformers (supported by the Scotch Education Department, established in 1885) favoured distinct secondary schools (with preparatory departments) characterized by a rigorous classically based curriculum serving the occupational ambitions of an élite – mainly the increasingly professionalized middle classes. The alternative, traditionalist, view was that elements of a broadly based secondary education should be widely available in public schools at little cost, growing naturally out of elementary work and not necessarily hived off into separate schools. This view found support in the reports of several official commissions: thus in 1881, one argued that 'not only is it possible to combine thorough elementary teaching with instruction in the higher branches but any separation is detrimental to the tone of the school and dispiriting to the master'.[19] Not until the turn of the century did the balance tip in favour of distinct elementary and secondary schools. Even then, though a social hierarchy of secondary schools did emerge, the strength of tradition was sufficient to ensure that a much larger proportion of children received post-elementary instruction than in England, and that curricular distinctions along class lines were largely rejected.

The tradition of schools embracing both elementary and advanced functions was upheld by the addition in 1873 of 'specific subjects' (including classics, modern languages, mathematics and science) to the curriculum of the ordinary board schools – thus providing older pupils with a kind of lower secondary education. But the movement for the creation of discrete secondary schools was advanced by the conversion in the 1870s and 1880s of many urban hospitals (endowed charity boarding schools) into large prestigious middle-class fee-paying day schools (with a limited number of free bursaries) which were strongly academic. Other endowments were used to create new schools. In addition a number of burgh schools already providing mainly secondary instruction became public fee-paying higher class schools under the school boards (which unlike the English boards could legally provide secondary education, though not fund it from the public purse). Then from the 1880s some urban boards established fee-paying schools along the lines of English higher grade schools (sometimes adopting that nomenclature).

Into the 1890s full secondary education was mainly represented by private and endowed schools. In that decade, however, the growth of white-collar employment in Scotland led to increased lower middle-class demand for secondary education, and this was met by the provision of state money for technical and secondary education. Secondary education committees, set up in counties and the main cities, used the funds to establish bursaries and subsidize higher class, higher grade and endowed schools. Some new schools were established, particularly in rural areas, and higher or secondary departments attached to elementary schools developed – their existence alongside distinctly secondary schools keeping the parochial tradition alive. At the same time more academies, higher class and endowed schools were absorbed into the state system. Thus public secondary education of various kinds became more widely available and, since much of it was free, caused many small private schools to disappear. The traditional position was further strengthened in 1892 by the success of pressure to open the Scottish Leaving Certificate (inaugurated in 1888 for pupils in higher class and other secondary schools) to candidates from board schools and by the replacement in 1899 of specific subjects by a liberal secondary syllabus for 'advanced departments' of board schools. By 1902–3 nearly 400 schools, including many small rural ones, had such departments and about 70 per cent of all Leaving Certificate candidates were from schools other than the higher class or higher grade schools. By 1905 public schools were providing as much secondary education as non-public ones.

The Scotch Education Department and other supporters of centralized secondary schools regarded this plurality of provision as chaotic and the Department persisted with its policy of bringing an end to the traditional system. In 1899 the government had inaugurated another raft of higher grade schools under the school boards, intending to provide the artisan class with scientific and technical instruction. Then, in 1903, under terms of the 1901 Education Act, the advanced departments of the board schools were abolished. The school-leaving age of 14 was enforced more rigidly and 12-year-olds offered either vocationally orientated supplementary courses or transfer to secondary schools proper.

Increasing distinction between elementary and secondary schools was accompanied by the abandonment by the Education Department of its attempts to create a hierarchy of secondary schools with distinct curricula for different social groups. The development of higher grade schools as scientific and technical institutions had proved unpopular with existing schools as unfair subsidized competition. It was disliked, too, by radicals who objected to rates funding middle-class education and by parents who regarded vocational education as inferior. The

Department, therefore, sought to assimilate these higher grade establishments into the general body of secondary schools, imposing a common curricular pattern through its control of grants and its requirement
that all such schools should teach to the Scottish Leaving Certificate.
This paralleled the decision (noted in the preceding section) that the
English public secondary schools should embrace the liberal curriculum
of the grammar and Public schools. Thus all Scottish secondary-school
pupils could follow courses leading to the professions and the universities.

Scottish secondary education, as it evolved from the later nineteenth
century, while predominantly middle-class, was none the less more
broadly based than that of England. Though not differenced curricularly, schools, especially in the larger cities, ranked in esteem according
to social divisions within the middle classes. The fact that all (including
those catering for the professional classes) were day schools, however,
linked even the most prestigious with the local community and made for
greater homogeneity within the middle classes. There was a 'hierarchical continuum' regulated by levels of fees, rather than the social gulf
which separated English boarding schools from other schools and from
local communities.

Cohesion of secondary schooling was also strengthened when, led by
some élite urban schools, like Edinburgh Academy, Scottish secondary
schools began to promote the corporate characteristics which had
spread from the English Public schools to secondary schools throughout
England and Wales. Emphasis on the development of character as well
as intellect, and of a collective *esprit de corps*, was bolstered by school
magazines, uniforms, cadet corps, and competitive games to create a
common ethos, incidentally reinforcing the social division between secondary and elementary schooling. Yet this aspect of anglicization was
tempered by a less obsessive attitude to athleticism, an absence of the
emphasis on religion and the fact that Scottish schools were virtually all
day schools and more open to parental influence.[20]

All this is not to suggest that the experience of schools at the bottom of
the Scottish secondary hierarchy was not very different from that of the
élite city schools. Some public higher class schools suffered from grud-
ging support from the boards and from competition from the non-
public schools. In the 1870s and 1880s they were also adversely affected
by the attraction of the 'specific subjects' in the board schools, which
often satisfied the needs of some lower middle-class parents. And
though the higher grade schools could prepare for the professions

and universities, many artisan and lower middle-class pupils tended to leave about age 15 for commercial occupations.[21]

Before the 1890s, relatively few working-class children obtained free secondary education. Those who did often received a truncated one. Some (mainly small-town) higher grade schools provided only three-year courses, while board-school children choosing secondary rather than vocational schooling from 1903 often failed to complete the full course. Advancement by merit was more limited in fact than theory, and often middle-class groups were the chief beneficiaries of bursaries and scholarships, while, as universities raised entry standards, access to them became more difficult for those who had not followed a full secondary-school course.[22]

Yet, though the bulk of the working classes received only elementary education, secondary education in Scotland remained relatively open to the talents. While it did not become universally free until 1918, numbers of bursaries multiplied from the 1890s and education in most higher grade schools was free or quite cheap. By about 1912 some two-thirds of public secondary schools provided free tuition and in a number of counties it was totally free. Around 15 per cent of Scottish elementary-school children proceeded to secondary education – more than three times the proportion in England.[23] By 1900 secondary schooling was also geographically accessible to most Scottish communities and Scotland remained unusual in the large number of small schools able to prepare pupils for university entrance in competition with larger, more prestigious and more expensive institutions. Even though scholarship schemes favoured middle-class children, in the early twentieth century there were more working-class Scottish undergraduates than in the 1860s.[24]

### Secondary Education for Girls

This period saw important developments in girls' secondary education. In England and Wales, in the 1860s, there were no girls' grammar schools and only a handful of academically orientated pro-prietary schools. By the 1890s there were over 218 endowed and proprietary schools for girls and by 1914, following the 1902 Act, there were 349 girls' and 237 mixed secondary schools receiving government grants, besides large private establishments. Admittedly the almost entirely middle-class pupils at these schools represented a small number even of their own class, the vast majority of whom, even in 1914, were still educated at home or in traditional private schools. Nevertheless, as many places for girls as for boys were created in the Welsh intermediate schools following the legislation of 1889, and the 1902 secondary schools broadened the social intake in England and Wales generally for girls and boys. The network of largely successful academic girls' schools thus created by 1914 represented the first stages of a revolution in female education.[25]

Much of the success of the new schools stemmed from the determination of outstanding headmistresses and their staffs (backed by their professional associations) to reject the idea that intellectual study would be harmful for girls' health and to adopt an academic curriculum. Though they disagreed over whether to accede to pressure in the 1890s for the inclusion of domestic science, they generally avoided a curriculum intellectually inferior to that of boys.[26] Parity was advanced by the admission of girls from the 1860s to the same public examinations as boys, an achievement owing much to pressure from headmistresses and others and, particularly, to the feminist campaigner, Emily Davies.[27] These examinations provided external standards and proved 'one of the most important levers in raising the whole level of women's education'.[28]

Reform was not, however, predominantly the fruit of a feminist attack on an existing male fortress, but the outcome of the general movement for sound middle-class schooling. The same shift from small unsystematic private schools to corporate proprietary schools, and the better use of educational endowments, took place for both sexes, even if more slowly for girls and, as noted, the 1902 Act applied to both boys and girls. Equality of provision was advanced less by feminists than by sympathetic and influential male academics, clerics and public figures, and by fathers. A daughter's intellectual education represented for some professional men an indication of élite status, while, for the growing number of professional, clerical and business men whose incomes were precarious, it provided insurance against their daughters having to earn their own livings. Many men actively supported individual girls' schools and the Girls' Public Day School Company (later Trust) (founded 1872), which established over thirty schools by 1896, was largely administered by men.[29]

Most significant, however, was the contribution of the male public servants of the Endowed Schools Commission, who showed a missionary determination to establish girls' grammar schools. By 1900 they and their somewhat less enthusiastic successors after 1874 (the Charity Commissioners) had established over ninety such endowed schools. Though these were very unevenly distributed and grammar-school education was still enjoyed by three times as many boys as girls,[30] this marked a considerable advance and was patently not achieved, as has been claimed, 'largely by private effort'.[31] Further public input, represented in the Welsh Intermediate Education Act and the 1902 Education Act, resulted in an almost tenfold rise in the number of girls in recognized secondary schools by 1914.[32]

Moreover, though most middle-class girls were still catered for in private schools down to 1914 and beyond, these schools were also affected by the reforms – though to what extent is under-researched. Some private schools continued to emphasize ladylike 'accomplishments' and to scorn systematic academic study. But an increasing number, including, especially, denominational schools, attracted well-educated staff, motivated to the development of the intellect. These schools achieved very high academic standards, with curricula embracing Latin and some mathematics and structured approaches to history, geography and modern languages – though not often science. To varying degrees they emulated the structures and ethos of the corporate institutions, preparing girls for public examinations and university entrance while maintaining the ideal of a distinct female education.[33]

The aims of most agents in these changes were conservative rather than revolutionary. Some female educational reformers were active in other women's movements, but many were indifferent or even hostile to any fundamental change in women's position in society. Thus input from feminists who believed in educational reform primarily as a means to advance female emancipation was limited. Intellectual education for girls was not yet intended to produce emancipated females competing with men for careers, but to allow middle-class women, freed from household duties by labour-saving devices and more servants, to develop intellectual and personal attributes enabling them to fulfil their traditional roles as wives and mothers more effectively. It aimed also to prepare women to assist intelligently in voluntary social work and to act generally as guardians of liberal culture. The curriculum, though determinedly academic, stressed the literary and the humane without neglecting the development of ladylike attributes – reflecting the view of headmistresses, parents and male-dominated committees that girls' and boys' education should not be identical.

Such an outlook was manifested in the emphasis on botany in science teaching, the transformation of ornamental accomplishments into serious study of music and art, the linkage of physical education to hygiene and anatomy, and, from the 1890s, in the growing emphasis (unpopular among more academically minded heads) on domestic science, which had been accepted in the state secondary schools as a partial substitute for science.[34]

Religion was also an important moving force. The new girls' schools modelled themselves to varying degrees on the corporate ethos of boys' Public schools, emphasizing character training in a religious and moral environment. Some girls' proprietary schools were Quaker, Methodist and Roman Catholic foundations, others Anglican: the Church Schools Company (founded 1883) set up over thirty schools by the end of the century. Though most girls' high schools were non-sectarian or interdenominational, many male and female supporters and headmistresses were activated by religious, often evangelical motives, seeking to give Christian meaning to women's lives.[35]

By 1900 secondary schooling for girls was accepted by the governing and middle classes, and though no radical change in women's status was intended, and did not immediately occur, a firm basis for such a revolution was laid. The entry of increasing numbers of well-educated girls into voluntary public activities and higher education converged with certain demographic and economic factors to influence, over time, women's general emancipation and to fuel further demands for female education. While most better-off parents did not envisage their daughters taking paid employment, reduction (from the later nineteenth century) in the proportions of males in the population (particularly within the middle classes) created the prospect of permanent spinsterhood for many middle-class women and the need to earn their own living. Though girls' schools generally rejected specifically vocational training, they provided the necessary intellectual and personal basis for entry into employment – just at a time when openings for women increased. Many lower middle-class girls from public secondary schools took jobs from necessity; others increasingly from choice. Before 1914, however, most took up modestly paid clerical posts, teaching and other jobs which did not compete with men. Entrepreneurial activities remained male preserves and only a few women aspired to the higher professions and the more prestigious posts in civil and local government.[36]

In Scotland girls and boys had traditionally been educated together in the burgh and parish schools and, outside the cities, mixed secondary schools remained the norm. Though in practice few career opportunities existed for the 'lass of parts' before the 1880s, and the universities were not fully opened to women until 1892, girls of middle- and artisan-class backgrounds had equal access with boys to secondary education, a practice inhibiting too great curricular differences between the sexes. Scottish parents at all levels of society regarded academic attainment as a commendable attribute in wives and mothers. So, though domestic subjects for girls were injected into public secondary schools from the 1870s, many tended to look unkindly on them and to prefer academic to practical instruction, and girls took the Leaving Certificate alongside boys.[37]

Many upper middle-class Scottish parents, however, continued into the twentieth century to prefer small private girls' schools which existed in large numbers, especially in the largest towns where the most prestigious schools took only boys. But intellectual education for girls was strengthened, as in England, by the appearance of well-structured academic secondary schools, and from the 1870s several developments caused a shift from private schooling. Some large, socially exclusive, proprietary day schools for girls were established, especially in Glasgow and Edinburgh, modelled on those of the Girls' Public Day School Company in England, while for the wealthy, St Leonard's College, a girls' boarding school on English Public-school lines, was founded at St Andrews.[38] Additionally, the reform of educational endowments (achieved more easily than in England) enabled the creation, especially in the main towns, of further large academically orientated girls' secondary schools. These were often able to charge lower fees than the private schools, and this, combined with the opening of Scottish universities fully to women in 1892, further stimulated the shift towards larger academic institutions. Smaller private schools, however, still remained significant in urban areas.

These developments affected mainly the middle classes, but from the 1880s bursaries from elementary schools and the creation of higher grade schools opened secondary education to girls somewhat lower down the social scale. Demand for female secondary and higher education was also stimulated from the 1870s by feminization of the traditionally male Scottish teaching profession. Growing opportunities for men in commerce and the civil service coincided with the lower cost of employing women at a time when school finances were stretched by rising pupil numbers. Secondary schooling also had the attraction of giving girls the means for independence and careers other than in teaching.[39]

In 1871 almost identical proportions of Scottish boys and girls aged 14–17 were at school, but by 1901 a higher proportion of girls than boys attended. These were still mainly middle-class children, but the breadth of the Scottish system, including the continued availability of post-elementary education outside secondary schools proper, make it likely that lower middle- and upper working-class girls were better catered for than their counterparts in England. By 1900, 21 per cent of women students at Aberdeen University and 28 per cent at Glasgow were working-class, and in 1902 over half of the female matriculants at Aberdeen had been educated solely at public elementary schools.[40]

## Higher Education

Between the 1860s and 1914 British university education was transformed consequent on profound changes in society: the waning influence of the Church of England and the landed gentry, the growth of a prosperous urban middle class, the merging of the great landowners and the new plutocracy into a new élite, the expansion of public services and the professions, and a modest spread of meritocracy as educational qualifications became the key to advancement.[41] The ancient Scottish and English universities were reformed, London University expanded and new provincial university institutions developed. Student numbers increased and higher education was broadened in scope to meet the secular needs of society, beneficially affecting standards in the public services and the professions.

The mid-century reforms at Oxford and Cambridge had limited effect, but academic eclipse by newer institutions was avoided as parliament from the 1870s imposed further changes on them, resulting in new posts and specialized studies in law, history, physiology and engineering. Fellowships were opened to dissenters and a teaching body of high repute in research and scholarship developed.[42] For many of the middle classes, however, Oxbridge education remained both limited and expensive, and the fourfold increase in British university student numbers, 1861–1911, stemmed mainly from the growth of institutions other than Oxbridge (and from the influx of women, discussed below),[43] so that by 1900 Oxbridge accounted for only one-third of English university students.

Most significant in this expansion was the growth of London University, the extension of its function as an examining body for institutions at home and abroad and the opening of its external degrees to individuals (see Chapter 3). From 1898 London became a teaching university, having by 1914 – in addition to King's College and University College – thirty-one schools (including Imperial, East London, Bedford, Westfield and Royal Holloway colleges and the London School of Economics) and another twenty-five specialist institutions concerned with agriculture, medicine, theology and teacher training. In another thirty institutions (including Goldsmiths and Birkbeck colleges) the university had recognized teachers.[44]

Also of great significance was the establishment, between 1870 and 1894, of university colleges (originating in local science colleges or the university extension movement) in some ten English and three Welsh centres and at Dundee. At first much of the work of these civic colleges was at a modest level with many part-time students. Only a minority of students took degrees (and those often London external qualifications). By 1914, however, many of these institutions had become full universities most of whose students were full-time undergraduates. The Victoria University, embracing Owens College, Manchester and colleges at Leeds and Liverpool, became three separate universities in 1903–4, while the Welsh colleges joined as the federal University of Wales in 1893. Expansion went with a broadening of the curriculum, and university teachers emerged as an autonomous profession dedicated both to teaching and research.

Though initially it seemed that the newer university institutions would develop as higher technical establishments on the German model, a permanent bifurcation of British university education was avoided by a calculated change of direction by the civic institutions from the 1880s. They responded to the growing demand for liberal and professional education and became multifaceted university establishments. Like London, they gave more attention than Oxbridge to pure and applied science, often absorbing existing medical schools, but they also embraced traditional disciplines and modern specialisms in the arts and social sciences. Thus, while at Manchester in 1889–90 some 50 per cent of students were reading pure sciences, about 30 per cent were studying arts subjects and only 6 per cent technology. By 1914 one-third of students at the newer English universities and two-thirds in Wales were reading arts, compared with 17 and 11 per cent studying applied sciences. Curricular convergence was also furthered by a limited development of scientific and professional studies at Oxbridge. One consequence of all this was the separate (but extensive) development of technical and vocational education in other institutions and greater homogenization of British university education – reinforced by Scottish developments.[45]

Scottish universities shed school-level work and from the 1860s and particularly the 1890s gradually replaced their general humane curriculum by a more flexible system of specialized honours courses in arts, science and applied science. These changes, sometimes deplored as anglicization, are better seen as part of a widespread shift from general to more specialized study, evidenced also in the newer English universities, and to some extent at reformed Oxbridge, and facilitated by improved secondary schooling. English and Scottish university education thus converged to meet the educational needs of the British middle and professional classes. The new universities of the Empire, too, modelled themselves less on Oxbridge than on Scotland, London (itself influenced by Scottish practice) and the English civics.[46]

This revolution in higher education had several sources. Before 1900 the demand of industry for applied scientists and managers provided some impetus to the newer institutions, though these needs were met more by training on the job and institutions other than universities (see Chapter 7). From 1900, however, university research contributed more to industrial development, while commerce, and to some extent industry, began tentatively to recruit graduates. Industrialization affected university expansion much more significantly, however, by contributing to the growth of an affluent society which demanded better administrative services and improved general and professional education.[47]

Diversification and expansion of the professions created demands for well-defined preparation and formal credentials, reflecting the waning influence of family and patronage and the growth of middle-class ideals of certificated expertise and selection by merit. Higher education consequently assumed provision of specialized education for the professions, especially law and medicine. Again, the advent of the corporate state and an expanding Empire multiplied opportunities in central and local government at home, and for administrators, doctors and so on in the colonies. This, combined with a general expansion of responsible white-collar employment, increased demand for graduates, not least in the arts. Changes in Scottish university practice derived partly from the wish of the Scottish middle classes to be able to compete equally in Britain and the Empire in all these fields.[48]

The extension of higher education to women was also a significant ingredient of change both in the universities and in society. They were admitted to the new civic colleges (including the University of Wales) from their inauguration and allowed to graduate at London from 1878, Manchester from 1883 and Durham from 1895. The ancient Scottish universities catered for them from the 1860s and permitted them to graduate from 1892. From 1870 female colleges were established at Oxbridge – where women were gradually integrated into academic life, though not formally admitted to degrees until 1920 (Oxford) and 1948 (Cambridge). By 1910, 20 per cent of British university students were women.[49] This revolution stemmed from women's urge to demonstrate intellectual parity with men, the work of female educationists and educational associations, support from male academics, liberal intellectuals and provincial business figures, as well as from the indulgence of middle-class parents. College education, often felt by the business classes unnecessary for sons, gave social cachet when enjoyed by daughters, adding intellectual to artistic accomplishments. The increasing possibility that daughters might have to earn their own living, however, led many to seek higher education as a grounding for employment. In fact many did obtain paid jobs – especially as school teachers and governesses.[50]

Prospects of access to public life or traditional male occupations, however, played little part in these developments for, aside from school teaching (and, for a tiny number, medicine), the professions, politics and business remained virtually closed to women until after 1914. Feminism, likewise, played a minor role and the contribution of female higher education to women's emancipation generally is controversial. Higher education advantaged women mainly in 'female' occupations, driving a wedge between highly educated and other women, rather than promoting feminist solidarity. Until after 1914, most female graduate employment was in school teaching, an outlet also serviced by the women's teachers' colleges which were established in this period, and provided an alternative educational experience for intelligent middle- and artisan-class girls.[51] Teacher training, whether in the civic universities (where it was introduced from 1890) or in other colleges, was particularly significant both in the social advancement of the lower middle and working classes generally and in provision of advanced education for able girls. Students in training increased from some 2,000 in 1861 to over 12,000 in 1911.[52]

The fortunes of universities and secondary schools were interrelated. The Oxford and Cambridge Local Examinations (established 1857–8) strengthened the influence of the universities on the school curriculum, helped to prepare and identify future able undergraduates and earned the universities good will. They also (like the Scottish Leaving Certificate, established 1888, which they influenced) benefited secondary education by providing tests impartial to the social standing or sex of the examinees, and success in them became generally accepted as a valid indication of educational attainment.[53]

Again, the schools multiplied potential undergraduates and, by creating a demand for teachers, stimulated university arts as well as science departments – even to the extent of ensuring the survival of some civic universities. The civics also owed much to funding provided by local employers, private benefactors and societies (among them women's bodies) activated by civic or regional pride and a general belief in the benefits of spreading higher education. From the late 1880s, pressures from within and outwith the universities led to government grants, without which development of university education other than in London, Oxbridge and Scotland would have been much restricted. Only successful Welsh pressure for government funding for the University of Wales ensured its survival for, though it became a symbol of national unity, the rhetorical support given by Liberals and nonconformists was not matched by local funds. Welsh industrialists were lukewarm and dissenters' money was channelled rather into chapels.[54]

The expansion of university education and changes in its nature were accompanied by a diversification in the social background of students and their subsequent careers. In English universities as a whole, growth in proportions of students from professional and administrative families was the most evident development, though the extent and nature of social diversification varied considerably. At Oxbridge the dominance of students from landed and clerical backgrounds diminished progressively as numbers from comfortably-off professional and business families rose, reflecting the merging of old landed and new upper middle classes into a new ruling élite. But otherwise change was limited. On the eve of the Great War there were very few lower middle-class and virtually no working-class students at Oxbridge. Those from Public schools greatly outnumbered those few on scholarships from state secondary schools, while grammar-school entries had been restricted by the abolition of reserved scholarships in the 1850s. The newer English institutions, however, from their beginnings, attracted more students from business and professional backgrounds, including a substantial minority from the lower middle and artisan classes. Between 1900 and

1914 increased numbers of scholarships and expansion of teacher training resulted in a considerable body of working-class students at some civic colleges. At Nottingham in 1911, for example, 73 per cent of those destined for school teaching and 24 per cent of other students were from the lower middle and manual working classes.[55]

Scottish and Welsh university education had a broader social base than the English civic colleges. The danger that the entrance examination instituted for Scottish universities in 1892 might disadvantage the less well-off was obviated by improved secondary schooling and a proliferation of scholarships, and the universities remained basically meritocratic rather than élitist. By 1910 some 30–40 per cent of students at Glasgow and Aberdeen universities were of the lower middle and labouring classes. By 1914, in the Scottish universities as a whole, perhaps one-third were from the (mainly skilled) working class.[56] In Wales the effect of improved secondary schooling was to increase the numbers of college students from lowly backgrounds. The proportion from manual working-class (including mining) families rose from one-quarter in the early 1870s to one-third in 1910, by which time one-quarter came from the lower middle class.[57]

Changes in the social composition of the student body affected graduate career patterns. At Oxbridge proportions of those returning to landed estates and going into the Church fell as those entering professions and administration (and, to a very modest extent, business) rose. The balance thus shifted from returning the young of a narrow ruling class to their origins to, increasingly, redistributing sons of a broader élite to an expanding number of higher occupations, thus gaining for Oxbridge a more significant role in national life. Generally, however, the role of the older universities in élite creation was limited. Normally an Oxbridge education reflected rather than bestowed élite status, which was based on wealth and family. It was not essential for many élite occupations and only a minority of the ruling establishment received it. Nevertheless, for a few less well-off middle-class students it did give access to élite positions and from the mid nineteenth century the universities, especially Oxbridge, did expand the pool from which the dominant élite was recruited.[58]

The extent of the spread of university education must not, however, be exaggerated. Between 1861 and 1911 the percentage of university students in the population rose only from 0.02 to 0.06 in England and 0.1 to 0.14 in Scotland. By 1911 students in Wales represented some 0.07 of the population of the principality.[59] Nevertheless, by 1900, a basis had been laid for advance and British universities stood poised to enter into what Michael Sanderson has called their twentieth-century role of 'fire and crucible of social change and mobility'. The newer English universities, with lower fees than Oxbridge and local recruitment, were particularly significant in providing opportunities for social and occupational advancement to a growing spectrum of the middle and artisan classes. Scottish universities had for a long time sent many clever lower middle- and working-class students into teaching, the law, medicine and the Church, and from mid century provided access to a broadening range of middle-class occupations. The Welsh colleges, with even larger proportions from lower social groups, concentrated on the liberal arts and medicine rather than pure science or technology, and by the early twentieth century were sending over three-quarters of their students into medicine, the churches and, especially, school teaching. This trend was accentuated following the introduction of local government scholarships after 1902.[60] Meanwhile, out of the university extension movement of the later nineteenth century grew the Workers' Educational Association (founded 1903), which in association with the universities brought a taste of advanced liberal education on a part-time basis to a sprinkling of the working classes not otherwise touched by intellectual study and to some middle-class women.[61]

### Segmentation or Convergence?

Historians seeking a conceptual framework for the development of British secondary and higher education, between 1870 and the outbreak of the Great War, have been attracted to theories portraying it as part of a general western European process of hierarchical systematization, reinforcing social stratification. While the masses received only elementary schooling, parallel segments of secondary and higher education were developed – differentiated by social class, curriculum, student age range and level of teaching. Thus, the argument goes, in England and Wales, the ruling élite enjoyed a superior liberal education in the Public schools, the first grade grammar schools and (into early adulthood) Oxbridge, while a small minority of students lower down the social scale were provided with a less prestigious (basically modern or scientific) secondary schooling in lesser grammar, higher grade, Welsh intermediate and (from 1902) state secondary schools. Most of this latter group left school by their mid teens, though some might attend part-time technical colleges and a very few the civic universities, which had a scientific and technological bias. Scotland moved in the same direction, as much secondary education became functionally distinct from elementary and in the cities socially stratified.[62] There is an implication, too, that the 'inferior' segment was consciously created by the ruling élite to perpetuate and reinforce its own hegemony – an inegalitarian policy, antagonistic to all but a minimal degree of social mobility. The 1902 Education Act is seen as involving deliberate destruction of the higher grade board schools, 'one of the most relevant and forward-looking developments in English educational history',[63] which threatened to evolve into a system of high-quality secondary education with a broad social intake and modern curricula under local, democratic control.

But because educational institutions quite naturally tended to reflect existing social stratification, it does not necessarily follow that they were designed or manipulated to perpetuate it. In England and Wales the separate investigations of the 1860s into elementary, grammar and Public schools, and subsequent social gradation of the grammar schools, recognized existing divisions rather than initiated them. Indeed, the complexity of developments in British elementary, post-elementary and higher education from the 1860s, revealed in earlier sections of this chapter and in Chapter 5, suggests the need for caution before acceptance of attempts to fit them to a common international matrix. By the 1880s and 1890s it was no longer possible to regard the English and Welsh public elementary schools as exclusively working class: especially in some urban areas the lower middle classes dominated some schools as well as making use of higher grade and grammar schools.[64] Moreover, facile segmentation theories take no account of the heterogeneous mass of private schools, curricularly diverse and not susceptible to external manipulation, which catered for large swathes of middle-class and upper working-class English and Welsh children. They fail, too, to embrace the extension of secondary and higher education to females, a large and previously educationally deprived social group. Neither do they show appreciation of the considerable overlap between British universities and other institutions of post-school (particularly technical) education. Moreover, in Scotland, not only is it clear that there was no 'hermetic seal' between elementary and secondary education, but it is equally evident that there was also 'no real segmentation within secondary education'.[65] The Scottish day schools (including many board as well as secondary schools) and universities had a relatively broad social intake, and were never overshadowed by Public-school education or Oxbridge.

Most significantly, development of institutions characterized by distinct curricula related to social class (emphasized as an essential ingredient of segmentation theories) was conspicuously absent both at secondary and university levels in Britain. Though the reformed grammar schools in England and Wales varied according to local circumstances in social composition, prestige, the degree of emphasis on the classics and success in competition for Oxbridge bursaries, these were differences of degree rather than kind. They were mitigated not only by common adherence to a basically liberal curriculum, but also by the tendency for secondary and private schools generally (as well to an extent Scottish schools) to adopt much of the organization and ethos of the Public schools. So, just as in the Scottish secondary schools and universities there was little curricular differentiation, such a development was deliberately rejected in the state secondary system and by the universities in England and Wales.[66]

Convergence within the university sector was assisted by colonization of the English civic universities by men from the ancient English and Scottish universities, by the unifying effect of the professionalization of university teaching and by the adoption by the newer institutions of the intellectual values and some of the ethos and trappings of Oxbridge.[67] The view that by the Great War the civic universities were 'at the intellectual summit of British higher education'[68] may be somewhat exaggerated, but certainly by then the civics aimed at the same peak as older institutions. In British universities a hierarchy of esteem existed, based on general levels of attainment (and, between Oxbridge and the rest, social standing), but rigid bifurcation had been avoided and adaptation towards a future single model advanced. Diversity in the provision of particular specialist studies represented variety within a body of institutions basically similar, rather than a clear division into two distinct types.[69] Though the social make-up of the student bodies of Oxbridge and the civics differed considerably, it is significant that, as early as the 1890s, some 26 per cent of students in the federal Victoria University (Manchester, Liverpool, Leeds) were from Public schools (including even some from the 'great' schools) and at Manchester in 1895, 36 per cent of new students were from grammar and Public schools.[70]

This convergence represented initial stages in the democratization of cultural capital.[71] Condemnation of the Victorian and Edwardian

governing classes for failing to provide general access to equally prestigious types of secondary and higher education (only a decade or so after
achieving universal free elementary schooling) is hardly reasonable.
The logical implications of absolute equality of opportunity (such as
the abolition of the family) are unacceptable even in late twentieth-
century democracies and its achievement has proved unattainable
even in modern Marxist regimes.[72] Naturally, changes in the social
composition of secondary schools and universities occurred gradually,
and first to benefit were the better-off. Numbers of working-class students in secondary and higher education were, as noted above, relatively small before 1914. But a continuing process had been launched.
The underlying aims of Scottish education had always been democratic
rather than élitist, and pre-1914 liberalism supported democratic educational policies in Britain generally. The progressive extension of secondary, technical and higher education to social groups not previously
covered was deliberately fostered by governmental financial assistance
and, especially in the early twentieth century, by proliferation of scholarships which began to breach the barrier between elementary and secondary schooling.[73]

    There might seem to be a stronger case for believing that segmenta-
tion occurred between higher and purely technical education, particularly as the new universities rejected a role confining them to science
and technology. The technical institutions recruited mainly working-
and lower middle-class students who frequently attended part-time and
would have found it difficult financially to follow full-time university
education. To some extent, however, both class and curricular differences in the pre-1914 period were blurred. The civic universities often
retained vocational training (some of it part-time) for a minority of
students (of the same ages as in the technical colleges) well into the
twentieth century, and most British universities (including Oxbridge)
developed particular technological specialisms (Chapter 7). Offspring of
the artisan and lower middle classes, moreover, entered both technical
and higher education, particularly the Scottish and newer English and
Welsh universities.

    The distinction between much of the scientific and technical educa-
tion offered by the universities and most of that purveyed by the purely
technical institutions, lay in the level of instruction, the way it was
organized and the nature of the topics studied. The bulk of the instruction given in the technical colleges had a practical bent and was academically at a lower level and less intellectually demanding than the

advanced scientific and technological work of the universities. But it had been developed to meet perceived national economic needs, the demands of the market and the belief that more skilled technicians were required than graduate scientists. It was not obviously the child of sinister social or political motives, consciously conceived to provide an inferior, curricularly differenced type of post-school education into which to divert working-class youths.[74] Indeed the technical institutions provided (as is discussed in detail in Chapter 7) excellent technical and technological instruction at a number of different levels. The provision of part-time instruction for those in industrial employment was not necessarily inferior to full-time education in the advanced technical institutions common on the continent – indeed, for reasons expanded on in the next chapter, it may well have been superior. Moreover, while British technical institutions trained the bulk of their students as technicians or craftsmen, offering an alternative avenue for upward social mobility to that provided by the secondary schools and universities, at the highest level they overlapped or complemented the universities. Some of the work they undertook, especially in branches of engineering, was the equivalent of what was undertaken by institutions of higher education on the continent, and was held in high esteem. At the same time, the colleges of London University and the civic university institutions continued to undertake a great deal of sound work at sub-degree level.[75]

There is, therefore, a strong case for believing that the development of secondary, technical and higher education, 1870–1914, is better summarized as an initial stage in the process (still incomplete) of democratization, convergence and 'inclusion', rather than as a process of segmentation. The gradual introduction and extension of compulsory elementary education was followed by first steps in the creation of a variety of kinds of post-elementary education in which a neat equation of curriculum with social class in a highly differentiated hierarchical system is difficult to discern. Changes which were introduced reflect the strength of progressive intentions in ruling circles, and belie the picture of a system manipulated to restrain rather than extend educational opportunity.[76]

# 7

---

# SCIENCE, TECHNOLOGY, EDUCATION AND THE ECONOMY FROM THE 1850s TO 1914

## Education and Britain's Economic Fortunes: the Debate

There is a broad division between historians who link apparent defects in education (particularly scientific and technical education) in this period with a perceived decline in Britain's economic fortunes, and others who doubt whether, in fact, any avoidable decline occurred, whether any particular link existed between education and economic performance and whether, anyway, there is not (from the point of view of its contribution to the economy) more to praise than to blame in contemporary educational provision.[1]

A widely promoted thesis posits a Britain at the height of its economic dominance in 1850, yet beginning to slip into a long period of relative decline persisting into the late twentieth century and owing much to factors of a cultural and educational nature. These included the failure of the state to provide systematic elementary, technical and scientific instruction; the development among the middle and upper classes of a culture (nurtured by their educational experience) deeply antagonistic to industry and business; and the inertia of the bulk of industrialists who were suspicious of formal technical training, incompetent in business acumen, unwilling to embrace innovation or enter new fields, and generally lacking the spirit of enterprise which imbued their forefathers. New science-based industries and technologies were ignored, unfamiliar markets went unexploited, banks failed to fund domestic industry and capital flowed abroad. All this, the argument goes, contrasted strongly with the state of affairs in emerging rival economies. Especially in Germany and France, state-funded systems of scientific and technical education at secondary and higher levels boosted industry by providing it with sound technicians and high-grade scientists and researchers. In Germany compulsory elementary schooling provided a soundly educated workforce. Consequently the British economy expanded at a slower rate than those of its more competent competitors, and indeed than it had done itself in more successful times.[2]

Both the waning of the entrepreneurial spirit and the lack of scientific and technical knowledge among industrial leaders are blamed particularly on the English Public schools and ancient universities. For reasons of social ambition, successful entrepreneurs increasingly sent their sons and grandsons to Public schools steeped in the conservative traditions of rural landowning, the armed services and the Church of England. These schools were contemptuous of manufacturing and business, scorned innovation and material change and provided, as did the universities, a largely classical curriculum, holding science in low esteem and regarding practical subjects as beyond the pale. Usually situated in the rural and Anglican south of England, far from the manufacturing districts, these boarding schools were instrumental in instilling in 'the sons of rough and warty pioneers . . . a dislike for the pursuits which had made the country rich and powerful'.[3] The result was a 'haemorrhage of talent' as many such boys shunned industry and trade for the professions, other gentlemanly pursuits and the civil service (where they imbued government with the same anti-industrial bias). If they did return to the manufacturing and business world, it was as half-hearted incompetents, avoiding innovation and risk and with all the attitudes necessary for successful entrepreneurship stifled.[4]

Grounds for this pessimistic picture are not lacking. British industrial supremacy was shown to be under threat as early as the international exhibitions of 1851 and 1867, and by the later decades of the century Britain no longer so manifestly surpassed its rivals in industrial output and commercial activity. It is true, too, that the incorporation of science into school and university curricula and the expansion of technical education was a slow business, and that British governments played a less dominant part in organizing such activity than did those of continental countries.[5]

In the later 1860s the Clarendon Commission on the 'great' Public schools found that 'natural science is with slight exceptions practically excluded from the education of the higher classes in England', while the Taunton Commission on the grammar schools reported that in those 'the place of science is an unsettled and unsatisfactory one. In very few schools does it form part of the regular curriculum.' Although, between the 1870s and 1914, science did find a place in the Public and grammar schools, often it was only perfunctorily addressed by many pupils, and by some not at all. As late as 1875, in the 128 English Public and grammar schools responding to a Royal Commission enquiry, science was taught in only sixty-three, and of those only thirteen had a laboratory. Of some 9,000 boys in the sample, fewer than 2,500 were studying science at any level and many of those were devoting very small proportions of their time to it. Even in the 1880s only twenty-five boys out of 320 were learning science at Uppingham, and at Radley the laboratories were used for storing hampers and no science was being taught. Higher grade schools, established in the 1890s with a scientific and technical bias, were superseded from 1902 by state secondary schools on which (as described in Chapter 6) the government from 1904 imposed a liberal curriculum, reducing the scientific bias (especially for girls) and eschewing technical training.[6]

Down to 1914 and beyond, the Public schools and some grammar schools were influenced both by the multiplicity of Oxbridge scholarships in classics and the paucity of those in science, and by their recruitment of staff from universities where science only slowly achieved a significant place. At Oxbridge science was for long poorly funded and attracted few students (and those were often destined for medical careers). Finance for extending science teaching at Oxford was adversely affected by the agricultural depression, which depleted college revenues, and, between 1850 and 1900, pure science accounted for only 9 per cent in the public examiners' lists (compared with history: 37 per cent, classics: 39). The theoretical study of technology found even slower acceptance in the ancient universities.[7]

The English Public schools preferred not to teach 'useful' or what they regarded as purely factual subjects (science) but to train the mind (for which classics and the humanities were considered admirably suited) and to form the character of the ruling élite for leadership in society, government, the armed and civil services and the Church. Such an outlook was reflected in some grammar schools, particularly in the more substantial ones where parents were influenced by the social and professional advantages of a traditional education.

In Scottish schools classics was not so dominant, but they, too, tended to ignore technical instruction, and science was established as a significant subject only in the later decades of the century. The Scottish middle classes generally sought a liberal education suitable for careers in the churches, medicine, teaching and the law and for superior posts in commerce and banking, rather than in industry. Technical education was regarded as fit only for artisans. Moreover, as in England, lower middle-class and upper working-class parents wanted clerical jobs for their sons and favoured liberal and commercially useful subjects. Of some 14,000 burgh school pupils in 1866, 92 per cent were studying 'English' subjects, 75 per cent writing and arithmetic and 25 per cent Latin; science was almost completely neglected. The more distinctly secondary schools, developed from the 1870s, paid more attention to science, but parental demand ensured that modern and commercial subjects and Latin continued to dominate. Such a bias found support in the Scotch Education Department and the Scottish churches. Even Simon Laurie, a member of the Scottish Association for the Promotion of Technical and Secondary Education, warned in the 1890s of too much emphasis on technical subjects, claiming that the 'Shorter Catechism has done more to make Scotland efficient in the world's work than mathematics and chemistry can ever do'.[8]

It is true, too, that British governments left technical training to a disparate array of voluntary and local government institutions, all independent of one another, catering largely for part-time (usually evening) students. The governments of Germany, France and to some extent the United States, on the other hand, directly organized and generously funded technical and scientific education at all levels and sponsored research. From the early nineteenth century France had a system of full-time technical training establishments and vocational schools, and the German states widespread elementary schooling topped by trade schools, modern secondary schools and polytechnic colleges. These last developed into advanced technological institutes (*Technische Hochschulen*) in the 1860s, attaining university status in 1892. They built up impressive scientific and technological faculties with close ties with industry, and by 1910, since science was also taught in the traditional universities, Germany had more than eight times as many university science and technology students as did England. In the United States, land grant colleges covered practical and technological subjects, the older universities embraced applied science, and the Massachusetts Institute of Technology was established in 1862. In the 1890s, with only twice

Britain's population, the States had ten times the number of engineering students.[9]

This pessimistic picture is supported by the record of contemporary opinion. Failure of British governments to match overseas educational provision evoked criticism in the nineteenth century from a 'scientific lobby' of academics, politicians, industrialists and organizations. These last included the Society of Arts, the Royal Society, the British Association for the Advancement of Science (established 1849), a parliamentary committee of MPs and Lords, the so-called 'Cambridge network' of scientists seeking expansion of university science, the 'X Club' (founded 1864) of influential scientists and the National Association for the Promotion of Technical (*later* and Secondary) Education (founded 1887) and its Scottish counterpart (1893). Their views, vociferously promulgated in numerous publications and speeches, and their evidence to various official investigations (into the Great Exhibition, scientific and technical education, elementary education, the universities, the Public and endowed grammar schools and the Great Depression) stressed a causal relationship between Britain's supposed deficiency in technical and scientific education and its apparent economic difficulties.[10]

This simple linkage of economic decline with educational and cultural deficiency has for long been supported by many economic and educational historians, and has proved attractive to historical popularizers as well as to politicians and pundits seeking an explanation of Britain's supposedly poor economic performance in the later twentieth century. Though the matter is still contentious, this view seems, on balance, to present an interpretation of complex developments which is inadequate, especially for the period before 1914.[11]

The thesis of a uniquely British anti-business culture is largely mythical. Hostility towards capitalist enterprise was common in Europe but probably less evident in Britain than in other advanced communities. Enthusiasm for science and its practical application was widespread among the British middle classes, and professional scientists and engineers enjoyed respect and influence. The landed classes often had strong interests in mining, manufacturing, transportation and urban development: some 85–90 per cent of leading men in the steel industry, 1850–1950, for instance, were from the top social stratum (including aristocracy and gentry). In contrast Prussian landowners were much more antagonistic to business and industry, and recent research has stressed Germany's 'anti-industrial value system' and the low esteem of practical education among the ruling élite, which, until the late nineteenth century, consisted largely of the 'non-entrepreneurial', 'non-economic' upper middle class.[12]

The allegedly detrimental influence of the English Public schools and Oxbridge on the middle classes, entrepreneurial enterprise and the overall economy, most vehemently promoted by M. J. Wiener, is now criticized as based on 'a collection of generalizations and one-sided prejudices'.[13] It is a thesis which overestimates the possible influence of the Public schools. Those investigated by the Clarendon Commission in the 1860s had only 2,741 pupils, and even by 1900 there were only some 20,000 boys in the sixty-odd schools by then recognizable as Public schools.[14] Even fewer attended Oxbridge. Moreover, the view that entry of industrialists' sons into the Public schools became a 'flood' after mid century is highly dubious: in the 1860s probably fewer than 4 per cent of middle-class boys attended them, and by 1900 only 7 per cent, most of them sons of professional men. This was far too low a proportion to have instilled anti-business attitudes into the middle classes generally. The penetration of the Public schools by a few of the industrial middle class did not come until after 1860, and then on a small scale, so that the great mass of industrial leaders down to 1914 were not Public-school men.[15] And among the few thousand students at Oxbridge there must have been very few indeed.

It follows that there can have been no great 'haemorrhage of talent', with scions of successful entrepreneurs seduced into non-productive occupations. Indeed research shows that most Public-school pupils from professional and business families followed their fathers' callings with little shift from business to the professions, though at the same time increasing proportions of Public-school boys as a whole were entering business. All of this throws doubt on the thesis of generational decay and the picture of the Public schools as divorced from the economic world.[16] Where there was migration from business families to the professions it often reflected a career choice by younger sons, 'haemorrhage' here being but 'a persistent demographic illusion' created by business shedding superfluous family members. The likelihood that those less likely to succeed in business were (providentially for the economy) among those so diverted turns the 'haemorrhage' argument on its head.[17]

The allegation that Public-school boys who did enter the business world were half-hearted incompetents is also difficult to maintain. Many who took this road did, in fact, do well in the financial, commercial and service industries, contributing to the diversification from manufacturing which ensured the continued health of the economy.

Similarly, those who followed careers in the law, the armed services and the civil and colonial civil services contributed indirectly to an economy which relied on stable administration at home and in the Empire and on well-policed oceans and well-protected colonies. In all these areas the general intellectual education of the Public schools was preferable to specialized scientific knowledge. It is noteworthy, too, that initiative in decision making, self-reliance and leadership qualities, so energetically developed by the schools, were the very characteristics of effective entrepreneurs and creative individuals generally.[18]

The 'cultural critique' of Wiener and others is thus to many scholars no longer acceptable as an explanation of changes in Britain's economic fortunes, and it seems probable that the 'hypothesis of the negative influence of the Public schools on economic growth must be rejected *in toto*'.[19] Such a critique, anyway, ignores the development of English and Welsh secondary and university education outside the Public schools and Oxbridge, as well as the Scottish educational experience, all of which have been explored in Chapter 6.

In Scotland only the aristocracy and a few of the very rich middle classes patronized the English Public schools or the handful of Scottish boarding school imitations. Virtually all middle-class Scottish parents, including the well-off and professional, sent their children to publicly controlled local secondary schools, or (especially in the larger towns) proprietary or private schools not essentially different in ethos. In all these day schools, pupils remained in their family and local community, not isolated in any artificial anti-business environment and with no pressure to reject the economically productive pursuits of their parents. Certainly parents rejected vocational and science-based training, preferring a general literary–commercial education, but this stemmed not from aristocratic influence or social snobbery but from ambition for careers for their sons in commerce, finance or the Kirk (or teaching or white-collar work in the case of the lower middle and artisan classes). In the Scottish schools and universities, certainly, there was nothing of the rejection of the modern economic world which Wiener purports to find in the English Public school and Oxbridge.[20]

**Technical and Scientific Education in Germany, France and Britain**

The alleged economic eclipse of Britain by her rivals rests partly on the assumption of relative backwardness in scientific and technical education.[21] But just as the level of esteem in which other countries held scientific and technical education has been exaggerated, so too has their superiority in those fields and the impact of such education on their economies.[22] In France only a tiny minority of the industrial labour force received vocational training, and any effect of that on the French economy before 1914 must have been marginal. At a higher level, a secondary education based on the classics, philosophy and pure mathematics was necessary for entry into the *grandes écoles* and administrative careers, to which greater prestige attached than to industrial or commercial occupations. Between 1880 and 1913 numbers awarded the science baccalaureate actually fell, and in 1900 only 13 per cent of university students were in science faculties. Moreover, university science was concerned mainly with medicine while the curriculum of the prestigious engineering establishment, the *Ecole Polytechnique*, was dominated by pure mathematics. That institution concerned itself mainly with supplying state mines and the army with engineers, and its students regarded employment in industry as a last resort: between 1880 and 1914, 74 per cent of its graduates went into the army.[23]

In Germany the quality and impact of state elementary education was more limited than once thought. It did not lead to secondary education and many continuation schools provided remedial rather than vocational training, and, anyway, even in the 1920s, most of the industrial workforce was not engaged in activities 'driven by science-based technology'.[24] In the late nineteenth century some 7 per cent of Germans attended secondary schools, and the curriculum of the most prestigious of those was strongly classical. Most German entrepreneurs with secondary education came from these classical *Gymnasien*. Yet, as Sidney Pollard has pointed out, these institutions 'did less for future business entrepreneurs' than the English Public schools, rather doing 'their best to ensure that a large proportion of the most intelligent and most influential [of the] population looked down with contempt on science and technology'. The curriculum of other secondary schools was of a general humanistic kind, and even those which grew out of earlier trade schools were, by the 1880s, spending only between 7 and 18 per cent of their time on science. Only 2 per cent of secondary-school pupils proceeded to higher education, of whom four-fifths were from the classical *Gymnasien*. The traditional universities concentrated on classics and the humanities and overproduced arts graduates. They resisted the inclusion of applied science in their curricula and disdained vocational training. As late as 1914 only 30 per cent of students, in these and the

*Technische Hochschulen* together, were studying science and technology, and that included medical students. Moreover, only a tiny number of science and technology graduates went into industry; the majority went into state employment – many engineers were engaged in the construction of public buildings, railways, roads and canals. As for research, the Prussian victory against France in 1871 is said to have owed more to foreign (especially British) technology than to German research. From then on the government did support research aimed at strengthening Germany industry, but often with military and naval purposes in mind.[25]

The thesis of German and French superiority in scientific and technical education owes much to uncritical acceptance of the views of the Victorian science lobby by historians – themselves perhaps over-influenced by the rhetoric of the dirigist economic and educational policies of the post-1945 period. They have concentrated too much on Oxbridge and the Public schools, ignoring the English private schools, underrating the contribution of the newer institutions of higher and further education and the Scottish universities, and failing to acknowledge possible merit in the policies of British governments or in the attitude of employers, educationalists and others to vocational and technical training.

At least until the end of the nineteenth century, the bulk of the English and Welsh middle classes attended private schools. Of these, many boys' schools carried on the tradition of the eighteenth-century academies, teaching not only the arts but pure science as well as technical, commercial and practical subjects, thus being recently judged 'major agents of change, playing a substantial part in determining the curriculum of the modern secondary school'. Moreover, from the 1870s onwards, the reformed grammar schools generally did pay more attention to science than formerly, and some in larger cities (such as Manchester Grammar School, King Edward's at Birmingham and the grammar schools at Bradford and Exeter), devoted substantial resources to it.[26]

School-level scientific, technical and vocational education was further advanced by the interrelated activities of central and local government. Throughout Britain the board schools included science in their curricula. From 1872, grants from the Department of Science and Art (established in the early 1850s to promote scientific and technical education) went to 'organized science schools' working for its examinations. These grants benefited evening institutions, grammar schools and the higher grade schools, which emphasized science within a modern curriculum. Additionally, during the 1890s, the technical instruction committees (see Chapter 6 and below) are said to have revolutionized the teaching of science in secondary schools. They channelled considerable sums from local rates and money allotted them from the excise duties, detailed below, into science and technical education in existing secondary classes and schools, including some grammar schools, and also established scholarships for elementary-school pupils.[27]

As already suggested in Chapter 6, it seemed possible that the higher grade schools might have developed into a major sector of English and Welsh state secondary schooling along the lines of the continental technical and vocational schools. This would have provided the upper working and lower middle classes with a decidedly technically orientated education quite distinct from the liberal curriculum of the middle-class secondary schools. That this did not happen marked not a rejection of science, but a recognition that, at school level, liberal education embracing science would better serve national needs. The curriculum of the maintained secondary schools, which succeeded the higher grade schools, from 1904 included science as an essential element – but within a general modern syllabus. They generally avoided purely vocational training. Official policy was influenced here by the views both of contemporary educationalists and of some leading scientists and their organizations. This ensured that secondary schooling in the years before 1914 (destined to be increasingly available to the most talented of the nation's young), was general, liberal and modern, serving the multifarious needs of a modern economy, rather than a restricted training serving only manufacturing.[28]

Scottish public and parental opinion continued to be particularly opposed to narrowly technical, scientific or vocational training, preferring a traditionally liberal education. Thus, in Scotland, even the higher grade schools of the 1880s embraced science only as part of a general modern curriculum. Very few technical schools were set up by school boards under an Act of 1887, and attempts from 1899 to develop new higher grade schools with a technical bias had little success.[29]

Instead of maintained secondary education in Britain being developed as strongly vocational and technical, these areas of study began to be catered for at school level, from the early 1900s, in England and Wales in elementary, higher elementary and central schools. In Scotland they were provided in supplementary courses in elementary schools and in urban central schools. None of these developments can, however, have had much impact on the economy before 1914, and any possible consequences of failure to build on them to provide training for the less academic child belong to a later period.[30]

At the further and advanced level of scientific and technological education, too, British developments differed from continental ones, though it is doubtful whether they were less successful. The scientific instruction in the mechanics' institutes and the host of other voluntary adult education establishments found in Britain in the first half of the nineteenth century and later, though often sound, lacked structure and was usually at a fairly elementary level. In response to foreign industrial competition, therefore, British governments from the 1830s, and more particularly from the 1850s, began to toy with the continental system of state provision. From 1837 a central and some provincial government schools of design were established. This was followed in the 1850s by an attempt to create, under the aegis of the Department of Science and Art, a national science centre and provincial English and Scottish science schools. The plans for a national science centre, however, were only partly fulfilled and it had a limited success, while all four of the provincial science schools (at Aberdeen, Birmingham, Bristol and Wigan) had failed by 1860.[31]

Government policy consequently shifted away from the continental model of direct control, to a more flexible one of indirect influence. The establishment and maintenance of all types of adult education were left to voluntary effort, and technical education generally developed in institutions providing part-time tuition for students already in work. The government influenced the content of instruction through a system of examinations in theoretical aspects of science and technology and grants for institutions preparing students for them. The well-organized syllabi devised by the Department of Science and Art were adopted in many schools of art and science, teacher-training colleges, mechanics' institutes and so on, as well as in elementary and secondary schools. Government thus ensured certain levels of achievement, without itself owning institutions, employing teachers or directly controlling students. It also exerted pressure on the City and Guilds of London to complement government exams by a more vocationally and technologically orientated system of examinations: numbers registered for these rose from 2,500 in 1880 to over 34,000 by 1900. The City and Guilds also founded Finsbury Technical College in 1883, to which were added from the mid 1880s independently controlled London polytechnics, numbering eleven by 1896 with 36,000 students.[32]

From the late 1880s a means of further expanding scientific and technical education without direct government control was found. The Technical Instruction Acts of 1889 and 1891 (England and Wales) and 1892 (Scotland) permitted the raising of local rates for technical education, while Acts of 1890 and 1892 provided extra funds for it from the excise revenue ('whisky money'). This very considerable injection of public money distributed to local government technical instruction committees, resulted in extra money for a large number of existing institutions. It also made possible the establishment in many towns of well-financed technical colleges or institutes – under the control of local councils (or in Scotland of other bodies), but each independent of one another.

Most instruction in the new establishments was of a further rather than a higher kind and students were mainly part-time. But standards were generally good and some colleges in large English cities embraced advanced technological work. From 1895 at least to 1918, the bulk of English engineers were trained in municipal institutions through very successful full- and part-time courses for students of age 16 upwards.[33] Some of these English institutions, and others in Glasgow and Edinburgh, had ambitions to become British *Technische Hochschulen*. That they were unsuccessful in this was partly due to the emergence of London University and of the English civic university colleges which, unlike the German universities, developed strong science and technology departments from the start. The technical school in Manchester was absorbed by the Victoria University of Manchester; Imperial College (which might well have developed into a high-grade technical university) became a college of London University in 1907; and, in Scotland, the Royal Technical College affiliated with the University of Glasgow in 1913. Advanced scientific and technological work in some other municipal colleges, like those in Birmingham and Liverpool, and at the Heriot Watt College in Edinburgh, was given up or did not develop.[34]

The government (which gave grants to the independent university colleges from 1889) refused to fund university institutions devoted solely to technology, and for this and other reasons the embryonic provincial universities developed, like London University, as multifaceted institutions. Though they had something of a bias towards science and technology, they stressed the need for applied studies to be firmly based in pure science.[35] So Britain was 'saved from the dual form of higher education such as existed in Germany...and thus avoided... a "second rate" stigma', being attached to institutions dealing with technology – but without the advanced study of science and applied science suffering.[36] Well before 1914 the civic colleges (some becoming full universities by the early 1900s) achieved high reputations in these fields, developing a mutually advantageous relationship with a variety of industries (especially local specialisms). The Yorkshire College, for instance, had strong interests in mining, textiles, agriculture and engineering. In London, King's College and University College were important for the pure and applied sciences, especially various branches of engineering, and much of their research and development was undertaken in conjunction with industrial firms. Imperial College, too, achieved an international reputation in applied science. In the late nineteenth century one-third of the graduates at Birmingham and Bristol went into industry, and about half of those at Newcastle. Though Cambridge and, particularly, Oxford still lagged behind in science and technology, they gained some ground from the 1860s and still more after 1900. Engineering and chemistry were established at a modest level at Oxford and by 1900 science had become an important field at Cambridge, which also developed engineering and other applied sciences. Indeed by then, 45 per cent of successes in the various Cambridge tripos were in natural sciences, mathematics and mechanical sciences, as against 25 per cent in classics. Between 1870 and 1910, numbers of English university graduates in science and in technology increased by factors of 61 and 72 respectively.[37]

In Scotland, preference for providing a broad spectrum of society with a general university education slowed progress in undergraduate and advanced work in science and technological specialisms, though Glasgow University was traditionally involved with industry. Structural changes in Scottish secondary and university education in the later nineteenth century, however, raised general standards. Science teaching was strengthened and the universities became significant centres for physics and engineering – as world-wide demand for Scottish engineers testified. From the 1890s, science faculties were established in the four ancient universities and, by 1914, Scottish institutions were producing more BScs than most other British universities.[38]

Only in Wales was any great expansion of university scientific and technological education lacking. There the general cultural atmosphere was antagonistic to industry and commerce and the university colleges concentrated on general instruction, seeing themselves as agencies of Welsh religious and cultural development rather than as contributors to economic advance (except in agriculture).[39]

All in all, it is doubtful whether Britain lagged significantly behind her continental rivals in technical education at any level, or that British governments were half-hearted in supporting it. Between 1870 and 1914, governmental financial support for this area of education, though largely indirect, was considerable, while private sources contributed much more than in Germany. Total British educational expenditure was certainly no lower than Germany's in this period, and the consequent overall expansion of technical education of all kinds was, in Sidney Pollard's words, 'breathtaking... [and] there was nothing in Germany to compare with the incalculable stimulus given to science teaching at several levels, ultimately to hundreds of thousands of students, by the grants of the Department of Science and Art and the City and Guilds of London'.[40] 'What needs to be explained,' another scholar suggests, 'is not the decline or even the non-emergence of technical education but its rapid expansion.'[41]

By 1900, Britain was considered to have caught up with Germany in technical education at the lower and intermediate levels. At university level, Germany continued to lead in chemistry, but Britain was probably superior in advanced physics and in many branches of applied science. Imperial College was in no way inferior to Charlottenburg, the much-vaunted German technological institution, and prominent British scientists claimed that Cambridge, King's College London and Manchester were far superior seats of scientific education to the *Technische Hochschulen*. German scientists, indeed, acknowledged that Germany had nothing 'to touch Cambridge in physics, Sheffield and Birmingham in metallurgy, and Leeds and Manchester in textile chemistry and dyeing'. The record of London University in positive support for research and development in industry in the years before 1914 was, it has been said, 'one of outstanding achievement'.[42]

The common verdict that, in Britain, there was 'no overall plan' for technical and scientific education and research, and 'the central government is to be blamed',[43] must also be considered facile. The governmental abandonment of early attempts at direct control along continental lines, described above, did not denote neglect. Though direct state influence was minimized, financial aid was concentrated at the lower and intermediate levels on the part-time instruction of artisans and youths in technical and scientific principles (rather than on vocational training or more advanced work), such provision being allowed to respond *ad hoc* to local industrial needs. Vocational training was left to employers and more advanced work and research to independent universities, industrial firms and others. The lack of expertly manned research departments in British firms before 1914 is probably exaggerated. Often also underestimated is the achievement of a flourishing body of voluntary associations and institutions in encouraging and financing research and study, establishing professional qualifications and spreading scientific and technological knowledge.[44]

British practice proved more flexible than the system (in France, Germany and the United States) of training individuals for specific tasks, with particularized courses for scientists, engineers, researchers, managers, foremen and different kinds of craftsmen. Demand-led British training was able to react quickly and successfully to market requirements for both artisans and engineers, and avoided over-production of specialized personnel (as occurred with engineers in Germany and the United States after railway construction slackened). The less rigid, less hierarchical, and decentralized British system permitted greater workforce mobility at advanced as well as at lower levels. Whereas in Europe the focus of technical instruction was on those above the level of rank-and-file workmen, British evening classes placed particular emphasis on the development of working-class youths to enable them to rise to positions of foremen, draughtsmen and so on.

Moreover, at a more advanced level, entry into the top ranks of engineering did not require the formal qualifications demanded in Germany and the United States. Though in 1914 the *Technische Hochschulen* had four times as many full-time engineering undergraduates as there were in England, this reflected the preference of British employers, the Institute of Mechanical Engineers and, therefore, of British students for the mixture of academic and practical training offered by part-time short courses in technical colleges. Most English engineers were thus not graduates, but had a high reputation and found a world-wide market.[45] Not surprisingly, an American observer in 1929 identified the chief legacy of British policy in this period as the 'magnificent system of local technical institutions, devoted principally to part-time instruction for industrial employees . . . [with] an ideal of "vertical mobility" which is almost wholly lacking in the sharply stratified schemes of continental countries'.[46]

The practice followed in Britain in this period, moreover, equates well with modern human capital theory in its distinction between general or theoretical education (of value to the individual) and specific training (benefiting a particular employer). Governmental policy of assisting the first but leaving the second to employers stemmed 'not from stupidity on the part of British entrepreneurs and politicians, but from the nature of the competitive market system to which Britain at the end of the nineteenth century was a good approximation'. The continental system, driven by national pride or 'reasons of statecraft', interfered with the proper working of the market and, if it increased technical education, did so indiscriminately and at the expense of distortions elsewhere, probably through the taxation engendered. Training on the job was more cost-effective: apprenticeship costs were borne by firms who recouped themselves from training fees and lower wages.[47]

Expert witnesses to the Royal Commission on Technical Instruction in the 1880s maintained that British workshop training was superior to that provided by continental vocational schools. Indeed, German industrialists admitted that their trade schools were rather an indication of backwardness – representing training as a substitute for experience in an attempt to catch up with the ingrained expertise of the British workforce.[48] One German manufacturer, indeed, concluded in the 1880s that 'the English were at the head of all the workmen he had ever seen. In practical knowledge of their work, in mechanical genius, they were better without technical instruction than the continental workmen were with it.'[49] Thus, in 1914, for example, the British shipbuilding industry's skilled workforce, trained on the job, was more productive than the formally trained labour of foreign yards.[50] British practice, in fact, was 'well attuned to the economic environment of the time' and certainly not inferior to the continental system.[51]

Again, the popular view that the quality of elementary education in England and Wales before 1914 lagged behind that of other countries, especially Germany, failed to provide an adequate basis for later technical training, and adversely affected the efficiency of the industrial labour force, is now challenged on several counts. First, it is unlikely that German elementary schooling (which had many flaws) was at any time much ahead of that in Britain, either in quality or proportions of the workforce covered.[52] By the later nineteenth century illiteracy in both countries was confined to a minority. Secondly, econometric research suggests that, even had Britain invested sufficiently in schooling to improve the quality and incidence of elementary education vastly, industrial performance would not have been significantly improved. For large numbers of workers in this period a need for even minimal literacy is doubtful. Moreover, very high levels of general education existed in Sweden, Finland and Japan at various times, but were accompanied by comparatively low income levels and lack of economic progress. It has been calculated that increased educational input over the nineteenth century added only a meagre 2 per cent to German economic growth, while between 1856 and 1873 education added only 0.3 per cent a year to British national income.[53]

Thirdly, after the introduction of compulsory education from the 1870s, existing elementary schooling sufficed to inculcate suitable behavioural attitudes, and though formal education doubtless helped to promote mental flexibility in the acquisition of new manual skills, the manual dexterity of British workmen was never in doubt and could be fostered by other means. As already noted, practical training in employment continued to turn out effective workmen. British employers (as noted in Chapter 5) recruited on the basis not of schooling but of family relationship to known steady workmen or personal recommendation, and promotion depended on performance on the shop floor. Fourthly, the importance of elementary education for the provision of clerical workers may also have been exaggerated. A relatively small proportion of the workforce was needed for white-collar work: only 4 per cent in England were so employed in 1901.[54]

Some historians would also contend that no clear connection between higher education and the economy has been demonstrated, and that present-day notions of science as a key productive force have been anachronistically extrapolated back into an earlier period, an error deriving from too ready an acceptance of the propaganda of nineteenth-century science lobbies seeking status and funding. Much of that contemporary criticism did, indeed, come from scientists whose disciplines (such as astronomy) had no relevance to industry. Recent investigations of France, Italy and Spain have found no obvious connection between past higher technical education and economic performance. Research on the German economy suggests that, except in the chemical industry (which accounted for only 2 per cent of German employment and 4 per cent of exports in the years before 1914), 'it would be hard to maintain that Germany derived much gain [or]... superiority over Britain...from her lavish...expenditure on science and technology'. All that can be justifiably claimed is that German technical education did not hinder industrial development.[55]

Neither heavy investment in research nor high-level education necessarily gave a commensurate economic return. Innovation was importable and Britain, Europe and the United States shared a common stock of significant technological knowledge. A small core of highly educated scientists and engineers, backed by others trained at a more modest level (part-time or on the job as demand required), might suffice for science-based industrial progress, while the increasing sub-division of labour in the later nineteenth century limited the need for extensive or advanced technological training.[56]

## The Myth of Avoidable 'Decline'

Both the view that educational factors were responsible for Britain's poor economic performance from 1870, and the alternative suggestion that if technical education was not lacking then the failure of industry to make use of trained personnel was to blame,[57] are based on dubious premises. They assume not only that Britain did do badly, but also that she could have improved her performance had more enlightened attitudes existed and better strategies been followed. Such assumptions are contentious. Clearly, given the inevitable development of populous civilized rivals, Britain could not have retained the absolute economic hegemony achieved as the first industrialized nation, but recent research casts considerable doubt on whether the inevitable relative decline was as severe as often alleged or that actual performance (at least down to 1914) could have been bettered.

The balance of opinion among economic historians suggests that Britain (in 1900 still the world's richest country) had an economy (at least before the Great War) that was fundamentally sound. Her productivity growth rate arguably matched Germany's and the USA's, and entrepreneurial deficiencies were no greater than in her rivals, while British economic performance was too good to reflect widespread entrepreneurial failure. Indeed, the best British entrepreneurs 'could hold their own with the very best abroad'. Scottish steelmakers and shipbuilders, for instance, were 'dynamic, imaginative, and driving men'. Technology was not significantly backward, nor were scientific knowledge or technically skilled workers particularly lacking.[58] There was successful innovation in numerous industries, and criticism of the quality of production techniques and overseas marketing, investment strategies and business structures is largely unwarranted.[59]

Moreover, Britain's economy was commercial and financial as well as industrial, and diversification of resources and entrepreneurial energy into those fields and into service industries in the later nineteenth century was an intelligent response to new opportunities, reflected entrepreneurial acumen and fuelled economic growth.[60] What is remarkable, it has been said, is not that Britain was overtaken by others but that it should have attained such a great lead and enjoyed it for so long.

So if, as Donald McCloskey has pointed out, 'there is little left of the dismal picture of British economic failure...[but rather the heartening one] of an economy not stagnating but growing as rapidly as permitted by the growth of its resources and the effective exploitation of the available technology',[61] then allotment of blame on educational (or indeed other) factors would be a *non sequitur* offering explanations for something which did not actually occur'.[62] The strength of such a verdict, though still contentious and perhaps requiring further research,[63] is clear, and, combined with rehabilitation of Britain's educational record, leads to the conclusion that British science and education was, at the outbreak of the Great War, 'a not unworthy component of what was still the richest and most productive economy in Europe'.[64] More generally, a flexible education system is likely to have contributed to the individualism and freedom of decision-making that produced economic success.[65] Even for the inter-war and post-1945 periods, it is arguable whether the British economy did particularly badly, or that, if it did, weakness in scientific and technical education (as opposed to failure of employers to use trained labour) contributed significantly to decline.[66] But that lies outside the scope of this volume.

# 8

---

# THE GROWTH OF A LITERATE CULTURE

The continuous rise in the proportions of brides and grooms able to write their names in the marriage register (outlined in earlier chapters) is not in itself evidence that those who signed in one decade were any better educated than those who did so in earlier ones. It can indicate only that progressively more people in their late 20s were attaining the same basic level of education. Yet common sense suggests that the growing proportions of each generation of the population receiving years of formal schooling cannot but have had a beneficial effect on the quality of education in the nation as a whole. One likely manifestation of this is the extent to which those who had learned their ABC put the skill of reading to use by becoming active readers. This chapter seeks to explore this, and to survey the various factors, other than formal education, which were involved in the development of a society in which the printed word became a significant part of the daily life of the various social classes.

No valid statistical evidence exists to provide a measure of the proportions of the population who actually made use of the basic skill of reading to peruse published material – for contemporary estimates of numbers of publications and of the size of print runs are neither comprehensive nor reliable, and cannot indicate how many people read each copy of a newspaper or book. Much inferential evidence, however, exists to suggest that the numbers of those who did read for one reason or another rose enormously in the period 1750–1914. The printed word became important in the lives of perhaps the majority of all classes, overlapping and then largely replacing or absorbing the traditional oral culture of the mass of working-class families – particularly in urban areas.

This process has been viewed in various ways. It has been stressed as the triumph of an enlightened culture, produced by the spread of formal education, over an ignorant and superstitious one (thus replacing a culturally divided national society by a more homogeneous one). It has been seen, too, as one means by which the working classes, previously divided between the literate and the illiterate, were brought together by the ability to read conferred by the schools, empowered to throw off ignorance and isolation and enabled to achieve a place in the political life of the nation and given opportunities for material advancement and personal development. More controversially it has been considered to represent the suppression of the indigenous oral culture of the people and its replacement by a culture of print dominated, like the public elementary schools, by the values of the ruling classes (in Scotland, anglicized values).[1]

While there may be elements of truth in all these views, they are too simplistic to provide a satisfactory overarching explanation of a momentous, if gradual, revolution in which complex economic, political, religious and social factors, tentatively examined in this chapter, were involved. Many of the multifarious aspects of the history of printing and publishing, literature, the press and libraries, all of which throw light on the spread of reading and which have been the subject of a great deal of investigation, cannot, however, be examined here.[2] The relationship between schooling, employment, upward social mobility and higher wages has been discussed elsewhere (see pp. 19–20, 59–61, 96, 160).

## Reading and Self Improvement among the Better-off

Before the mid nineteenth century the spread of reading, even among the middle classes, was inhibited by poor communications, which hindered the distribution of printed matter, and by the high price of reading material, which reflected costly production methods, small print runs and taxes on newspapers. Various attempts in the first half of the nineteenth century to promote the mass production of cheap books had limited success. Nevertheless, the expansion of the economy from the eighteenth century did result in a growing demand for technical and economic information which was met by an outflow of literature – specifically on farming, mining, manufacturing and commerce, technology and associated legal matters. The London newspapers (which circulated nationally) also provided business news, as did a thriving provincial press. The newspaper press grew enormously during the eighteenth century, providing an outlet also for advertisements, information on local events and human-interest items, as well as retailing national news.[3]

The national and provincial press also both catered for and stimulated burgeoning middle- and upper-class interest in national and local politics, especially in party politics, parliamentary affairs, governmental policy and the course of wars. Politicization of the press, already well established in the eighteenth century, was further stimulated in the first part of the nineteenth by contentious issues, like the extension of the franchise and the Corn Laws. Many newspapers supported, had connections with or were even promoted by particular political parties and campaigns. In particular, tory papers vied with those advocating parliamentary reform. Direct financial involvement by party organizations in newspapers, and governmental influence through the placing of official advertisements, tended to increase the resources of the press, broadened political awareness and increased the volume of reading matter.[4]

Until the later nineteenth century newspapers were central to the process of the increasing politicization of society through the printed word. Deeper treatment of political matters was provided by serious periodicals, while local single-sheet pamphlets relating to elections and other political issues probably reached a wide audience. However, though political content was not absent from the popular newspapers which emerged from the 1850s (for they often had a party, mainly Liberal, bias) increasingly the late nineteenth- and early twentieth-century press (of which more below) recognized that the enlarged newspaper readership was not exclusively interested in politics. From the 1880s party affiliation began to be eroded as the press developed as something of a fourth estate, but more particularly as an industry with sales its guiding star.[5]

Other factors were also significant in the spread of reading among the better-off. Particularly from the later eighteenth century, growing prosperity among the landed, entrepreneurial and emerging professional classes increased opportunities for leisure and encouraged interest in cultural and intellectual matters and in reading for enjoyment. These interests were catered for in part by the newspapers (which offered a varied diet including items relating to crime and sex) but also by novels, works on history, travel and biography and by numerous periodicals (among them *The Spectator,* the *Gentleman's Magazine* and the *Scots Magazine*). Serious reviews and magazines with broad interests, including education and social reform, proliferated in the nineteenth century, reaching a peak of influence among the intellectually inclined middle classes in the decades before the Great War.[6] Some represented particular political outlooks, like the whig *Edinburgh Review* and the tory *Blackwood's Magazine.* Others reflected the growing incidence of literacy among younger age groups. From the 1860s there appeared many periodicals, varying in quality from the sensational to the respectable, which were mainly aimed at the children and young of the upper working and middle classes.[7]

Urbanization had a greenhouse effect on reading for information and pleasure. From the eighteenth century, towns became increasingly important as centres for cultural activities, including printing and publishing, and for the distribution of literature to remoter areas. Large cities, especially London, Edinburgh and Glasgow, led the field, while Chester and Shrewsbury were important for supplying Wales. Towns also provided cheaper access to reading through circulating (commercial lending), subscription and other libraries and reading rooms, with those in Scotland tending to have a broader social membership than those in England.[8]

The reading public was further extended in the nineteenth century by a growth in the size and prosperity of that stratum of society straddling the lower middle and upper working classes. Small businessmen, artisans, shopkeepers, clerks and, from mid century, postal and railway employees, lower civil servants and teachers, were increasingly able to afford reading matter, and often needed access to printed information in their jobs. Their greater use of domestic servants as incomes rose brought more time for leisure pursuits, including reading.

It was these social groups, too, which made most use of railway travel, for holidays and commuting, and this also provided opportunity for reading. Railway bookstalls provided outlets for cheap literature, and trains made newspaper and book distribution easier and less costly. Railways enabled, for instance, the introduction of popular English Sunday newspapers into Wales and, from the 1850s, contributed to the proliferation of daily national and provincial newspapers and of monthly, fortnightly and weekly reviews. Better news-gathering arrangements, especially the exploitation of the telegraph, the formation of the Press Association in 1868 and its association with Reuters, created a cheap up-to-date news service for both the London and provincial press and made it increasingly possible to satisfy the widespread appetite for news. Consequently from the 1870s many comfortable middle-class families bought penny daily newspapers, and from the 1890s penny and halfpenny newspapers were enjoyed by increasing numbers of the lower middle class.[9]

The spread of evangelicalism in the Victorian period was another factor in the spread of reading among the respectable middle and better-off artisan classes. Puritanical objections to the stage, concerts, music halls, cards, billiards and so on, restricted acceptable leisure activities and enhanced the attraction of reading. Strict Sabbatarianism, involving the proscription (on the one day not dominated by work) of unnecessary travel and of physical activities and other pursuits permissible on weekdays, created a seventh day on which there was little to do other than to attend church and to peruse moral and religious literature. Such severe precepts were most readily followed by middle-class families but affected others, too, and led to widespread restrictions on Sunday leisure pursuits, apart from reading. This contributed to an enormous outflow of the moral and religious literature deemed proper fare for the Sabbath, and to the spread of bible study groups and the like. Almost 25 per cent of books published between 1816 and 1851 were religious in content, and the proliferation of religious and temperance literature reflected a voracious and broadly based Victorian demand. Sectarian and non-denominational presses produced vast numbers of publications, tracts, newspapers, magazines and journals, which were disseminated throughout Britain via itinerant preachers and places of worship.[10]

A literate culture was further promoted by the proliferation of voluntary societies, not only in the Scottish cities where they were a manifestation of the Enlightenment,[11] but in centres of population in Britain generally. In many towns, better-off citizens sought, through attending lectures and study groups and visiting libraries and newsrooms, to extend their general culture. Indeed the urban middle classes embarked in the nineteenth century on what might be considered a crusade of self improvement. The spread of scientific societies to meet both professional and more often social needs has been discussed in Chapter 4. Alongside these, many others – including literary, musical and historical societies – became common and statistical societies interested in social investigation were found in large cities – all stimulating discussion, publication and reading.[12]

## Reading and the Working Classes

The view, once common, that a mass active readership was the direct consequence of compulsory elementary education in the board-school era is demonstrably oversimplified (though that development may have had some impact).[13] The widespread provision in earlier decades of the nineteenth century of religious literature for working-class consumption (a matter explored more fully in the next section of this chapter) would have been pointless had not large numbers of such readers already existed. Similarly, and for the same reason, so would the efforts of the governing classes to restrict working-class access to 'dangerous' reading material. Duties on newspapers, newsprint and advertisements were progressively increased between 1776 and 1815, deliberately to price newspapers out of the reach of working men and particularly to restrict the spread of radical proletarian papers. In 1819 impositions were placed, too, on cheap periodicals carrying news. The reduction and final abolition of these taxes, which occurred between the 1830s and 1861 and is discussed in the next section, marked acceptance of the fact that by the mid century the habit of reading among the working classes was too entrenched to be controlled so arbitrarily. The extensive body of commercially produced secular literature, aimed at a working-class market, provides further support for believing that, long before the 1870s, many working people, particularly in Scotland, but also in England and Wales, were not only able to read, but that many of them put that skill to use.

Even so, before the mid nineteenth century, poverty, long working hours and poor housing, heating and lighting, combined with child labour, rural isolation and limited schooling to restrict the practice of reading among the poorer classes. At the same time the high cost of postage made the use of the written word for family communication impracticable for many working people. These difficulties were aggravated by the high cost of books and newspapers, enhanced in the case of the latter by the taxes noted above.

As the century progressed, however, rising working-class incomes and better living conditions led to more time being available for leisure activities, including reading. Opportunities for some kind of formal education increased, and child labour and the hours of female workers in some basic industries were progressively restricted; in the 1880s paraffin lamps began to replace candles even in farm cottages. Urbanization brought more working men into daily contact with posters and leaflets, while employers often passed on newspapers and other printed material to domestic servants, who as a class increased considerably in numbers in the nineteenth century.[14] At the same time the cost of reading matter fell. The price of books and newspapers was progressively reduced from the 1830s onwards as a consequence of technological improvements (including the steam press and cheaper newsprint), increased advertising income and growing realization by publishers of the commercial opportunities of mass production. As already noted, the burgeoning railway network cut the costs of distribution, and (consequent on a successful campaign explored below) newspapers were further cheapened from the 1830s by the reduction and eventual abolition of the taxes affecting them. Increased purchase of magazines, books and, above all, of newspapers by the better-off workers followed, and the 1890s saw the triumph of the cheap book movement.[15]

Demand for reading matter was stimulated, especially in the upper working and lower middle classes, by interest not only in religion but also in politics, as well as by an urge for self improvement and a desire for entertainment. Urbanization facilitated involvement in formal adult education (including mechanics' institutes, adult schools and later the university extension movement and the Workers' Educational Association).[16] Mutual improvement and other working-class societies, political associations, trades union, book clubs and so on, all helped to spread the literate culture. Many of these organizations developed libraries and the printed word thus became increasingly available and significant in the life of the growing artisan class. The introduction of the penny post in 1839 and the halfpenny postcard in 1870, moreover, led to a substantial, though gradual, increase in working-class communication via the written word.[17]

Probably the most significant factor in the spread of reading among the working classes, however, was their demand for educational and, to a greater extent, entertaining literature. There was a voracious appetite for fiction, and the pleasure it gave to many working men and women is well attested.[18] The reading matter traditionally favoured by them included almanacs, broadsheets and cheap booklets (chapbooks), the content of which was usually crude and sensational, sometimes humorous and often bawdy. It embraced scandal, violent crime, punishment, love, prostitution and sex generally, prophecy, magic, superstition, horror and the occult, but also history and folk tales. A large market for this sort of literature existed in the eighteenth century, and the traditional chapbooks and broadsides continued to be sold widely, by street hawkers and travelling chapmen, well into the nineteenth. Sales were particularly high in Scotland, probably because of the higher proportion of literates, but were widespread in England, too, with London the largest centre for the production of chapbooks. From the mid nineteenth century, as book-production costs fell, chapbooks and broadsides began to give way to cheap novels, the content of many (though certainly not all) of which was much the same – sensational, sentimental and salacious.[19]

The limited working-class market for weekly newspapers, which existed in the eighteenth and early nineteenth centuries, was expanded considerably from the mid nineteenth by the ending of taxes on the press, already noted. Then, from the 1880s a growing market for light magazines (like, for instance, *Tit-Bits*) and daily newspapers was created – less by the board schools than by further price reductions and the enterprise of businessmen discerning enough to seize the opportunities offered by mass circulation, advertising and popular content.

Though often supportive of working-class political radicalism, and prejudiced against the ruling classes, the established popular Sunday papers and the newer popular dailies (unlike the working-class radical press of the early part of the century, discussed below), were primarily capitalist ventures. Essentially commercial, they provided (alongside political comment and serious news) narratives, items of human interest, entertaining correspondence, serial fiction, competitions and prizes. Some added to their attraction by carrying advertisements for jobs. Their provision of sports reports from the later nineteenth century, and the advent of specialist sports papers, provided an added incentive for working men to join the literate culture.[20]

Well into the twentieth century, Sunday papers, like the *News of the World*, *Reynolds' Newspaper* and *Lloyd's Weekly News*, remained more popular than the dailies. By 1914, however, daily papers had become cheaper and their reading widespread if not universal among working- as well as lower middle-class families. The spread of education by the turn of the century caused the new journalism to raise its standards somewhat and to become more serious, though its content and vigorous style continued to show a clear descent from the street literature which it had largely displaced.[21] While the oral culture of the past did not disappear, and its content endured in popular literature, the balance by 1900 was well tipped towards the culture of print, particularly among the young. The triumph of popular journalism, however, contributed to the relative decline of the Welsh language press.[22]

Working- and lower middle-class interest in radical politics represented another influence on the spread of a literate culture, though it was an influence which has probably been exaggerated by educational and social historians. Literature reflecting a broad spectrum of working-class political viewpoints proliferated from the eighteenth century onwards. Some popular street literature had a political content, though often its message was hardly constructive. When it did not take the form of innocuous jingoism or mild criticism, it often indulged in tirades against the religious establishment, the aristocracy, the Crown, exploiting employers and the ruling classes generally – sometimes preaching violent retaliation against perceived oppression. Virulent literature of this kind circulated particularly during the anti-poor-law campaigns and the agricultural unrest of the 1830s. The Home Office collection of anonymous letters threatening rick burning, machine breaking and physical violence against 'oppressors', reveals a society in which the literate culture was beginning to embrace its poorest members.[23]

But from the eighteenth century onwards, alongside this blindly mutinous material, there circulated among the more serious of the working and lower middle classes a great deal of more substantial radical literature, based on critical analysis of the economic system and purveying serious practical views on political and economic change. Those who sought to improve the lot of their fellows through radical political action made much use of the printed word to spread their views and to organize their movements. They naturally tried to promote the spread of education among their followers, recognizing illiteracy as both suggestive of inferiority and a reason for denial of participation in the political process. Education was seen as a potential tool for change if utilized to do more than make the working man respectable and submissive: properly directed it could make him politically active and able to assume or participate in political and economic power.[24]

The mutual improvement societies, common in working-class communities throughout the later eighteenth and the nineteenth century, actively encouraged reading and the discussion of the printed word. Often they built up libraries and, down to the 1850s, they were frequently politically orientated.[25] Other organizations and movements, more exclusively political, also had a positive influence at various times on the spread of a literate culture. In the late eighteenth and early nineteenth centuries these included the corresponding societies, constitutional societies, Hampton clubs, secular Sunday schools, political protestants, and other groups stimulated by the example of the French revolutionists to seek democratic constitutional reform or revolutionary change. They included, too, the socialist trades union and cooperative movements and the working men's associations of the second quarter of the nineteenth century, and the Chartists and the promoters of the ten hours movement of the 1830s and 1840s.

Most of these movements produced their own propaganda, often as short tracts, and distributed the works of progressive political and social thinkers. Some created adult education institutions (halls of science, socialist mechanics' institutes, people's palaces and so on) with libraries, classes, lectures, reading rooms and study groups. Some, like the co-operative societies, established their own schools for children. Many working-class political leaders had been led to their views through self education, and maintained a strong belief that the power of workers would be enhanced through the knowledge attained by intelligent reading, especially in the fields of politics, science and economics. The publications of men such as Robert Owen, William Lovett, Richard Carlile and William Thompson demonstrate, too, the deep belief of the working-class radical movement that political advance required an educational system free of bourgeois and religious control.[26]

Among the politically minded working and lower middle classes there was an appetite for serious radical literature. The works of Tom Paine and William Cobbett sold in large numbers and were said to be read in humble homes throughout Britain. In Wales, trades union and political groups distributed periodicals via a network of institutions, pubs and newsrooms. In Britain, generally, scores of radical periodical papers (the most influential of which included the *Black Dwarf*, the *Poor Man's Guardian*, Cobbett's *Political Register*, the Chartist *Northern Star* and Glasgow *Patriot* and the *Voice of the West Riding*) preached left-wing causes and circulated widely, despite being open to prosecution for seditious libel or in some cases evasion of stamp duty, the most irksome of the taxes on the press.[27]

Nevertheless, though historians have tended to concentrate on political publications, the content of the majority of 'unstamped' (illegal) papers was entertaining rather than political.[28] Moreover, while newspapers aiming at working-class readers and supporting working-class radicalism can be traced through the nineteenth and early twentieth centuries, the abolition of fiscal restrictions on the press from the 1850s coincided with the collapse of Chartism and of the socialist co-operative and trades union movements and the advent of economic conditions more favourable to the lower classes. Working-class interest in politics diminished, and thus the influence of the radical political press on the spread of a reading public waned. Small circulation papers like the *Bee-Hive* supported trades union struggles in the 1860s, and from the 1880s papers like the *Clarion* and a spate of labour and socialist periodicals and pamphlets sought to address those workers newly enfranchised in 1884. But they catered now for a minority, were beset by financial difficulties and were eventually priced out of the market. A mass press needed expensive equipment and to be able to attract business advertisers. It thus developed in the hands of those who had capital and were anxious to provide readers with entertaining content without promoting extreme political views – which might deter advertisers. From the later nineteenth century the truly working-class press was the cheap Sunday and daily newspapers, which might support liberal and radical causes in their pages, but whose *raison d'être* was commercial rather than political. It was they who deserve the credit for much of the continued spread of reading among the working classes in the later nineteenth and the twentieth centuries.[29]

### Religious and Utilitarian Pressures and Working-class Response

The possibility of a literate culture spreading to large proportions of the working and lower middle classes was seen by the ruling classes in the eighteenth century and the first half of the nineteenth as a potential threat to social and political order. The initial response of governments to radical literature which openly questioned the validity of the existing social system was threefold: to advocate a restricted, largely religious schooling for the working classes; to attempt to suppress undesirable reading matter; and to sponsor literature countering radical views and supporting the status quo.

The perceived threat (certainly exaggerated)[30] of an uprising inspired by literature expounding French and American revolutionary ideas and other inflammatory political writings was met from the 1790s by prosecutions of the publishers of such material for seditious libel.

Radical political societies, like the corresponding societies, which distributed such literature and were centres for its discussion, were outlawed and the fiscal duties on newspapers were increased. Governments also sought to influence the press by means of subsidies from secret-service funds, the granting of pensions and other favours, and fees for the placement of official advertisements. The policy of suppression and restriction, however, not only failed to prevent the diffusion of radical political views but actually made the militant press more sought after. Legal restrictions were found difficult to enforce, and while some radical newspapers failed as duties forced price rises, survivors probably continued (through multiple readership of each copy) to reach more than their circulation figures would suggest. Deprived of advertising income by antagonistic businessmen and a hostile government, they felt no need to temper their radical message. More important, illegal publication and distribution of an 'unstamped' press, particularly from the early 1830s, also ensured that radical political views continued to be read. At the same time a boost was given to alternatives – particularly cheap fiction and the popular Sunday press, which could afford the duties and generally continued to carry political news and comment mildly supportive of working-class interests.[31]

Governmental efforts to restrict working-class reading were gradually replaced by middle-class attempts to influence its nature. Two broad pressure groups may be distinguished: one representing religious and moral sentiment and another influenced by Benthamite or Utilitarian principles. The first – appalled by the prevalance of crime, drunkenness and religious ignorance among the working classes, their interest in anti-clerical political views and their predilection for sensational and salacious literature – sought to replace such material by wholesome moral and religious publications. The other group, middle-class radicals led by men such as Henry, Lord Brougham, was predominantly concerned that working-class socialist and revolutionary literature should give way to material supportive of classical economic theory and of a political alliance of middle- and lower-class radicals against the entrenched privileges of the landed classes and the religious establishment. The Utilitarians also sought to replace both street literature and religious publications by 'improving' or 'useful' literature.

Both pressure groups deplored revolutionary politics, socialist co-operatives and Owenite trades union, but although linkage of scientific knowledge with religion (as in the 'natural theology' promoted by some Scottish social thinkers) was present,[32] generally the two groups were mutually antagonistic. Religious opinion disliked the secular views of the middle-class radicals, who, for their part, disapproved of evangelical sponsorship of a working-class reading diet centred on religious knowledge, moral improvement and acceptance of the political status quo. Rivalry for the minds of working-class readers, however, created a vast addition to the body of available cheap reading material.

In the nineteenth century, developing the work of Hannah More's moralizing *Cheap Repository Tracts*, aimed at the working classes of the 1790s, most churches and a host of religious societies, notably the interdenominational evangelical Religious Tract Society, the Church Tract Association, the British and Foreign Bible Society and the Society for Promoting Christian Knowledge, poured out millions of copies of cheap tracts, magazines, periodicals and testaments. These were distributed throughout Britain via chapmen and through shops, pubs and places of worship. The churches thus stimulated many respectable working-class folk to become active readers (though often discouraging 'idle reading' – that is fiction). In Wales, especially, religious reading matter became a focus of chapel life, and the London trade in books for the principality was dominated by religious societies.[33] Though much of this literature was cheap or free, demand was sufficiently strong to attract commercial publishers into the field, and the abolition of taxes on newspapers from 1850 reduced the price of some religious literature. Religious influence on reading habits was enhanced, too, by the establishment by the Church of England of church institutes with appropriate libraries, while the Society of Friends set up adult schools where bible reading predominated.[34]

The efforts of middle-class radicals were also far-reaching. They had an overwhelmingly optimistic belief in the potential of the printed word to create a general populace sufficiently well informed to eschew violence and revolution and to support moderate reform. The Benthamites supported universal secular elementary education, but the thrust of their educational programme was directed at adult artisans. They encouraged these men to improve their general intellectual standing through serious reading and to master the logic of classical political economy, particularly in relation to the new poor law and the iron law of wages – and thus to recognize the futility of trades unionism and socialism. They launched the mechanics' institute movement (with its *Mechanics' Magazine*) to provide centres for reading and instruction and promoted series of cheap self-improving books through the agency of the Society for the Diffusion of Useful Knowledge (SDUK) and journals like the *Penny Magazine* and the *Penny Cyclopaedia*.[35]

Brougham believed strongly in the educative and civilizing potential of responsible newspapers, cheap enough to reach the working classes. He supported a group of middle-class reformers (including Francis Place, Joseph Hume and George Birkbeck) who pressed parliament and campaigned generally for the abolition of the duties on newspapers, advertisements and newsprint. This attack on the 'taxes on knowledge' (as they were depicted) was paralleled by a campaign against the duties by working-class radicals led by Henry Hetherington, William Carpenter and John Cleave, whose weapon was open defiance of the law by flooding the market with unstamped newspapers. Though the two groups differed in political and economic outlook, and in the sort of newspapers they wanted the workers to read, their differences should not be stressed too strongly. There was overlap in membership and much cooperation in their efforts to achieve the 'free' press which both groups felt an essential educational tool to prepare workers for a role in politics.

Prosecution of unstamped newspapers continued to serve only to increase their attraction, and the governing classes were reluctantly persuaded by the middle-class radicals that cheapening newspapers would result in an increasingly literate workforce rejecting the socialist press in preference for respectable newspapers. From these, it was felt, working men would absorb responsible opinions and see the wisdom of supporting a sensible social order. Consequently the duties on newspapers and advertisements were reduced in the 1830s and abolished in the 1850s, while those on paper went in 1861. This was followed, as already noted, by a decline in the radical working-class press and the emergence of a mass popular press (including provincial daily, evening and, especially, weekly newspapers). These papers, though highly market-orientated, were generally sympathetic to reform and also promoted the cooperation of the classes under middle-class leadership.[36]

It is difficult to quantify the impact of middle-class efforts to influence the working-class readership. Much of the free religious and moralizing literature distributed among the poorer classes probably went unread. Cheap, wholesome but serious books appealed most to the middle and lower middle classes and the SDUK publications were often too advanced for the generality of workers. The didactic style of middle-class authors, their lack of understanding of working-class ambitions and problems, and their avoidance of issues significant to working men, created a barrier difficult to overcome. The knowledge they purveyed was, moreover, 'useful' in the mind-improving sense rather than for any provision of information or skills directly valuable in the job market.[37]

Yet there is plenty of subjective evidence that religious tracts and magazines were appreciated by some sections of the working class. Ambitious members of the skilled working class, as well as the lower middle class, activated by a desire for self improvement, did read the *Penny Magazine*, the volumes of the SDUK's 'Library of Useful Knowledge' and its equally serious 'Library of Entertaining Knowledge'. Though by the 1830s the sale of SDUK publications declined, and the Society was disbanded in 1846, this was in part the result of the advent of commercial rivals who exploited the market which the SDUK had revealed. The concept of producing cheap wholesome books for a mass market, publicized by the Society, was taken up with increasing degrees of success by commercial publishers in London and Edinburgh, such as Knight, Chambers and Murray. Thus was created a great expansion of readily accessible reading matter including wholesome novels, magazines and cheap reprints of works of travel, history, biography and general knowledge. For instance, *Chambers's Edinburgh Journal*, founded in 1832 'to elevate and instruct' the labouring classes, was soon selling 50,000 copies a year (30,000 in Scotland), while by the early 1860s Cassell had sold millions of penny publications. At the same time, second-hand bookshops, book clubs and cheap commercial libraries increased the availability of such literature. Though free public libraries were few and not a major influence before the early twentieth century,[38] libraries and reading rooms were often very successful ventures of the mechanics' institutes, friendly societies and other societies with working-class and lower middle-class memberships.[39]

Self improvement, however, remained a minority pursuit. Though middle-class promoters of both evangelical and 'useful' reading sought to discourage unwholesome sensational publications and also fiction generally, reading for enjoyment proved the main stimulus for the creation of a mass reading public. Traditional popular literature persisted in various forms. Its spirit was absorbed by the new popular newspapers, cheap novels and magazines which began to flourish after the mid nineteenth century. It was kept alive, too, in the 1880s and 1890s, by the new popular magazines of W. T. Stead, George Newnes and others, and in the penny and halfpenny newspapers (of which Harmsworth's *Daily Mail* is best known). By the early twentieth century the triumph of the popular provincial and national cheap press as sources of news and especially of entertainment must have contributed enormously to the growth in the size of the reading public. It is estimated that, between 1840 and 1900, newspaper circulation may have increased by up to two and a half million copies.[40]

## Literacy and Working-class Cohesion

British society as it had evolved by the eve of the Great War was much more literate than it had been a generation before – though whether it had thereby become more homogeneous is uncertain. Some historians have suggested that it replaced a society in which a great social divide existed within the working classes between the respectable schooled, pious, sober, skilled workers and the illiterate, irreligious, unwashed, fickle and often drunken labouring families who clung to a backward oral culture.[41] Such a picture is certainly less applicable to Scotland where working-class literacy and respect for learning was widespread and illiteracy reflected geography rather than social division. For England and Wales, too, it probably exaggerates both the impact of educational progress and the significance of literacy as a divisive factor in working-class life.

Though the distinction in prosperity and outlook between artisan and labourer was real enough, that between the literate and illiterate was not clear-cut – except in the Gaelic-speaking areas where the literate culture was predominantly that of an alien tongue.[42] Generally there were degrees of literacy, and these influenced the extent to which a person actively used reading and writing skills. Moreover, many families included within them both literates and illiterates. Long after compulsory schooling, generational overlap ensured that illiterate parents and grandparents lived with younger literates. Both before and after 1870, some literates were married to illiterate or barely literate spouses, while sibling offspring might embrace readers and writers as well as those with one or neither skill, sometimes without any discernible pattern of age or sex. Again, some skilled tradesmen were literate but others not – without apparent related differences in wealth or practical ability; and by no means all labourers were illiterate even in the eighteenth century. Consequently, many, if not most, illiterate working folk mixed not only with literate relatives and fellow workers, but with friends and acquaintances who could read and write. Newspapers, pamphlets and books contained illustrations which could be appreciated by the illiterate, and these, like notices and letters, were often read aloud to them, while letters were also written on their behalf. Thus, long before the era of compulsory schooling, the illiterate were not cut off from the literate culture which increasingly must have touched both literates and illiterates. The existence of a working class neatly divided into two mutually exclusive groups, literate and illiterate, is certainly a myth.[43]

Greater working-class homogeneity did result from the spread of the culture of print, but this did not emanate from the fusion of a previously illiterate mass with a literate élite. Rather the use of print gradually spread through groups in which literate and illiterate were already mixed. Particularly over the two or three generations from 1840, the printed word helped to break down the isolation of communities, encouraging geographical mobility and promoting awareness of national political and social movements (see p. 59). Working-class literature written by working-class authors and the use of the written word for distinctly working-class social and political purposes may have helped to shape collective identity and class solidarity. The spread of literacy created more effective trades union leaders and facilitated the organization of collective action.[44] Compulsory schooling eliminated any economic advantages previously enjoyed by those who were schooled, and weakened educational differences between labourers and artisans, between men and women, and between rural and urban dwellers. Thus, as virtually all young manual labourers became literate by the end of the nineteenth century, possession merely of basic literacy skills ceased in itself to facilitate upward social mobility.[45]

Moreover, though superstition and ignorance were diminished by the culture of print, the popular culture of the past was not extinguished. Readers had never been excluded from the oral tradition and, even in the later nineteenth century, the oral and literate cultures overlapped. Early working-class street literature had drawn on oral tradition, embracing the same interests, and, as already noted, its spirit was to some extent absorbed by the popular newspapers and fiction of the late nineteenth and early twentieth centuries. The nascent working-class literate culture thus merged with residual aspects of oral culture and thus reinforced class consciousness. In Wales, it is said, the easier distribution of the popular press of the later nineteenth century caused 'a cultural shift from a readership fragmented by ideology, language and region to one which resembled a more homogeneous social entity'.[46]

Some historians have argued, however, that working-class literacy, acquired largely through the commercially driven popular press and the public elementary schools, acted as a blinker on working-class political enterprise and outlooks. Both the schools and the popular press, it is suggested, purveyed an essentially bourgeois culture, supportive of middle- and upper-class hegemony, and the formal education provided was too limited and mechanical to encourage any originality of thought. The result, the argument goes, was that semi-educated working-class leaders accepted fundamentally the parameters defined by the ruling classes for social and political change.[47] This may be, however, to make too harsh a judgment on the early twentieth-century popular press, to exaggerate its influence and to underestimate the liberating influence of the mass of literature other than newspapers so much more readily accessible to all than had been the case in the past. It may seem, too, to place too much emphasis on the allegedly limiting influence of the pre-1914 elementary schools. What is certain is that the relationship between education, literacy and society was, and is likely to continue to be, extremely complex.

# NOTES

---

## 1 Elementary Education to the 1860s

1. Higginson (1974); Leinster-Mackay (1976a); Gardner (1984), 16–26; Jones, G. E. (1997), 21–2; Scotland (1969), i. 106–11, 262–5, 288–91.
2. Jones, M. G. (1964), 152–62; Sanderson (1972b); Sanderson (1974); Laqueur (1974); Foreman (1977). Simon, J. (1968) seeks to disprove the existence of a 'movement'.
3. Withrington (1962); Withrington (1993), 704.
4. Houston (1985), 74–9, 113, 124, 230; Scotland (1969), i. 90–103; Jones, M. G. (1964), Ch. 6; Anderson (1995), 9–12, 35, 88; Mason, J. (1954); Smout (1969), 461–3.
5. Seaborne (1992), 45–8; Jones, M. G. (1964), Ch. 7; Williams, G. (1961).
6. Jones, M. G. (1964), 314–21; Seaborne (1992), 115–16; Brown, G. C. (1981–3); Anderson (1995), 158; Laqueur (1976a), *passim*, q.v. for bibliography.
7. *Rep. R. C. on Education in Wales*, PP 1847, xxvii (pt I), 3; Seaborne (1992), 118: Laqueur (1976a), Chs 4 and 5. For Sunday schools as day-school substitutes, see pp. 25, 32, 57, 164n.10.
8. Laqueur (1976a); Stephens (1980), 228; Dick (1980); Davies, J. A. (1973), 9–10.
9. *Census of Education, England and Wales, 1851*, PP 1852–3, xc; *Census of Worship and Education, Scotland, 1851*, PP 1854, lix.
10. Stephens (1980), 227–9; Anderson (1995), 158.
11. Adult education cannot be covered in detail here: see Kelly (1992), 149–57, 200–5 and works cited and, for women, Purvis (1980); Purvis (1989), pt III.
12. Marsden, W. E. (1982), 182; Jones, M. J. (1997), 19–20.
13. Sanderson (1972a); Stephens (1987), 5–8, 257; Seaborne (1992), 133; Marsden, W. E. (1982), 181; Jones, M. J. (1997), 21–2, 28, 34.
14. Sturt (1967), 24–5.
15. Hurt (1971), Ch. 7 and 221 (quot.); Anderson (1995), 57–9; Sylvester (1974), 84–93. Literature on the Revised Code is too extensive to cite here: see refs in Stephens (1987), 273 n. 50.

16. Withrington (1997), 16–17, 32–4, 36; Scotland (1969), i. 278; Anderson (1995), 36, 96.
17. Anderson (1995), 32, 35–40, 45, 76, 78, 81, 86, 88–9, 92, 97, 121, 147, 152, 210–16, 312; Durkacz (1977); Scotland (1969), i. 242–9; Anderson (1983), 52.
18. Scotland (1969), i. 252–4; Anderson (1983), 10; Anderson (1995), 45, 81, 89, 93. Figures for 1851 are deduced from Anderson (1995), 75. Cf. Withrington (1997), 49.
19. Turner, D. A. (1970); Lawson and Silver (1973), 282–3; Gardner (1984), 19, 32, 161–4; Stewart and McCann (1967), 242, 256, 306–7; McCann (1966).
20. Clark (1969, 1977, 1982, 1982a, 1988); Ralston (1988); Balfour (1903), 53–9, 138–42; Hurt (1979), 56–9; Weinberger (1981); Anderson (1995), 95–6.
21. Drake (1970, 1976); Balfour (1903), 63–9, 142; McCrory (1981).
22. Evans, L. W. (1971); Robson (1931); Silver (1977); Seaborne (1992), 134–5; Hurt (1979); Sanderson (1967); Rimmer (1960); and pp. 87, 88.
23. Anderson (1983), 14–15; Anderson (1995), 24–5.
24. Rosen (1974); Silver (1965), 17–18, 20, 23; Johnson (1970), 98; Kaestle (1976), 178–81.
25. Cf. Anderson (1995), 25–6, 38–9; Withrington (1997), 48, 50.
26. Withrington (1997), 39–41, 52; Anderson (1995), 45–7, 49: Corr (1989).
27. Quot. Silver (1965), 43 (and cf. 46).
28. *Warwick Advertiser*, 18 Jan. 1845.
29. *Rep. Committee of Council on Education, 1870–1*, 28.
30. Johnson (1977); Silver (1975), 25–9; Colls (1976), 86; Goldstrom (1977); 93; Jones, M. J. (1997), 26.
31. Withrington (1997), 40–1; Anderson (1995), 25–6, 33–4, 41–3, 47.
32. Quot. Flinn (1967), 15.
33. Johnson (1976), 50; Stephens (1987), 132–7; Colls (1976), 92–5. Cf. Dickson and Clark (1986); Mitch (1993), 297.
34. Stephens (1987), 136.
35. Donajgrodski (1977); McCann (1977); Colls (1976); Johnson (1970): Paz (1981), 494; Digby and Searby (1981), 20–8.
36. Jones, G. S. (1978), 164 (quot.); Laqueur (1979); Donajgrodski (1977), Introd.; Paz (1981), 495; Anderson (1995). Cf. Reeder (1992), 33–4.
37. Thompson, F. M. L. (1981); Silver (1965), 30–1; Colls (1976), 96; Benson (1970), 16–17; Anderson (1992), 38–9; Stephens (1987), 56–7, 130–1, 135–8, 180, 224–5, 231, 235–6; Mitch (1993), 296–7; Rimmer (1960), 105–10; Heesom (1981), 139–40; Duffy (1981), 150; Evans, L. W. (1971), 15ff; and see p. 57.
38. Johnson (1976), 51–2; Paz (1981), 498; Goldstrom (1977), 107; Frith (1977), 78; Laqueur (1979); Silver (1965), 36.
39. Humphries (1979), 206; Stephens (1987), 48–50, 129, 224, 228–9; Frith (1977), 77, 86, 88; Laqueur (1976), 193–5, 197–8, 200.
40. *Rep. R. C. on Popular Education*, PP 1861, xxi (pt III), 30–1.
41. Simon, B. (1960), 275–6, 340–6; Simon, B. (1965), 122–3. For the private schools seen as the true 'people's schools', deliberately destroyed by the 1870 Act and compulsory attendance, see Gardner (1984). See also pp. 81–2.

42. Paz (1981), 496–7; Hurt (1979), Chs 2 and 3; and see p. 87.
43. Goldstrom (1972), 83–9; Goldstrom (1977), 101–4.
44. Withrington (1997), 43; Anderson (1995), 151–3, 155–6, 215; MacKinnon (1972); Withers (1982).
45. Hurt (1971), 35–8, 191–2; Perkin (1969), 294–5; Johnson (1977), 95–100; Paz (1980), 100–9, 127, 134; Ball (1963), 38–42, 45–61.
46. Humphries (1979), 172; Hurt (1971), 9, 147–85; Johnson (1970), 100.
47. Thompson, F. M. L. (1981), 196.
48. Goldstrom (1977), 107; Johnson (1977), 80; Thompson, F. M. L. (1981), 206–7; Royle (1971), 315–21; Tholfsen (1976), 262–3.
49. Simon, B. (1960), Chs 4 and 5, deals with these enterprises but ignores their almost complete failure.
50. Anderson (1983), especially Chs 1 and 5 and pp. 104–5; Anderson (1985); Anderson (1995), 32.
51. Quot. Anderson (1995), 69.
52. See pp. 59–60. The relationship between schooling and social mobility is controversial: see Sanderson (1972b); Sanderson (1974); Laqueur (1974); Mitch (1992), 22–36; Mitch (1993), 294–5; Vincent (1989), 126–34, 275–6.

## 2 School Attendance and Literacy: 1750 to the later Nineteenth Century

1. Laqueur (1976), 203; Withrington (1988), 171–2.
2. See West (1965), Ch. 10; West (1975), Chs 1–3; Withrington (1997), 33–4; and see pp. 82, 83.
3. Houston (1985), 74, 82; Withrington (1988), 164–71; Anderson (1995), 3–14; Smout (1969), 452–3, 461–6.
4. Withrington (1988), 178–9.
5. *State of Education in England, Scotland and Wales*, PP 1820, xii, 342ff. Cf. Stephens (1987), 352; Marsden, W. E. (1982).
6. Withrington (1988), 182; Anderson (1995), 108–11 and, for county figures, 306–7. Figures of attendance for Shetland and Orkney were combined: but Orkney's was high, Shetland's low.
7. *Census of Education, England and Wales, 1851*, PP 1852–3, xc; Stephens (1987), App. J. Welsh enrolments in *Rep. R. C. on Education in Wales*, PP 1847, xxvii, differ somewhat from those in the 1851 Census.
8. Stephens (1987), 12–13, 88–9, App. F; Stephens (1977), 43–6; Anderson (1995), 102–3, 108, 131. Cf. Withrington (1983), 61, 63, 65; Smout (1969), 451–2; and see pp. 57–8.
9. Sargant (1867), 85.
10. For Sunday schools as substitutes for day schools, see Stephens (1987), 26–7, 93–4, 156–7; Mitch (1992), 136–8, 147, 281n; Laqueur (1976a), Chs 4 and 5, App. 2; Field (1979); and see pp. 4, 25, 32, 57.
11. *App. Second Rep. R. C. on Employment of Children (Trades and Manufactures)*, PP 1843, xv (pt II), pp. C9–10.

12. For the following, see Stone (1969), 85; and refs in Stephens (1987), 3, 4, 269n; Stephens (1990), 553–4.
13. Stone (1969), 98; Stephens (1990) and works cited; Stephens (1987), 3–4; Vincent (1989); Anderson (1995), 15–16. Cf. Withrington (1988), 184.
14. Stephens (1990), 155; Stephens (1987), 271n; Houston (1985), 56; Houston (1982), 90; Anderson (1995), 14–15; *Rep. Registrar General of Births, Deaths and Marriages* (henceforth *Rep. R. G.*), *England and Wales*, PP 1880, xvi.
15. Stephens (1977), 43–6.
16. Houston (1985), 46–8, 56–7; Anderson (1995), 10–12; Withrington (1988), 181–3; Seaborne (1992), 46; and see p. 3.
17. Stephens (1987), 40–1, 121, 164, 232, and *passim*; Anderson (1995), 118, 128; *Rep. R. G., Scotland*, PP 1884, xx.
18. Anderson (1995), 86, 131; Stephens (1987), 323; *Rep. R. G., England and Wales*, PP 1873, xx.
19. Anderson (1995), 121; Stephens (1977), 42–3.
20. Stephens (1987), 42–8, 74, 89–91, 180–2 and sections 'Attitudes to education'; *Rep. Committee of Council on Education, 1867–8*, 96–7 (quot.).
21. Vincent (1989), 96–100.
22. Stephens (1987), 28, 37, 68, 237, 264–5, and *passim*; Stephens (1973), 7, 13; Anderson (1995), 38, 107–8, 118; Sanderson (1983), 12; Campbell, J. (1983), 26–8; Vincent (1989), 99–100; Bradshaw (1983), 8, 11, 12, 16–18; Grayson (1983), 58–9; Harrop (1983), 42, 47–8, 50; Anderson (1983), 5, 9; Webb, R. K. (1954), 107; *Minutes Committee of Council on Education, 1840–1*, 160.
23. Stephens (1987), *passim*; Anderson (1995), 107–9, 118; and see p. 32.
24. *First Rep. R. C. on Employment of Children . . . in Agriculture*, PP 1867–8, xvii (a) (pt I), 84 (quot.)
25. *Second Rep. R. C. on Employment of Children . . . in Agriculture*, PP 1868–9, xiii (a) (pt I), 37
26. Houston (1985), 78–83; Anderson (1995), 108; *Rep. R. G., Scotland*, PP 1884, xx; Davies, J. A. (1973), 15; Seaborne (1992), 87–97; Stephens (1973), 10 and n. 45.
27. Anderson (1995), 119; Hill (1836), i, 246 (quot.); *First Rep. R. C. on Employment of Children . . . in Agriculture*, PP 1867–8, xvii (a) (pt I), 52–3 (quot.).
28. The early paragraphs of this section draw on Stephens (1987), 11, 18 and *passim*; Vincent (1989), 16, 24–5; Stephens (1990), 557; Houston (1985), 57, 60ff; and Anderson (1995), 17, 101–2, 109–18, 306–7, without further citation.
29. *Rep. R. G., Scotland*, PP 1884, xx.
30. *Rep. R. G., England and Wales*, PP 1873, xx; Stephens (1987), 322–3.
31. Schofield, R. S. (1973), 453.
32. *Rep. R. G., England and Wales*, PP 1873, xx.
33. Vincent (1989), 101–4. Cf. Campbell, J. (1983), 33–4.
34. Anderson (1995), 103, 108–9, 112–15, 123–5, 141.
35. Stephens (1987), 18, 89, 99, 145, 153, 176, 178, 193–4, 199, 200, 203, 249, 334–5, 351.

36. Anderson (1995), 119, 121–2; Stephens (1987), 18, 145; Purvis (1980); Purvis (1989), 104, 126.
37. Vincent (1989), 104; Anderson (1995), 102, 109, 119–20, 141; Stephens (1987), 20–2, 318–19. Cf. Hurt (1979), 28.

## 3 Secondary and Higher Education to the 1860s

1. The initial paragraphs of this chapter draw on Anderson (1983), 1–5, 16–18, 136, 140, 144–8, 161; Anderson (1985), 178–85; Anderson (1985c), 87–92; Myers (1983), 80; Anderson (1995), 59; Balfour (1903), 210–13.
2. The Public schools (secondary boarding establishments) and the public (elementary) schools are distinguished throughout this book by the adoption of a capital P for the former.
3. *Third Rep. R. C. . . . into Schools in Scotland*, PP 1867–8, xxix, vol. i., 146 (quot.); Anderson (1985c), 87–92.
4. Roach (1986); Bryant (1969); Bryant (1986), Chs 4 and 5.
5. Tompson (1971), Ch. 1; Roach (1986).
6. Tompson (1971a), 32–9; Tompson (1971), Chs 3 and 4; Allsobrook (1986), 6–7, 111–17; Seaborne (1992), 147–9, 151; Roach (1986), 72–3; Tompson (1970); Sanderson (1962), 42.
7. Burn (1964), 197; Roach (1986), 28–9, 72–5, 81–2; Bamford (1967), 175; Sanderson (1962), 42; Balls (1967), 215; Tompson (1971), 10–15, 58–72; Tompson (1971a), 35–6, 39.
8. Bamford (1967), 175.
9. Roach (1986), 13 and Chs 2–5, 15, 16; Perkin (1961), 128–30.
10. Adamson (1930), 263.
11. For some exceptions, see Roach (1986), 82.
12. Roach (1986), 4–7, 103–9; Seaborne (1992), 169; Bryant (1986), 149–59.
13. Bryant (1986), 145–9. Cf. Theobald (1988). See also p. 111.
14. Roach (1986), 6–7 (and Chs 7–14 for detailed account); Archer (1921), 241–3, 252–3; Adamson (1930), 283–4; Burstyn (1980), 23; Bryant (1979), 22; Bryant (1986), Chs 4 and 5.
15. Bamford (1967), 4; Mack (1938), 28, 34, 73, 103, 118–20, 151–66, 192–9; Archer (1921), Ch. 3; Roach (1986), Chs 16–18; and see p. 101.
16. Roach (1986), 262–7; Mack (1938), 35–42; Bamford (1967), 165–8; Roach (1991), 120.
17. Shrosbree (1988), 216, 219–20; Mack (1941), 91.
18. Simon, B. (1960), 318.
19. Mack (1938), 400 (quot.); Mangan (1981), 2–3; Roach (1986), 211–14, 231–3; Bamford (1967), Ch. 2; and see p. 100.
20. Allen, E. A. (1982), 87–90, 107; Simon and Bradley (1975), introd. 5–7.
21. Digby (1982), 2, 14; Roach (1986), 298.
22. Simon, B. (1960), 335–6.
23. Roach (1986), 216–18. Cf. Mack (1941), 32.
24. Quot. Roach (1986), 38.
25. Sanderson (1962), 32. Cf. Bamford (1967), 197–8; Roach (1991), 14.

26. Balls (1967) and (1968); Roach (1986), 37–9, 54, 58–9, 96–8.
27. Balls (1968), 227. Cf. Roach (1991), 17–19.
28. O'Day (1982), 275; and see p. 63.
29. Anderson (1983), 27–37; O'Day (1982), 273–9; Chitnis (1976), 4–7, 37, 124, 146, 155; Chitnis (1986), 42–4; and see pp. 64–5.
30. Anderson (1992), 12–13; Perkin (1983), 207.
31. Perkin (1983), 208; Sanderson (1983), 40–1; Anderson (1983), 30–1, 149.
32. Chitnis (1976), 238–40.
33. Perkin (1969), 291; Carter and Withrington (1992), 3–4; Anderson (1983), 75.
34. Perkin (1983), 207.
35. Anderson (1983), Chs 2 and 3; Green, V. H. H. (1969), 95–6.
36. Sanderson (1983), 40–5; Simon, B. (1960), 84–94, 298–9; Armytage (1955), 197–206.
37. Sanderson (1983), 45–6; Anderson (1992), 13–14; Armytage (1955), 175–6, 212.
38. Stephens (1987), 44; Scotland (1969), i. Ch. 21.
39. Sanderson (1983), 46–7; Armytage (1955), 169–75; Bondi (1990), 115–20; and see pp. 66, 115.
40. Purvis (1991), 107–9; Bryant (1979), 22, 76.
41. Sanderson (1987), 47–8.

## 4  Education, Science and Industrialization, 1750s–1850s

1. Hartwell (1971), 227–8 and works cited; Bowman and Anderson (1963), 247–79. Cf. Tortella (1994), 11–16; Nunez (1990), 125–51. For supporters, see citations in Laqueur (1974), 101; Nicholas and Nicholas (1992), 11; Tranter (1981), 224; West (1978), 369–74.
2. Mitch (1993), 305; Sandberg (1990), 20, 21.
3. E.g., Hartwell (1971), 241–4; West (1978); Laqueur (1974), 102; Thompson, E. P. (1968), 787; Stephens (1987), 136–7.
4. Houston (1985), 218 and works cited; Laqueur (1974), 96–107; Minchinton [1957]; West (1975), 65–84.
5. Cipolla (1969), Ch. 3; Deane (1973), 64; Pollard (1965), 180, 211–12; Schofield, R. S. (1973), 452–4; Sanderson (1968), 131–54; Sanderson (1972b), 82–9; Sanderson (1983), 16; Stephens (1977), 3–4, 6, 58; Stephens (1987), *passim*. Cf. Eversley (1964), 135; Grayson (1983), 63.
6. *Reps. Commissioner on Population in Mining Districts*, PP 1850, xxiii, 12, 25–6, 33–4, PP 1851, xxiii, 9; Vincent (1989), 127–8; Stephens (1987), 92. Cf. *First Rep. Midland Mining Commission*, PP 1843, xiii, pp. xliii, cxxxix; Grayson (1983), 63.
7. Stephens (1987), 12–13, 27; Stephens (1977), 43–6; Mitch (1992), 138, 147; Laqueur (1976a), 258–60: *First Rep. R. C. Employment of Children in Mines and Manufactories, Pt I*, PP 1842, xvii, App., 183, 835–6, 859–60; *Rep. Commissioner on Population in Mining Districts*, PP 1845, xxvii, 33, 35; and see pp. 25, 27–31, 33–5.

8.  Anderson (1983a), 519, 525; Mason, D. M. (1985), 76–81; Anderson (1985a), 282–6: Webb, R. K. (1954), 108.
9.  Tranter (1981), 222–4; Nicholas (1990), 47, 66. Nicholas and Nicholas (1992), 12, 16–18.
10. Vincent (1989), 98; Stephens (1987), 5–10; Stephens (1977), 30–3; Grayson (1983), 55; Stone (1969), 103–5; Sanderson (1972b), 82; Bradshaw (1983), 8; Levine (1979), 371–2; Harrop (1983), 40; Schofield (1973), 446. Cf. Tranter (1981), 223; Sanderson (1974); Laqueur (1974), 99; Levine (1980–1), 28–9.
11. Harrop (1983), 40, 50; Stephens (1987), 7–8; *Rep. R. C. into State of Large Towns*, PP 1844, xvii, App., 86 (quot.); Scotland (1969), i. 269.
12. Schofield, R. S. (1973), 450–2. Cf. Vincent (1989), 96–100.
13. Pollard (1978), 128; Stephens (1987), 318–19, 322.
14. Stephens (1973a), 168–9; Stephens (1987), sections on 'Attitudes to education'. Cf. Cipolla (1969), 68.
15. Mitch (1992), 14–15 and App. A; Mitch (1993), 290–4. It is not clear whether Wales is embraced in Mitch's calculations; Scotland is not. Cf. Laqueur (1976b), 256.
16. E.g., Stephens (1987), 141–3, 243–4; Mitch (1992), 16.
17. Mitch (1990), 36.
18. Cf. Mitch (1993), 303–4, 307.
19. Laqueur (1976b), 268; Landes (1972), 340. Cf. Hartwell (1971), 231, 243; Houston (1985), 217, 219.
20. Stephens (1987), 42, 136–7; Laqueur (1976a), 220, 242; Pollard (1989), 141.
21. *Rep. Commissioner on Population in Mining Districts*, PP 1846, xxv, 38.
22. Significantly, controllers of domestic industries, where no direct management of workers was needed, never interested themselves in their employees' education: Sanderson (1967); Bythell (1969), 147; Stephens (1987), 231–2.
23. Houston (1985), 223, 228–9; Laqueur (1976a), 219–27 (quot.); Sanderson (1967), 266; Houston (1982), 101: Pollard (1965), 185–9. Cf. Johnson (1976), 47; Pollard (1963); Miller, P. J. (1973); and see p. 15.
24. Quot. Houston (1985), 225.
25. Cf. Houston (1985), 221; Stephens (1987), 124, 228; and see pp. 15–16.
26. Eversley (1964), 135.
27. Thompson, E. P. (1968), Chs 8 and 9; Deane (1967), 148; Landes (1972), 340; Boot (1995), 284 and refs in 283n. Controversy arises partly from different definitions of 'skill', a topic that cannot be pursued here: but see Morse (1980).
28. Mitch (1993), 302; Johnson (1976), 47; Foster (1974), 224–8; Mantoux (1928), 409–10, 454–6; Thompson (1968), Chs 8 and 9; Nicholas and Nicholas (1992), 12, 16–18.
29. Stephens (1987), 175–8, 199, 213–14, 228, 266.
30. Mitch (1993), 302–3; Ashton (1948), 121; Nicholas (1990), 49–50; Boot (1995), 299–300 and *passim*: Mathias (1969), 144; Tranter (1981), 224; Samuel (1977); Pollard (1989), 127. Cf. Berg and Hudson (1992), 42.

31. Mathias (1991), 33; Cardwell (1972), 76.
32. Quot. Musson and Robinson (1960), 224.
33. Stephens (1964), 213; Schofield, R. E. (1972), 147 (quot.).
34. Stephens (1964), 213–14; Schofield, R. E. (1963), *passim*; Schofield, R. E. (1972), 139–40; Schofield, R. E. (1967), 98; Schofield, R. E. (1956); Musson and Robinson (1960), 224, 227–8; Musson and Robinson (1969), 162.
35. E.g., Langford (1868), i. 33, 136, 246, 376, 378, 380.
36. Armytage (1966), 57–8; Wood (1994), 99; Musson and Robinson (1969), 57–8; Inkster (1991), 78–9.
37. Wood (1994); Green, V. H. H. (1969), 88–9; Chitnis (1976), 168; Pollard (1989), 127. For the early history of the movement, see Kelly (1992), Ch. 8.
38. Musson and Robinson (1960), 230–4; Armytage (1966), 384–5; Kelly (1957), Chs. 2, 4, 8; Kelly (1992), 118–20.
39. Kronick (1962), 73; Musson and Robinson (1969), *passim*; and see pp. 145–6, 147.
40. Musson and Robinson (1969), 31–6; Hans (1951), 47–53; Cardwell (1972), 20; Pollard (1965), 118–19; Mokyr (1993), 34; Pollard (1989), 124; Turner, G. L'E (1989).
41. Bamford (1967), 222–5; and see pp. 127, 128.
42. Hans (1951), Ch. 5; McLachlan (1931).
43. Armytage (1966), 391; McLachlan (1931), 117–25; Pollard (1965), 114–18.
44. Houston (1985), 219–20.
45. Quot. Scotland (1969), i. 160.
46. Sanderson (1983), 27; Pollard (1989), 126; Wood (1988); Armytage (1966), 390; Chitnis (1976), 4–6, 124, 142, 155; O'Day (1982), 275–9; Wood (1994).
47. Rostow (1975), 133. Supporters include especially A. E. Musson, E. Robinson, W. W. Rostow.
48. Ashton (1972), 117–20; Ashton (1948), 58; MacLeod (1988), 4–5 and *passim*; MacLeod (1992), 286, 288; O'Brien (1991), 9; Deane (1967), 127–8.
49. Rostow (1975), 133–4, 139, 152–3; O'Brien (1991), 10–12; Deane (1967), 124; Lilley (1973), iii, 169. Cf. Supple (1963), 35; Crafts (1981), 11–12; Mathias (1991), 34–5.
50. E.g. Babbage (1835), 379; and see Musson and Robinson (1960), 222.
51. Mathias (1969), 74–5; Mathias (1991); Musson and Robinson (1960), 227–9; Musson and Robinson (1969), *passim*.
52. Cardwell (1972), 21–3.
53. Cf. Coleman and MacLeod (1986), 602; Gillispie (1972); Mantoux (1928), 210.
54. Mathias (1969), 89–91; Fussell (1969); Flinn (1966), 76; Hall (1974), 136; Sell (1992), 110; Bryant (1986), 113–14; Pollard (1989), 184; Stephens (1964), 214; and see pp. 54, 70–3.
55. Rostow (1975), 132, 167, 174–5; Rostow (1973), 566–70; Tunzelman (1981), 149–50; Hartwell (1967), 160–1; Cardwell (1972), 25; Hall (1974), 144. For official British sponsorship of science, see Rothblatt (1983), 146–7, and below, pp. 133–9.

170        Notes

56. Gillispie (1972), 122–7 (quot.); Rostow (1973), 567.
57. Mathias (1991), 33–9; Hall (1974), esp. 132–3; Hawke (1993), 60–1; O'Brien (1991), 14; Checkland (1964), 73.
58. Cf. Fleming (1952), 3–5; Hall (1974), 139.
59. Landes (1972), 108, 111; Cardwell (1972), 21–2; Hankins (1985), 81–5; Gillispie (1972), 122–7; Taylor (1957), 167; Musson and Robinson (1969), 336–7; Hall (1974), 137–9; Gillispie (1957); Hardie (1972), 171–2.
60. Hall (1974), 141: Musson (1978), 127; Musson and Robinson (1969), 126; Cardwell (1972), 21–2.
61. Mathias (1969), 90–1; Tunzelman (1981), 149; Mathias (1991), 36.
62. Pollard (1989), 123.
63. Rostow (1975), 168–84: Crafts (1977), 438–9; Hartwell (1967), 290–1; Inkster (1983a), 654–5. But see Milward and Saul (1979), 35–9; Cameron (1985), 13n. See also Crafts (1977), 438–41; Crafts (1985), Ch. 3; MacLeod (1995), 3.
64. Landes (1972), 60–3; Hartwell (1967), 156; Harris (1970), vol. 7, 37–8; Landes (1993), 162; Crafts (1978), 613; McCloy (1952), 4, 101–2, 178–83; Roehl (1976), 250–1; Rostow (1978), 610–11; MacLeod (1995), 3.
65. Flinn (1966), 77; Mathias (1972), 90–1; Musson (1972), 57; Inkster (1983), 655–6.
66. Rostow (1975), 153–4; Morrell (1995), 311–16, 330–1; Jewkes, Sawers and Stillman, 14–15; Hall (1974), 142, 146; Mathias (1991), 36; Clegg (1980); MacLeod (1995), 3. But see O'Brien (1991), 36.
67. Inkster (1983); Gaski (1982). Cf. M. Berman, rev. *Journal of Social History* 5 (1972), 523; Morrell (1995).
68. Silver (1965), 30; Mathias (1972), 78–9; Musson and Robinson (1969), 23–5; Smout (1970), 82–3.
69. Musson (1972), 110; Musson and Robinson (1969), 24–5, 76; Checkland (1964), 77; O'Brien (1991), 15.
70. Hawke (1993), 61; Perkin (1969), 68–9.
71. Perkin (1969), 68; Cardwell (1972), 37: Emerson (1980).
72. Stephens (1980), 27–33.
73. Simon, B. (1960), 23.
74. Stephens (1964), 212, 215
75. Cf. M. Berman, rev. *Journal of Social History* 5 (1972), 525–6; Inkster (1976); Inkster (1983); Shapin (1972); Morris, R. J. (1980), 200–4; Mathias (1991), 37: Stephens (1964), 214; Simon, B. (1960), 24–6, 62–71. But see Schofield, R. E. (1963), Ch. 13. See also pp. 148–9.
76. Garner and Jenkins (1984), 142; Stephens (1980a), 47–51.
77. E.g., Simon, B. (1960), 255–7.
78. Kelly (1957), 226.
79. Stephens and Roderick (1972), 350.
80. Royle (1971); Laurent (1984), 588–91; Inkster (1985), 8; Russell (1983), 157–8; Kelly (1957), 218–20, 223–5, 243–5, 257, 259–60, 269–70; Kelly (1992), 157–8, 271, 276; Stephens (1980a), 47, 74–5; Anderson (1995), 159.
81. Shapin and Barnes (1977): for comment on the apparently serious suggestion in this article that failure of the institutes to engage in research

demonstrates that their interest in science was not genuine, see Russell (1983), 163–4.

82. Garner and Jenkins (1984), 151–2; Russell (1983), 162–8, 171–2; Laurent (1984), 585–6, 597–8, 606; Stephens (1980a), 52–5.
83. Stephens (1980a); Royle (1971), 305–7.
84. Royle (1971), 309; Garner and Jenkins (1984), 139, 149, 151–2; Inkster (1976), 297–8; Inkster (1975); Laurent (1984); Kelly (1957), 226–7, 236–40; Anderson (1995), 159.
85. Roderick and Stephens (1978), 54.
86. Roderick and Stephens (1978), 63; Kelly (1957), 271–6.
87. Flinn (1966), 81. Cf. Mathias (1969), 151. But see Crafts (1978), 613–14.
88. Perkin (1969), 71; Ashton (1948), 17–22; Hagen (1962), 295–309; Flinn (1967), 23–5; Pratt (1978) (for a useful bibliography).
89. Mathias (1969), 158; Mokyr (1993a), 34. Cf. Ashton (1948), 19.
90. Payne (1978), 182–3; Mathias (1969), 162–4; McClelland (1961), especially Chs 2, 3, 9 and p. 146; Bradburn and Berlew (1961); Flinn (1967), 19–21.
91. Payne (1978), 182, 665–6; Landes (1972), 23; Flinn (1966), 83–4.
92. Perkin (1969), 85 (quot.); Payne (1974), 33–4; Rostow (1978); Crafts (1978).
93. Perkin (1968), 137n; Perkin (1969), 72–3, 82 and Ch. 6; Flinn (1967), 23–5. For a dubious psychoanalytical explanation, see Hagen (1962), especially Chs 9–13; Hagen (1967); Flinn (1966), 86–7; A. Gerschenkron, rev. *Economica* n.s. 32 (1965), 91–3.
94. Flinn (1966), 89–90; Flinn (1967), 26–31; Perkin (1969), 84; Pritchard (1948), 26, 54, 329; Smout (1970), 74–83.

## 5 Elementary Education from the 1860s to 1914

1. Green, A. (1990), 31, 33, 109–10, 208, 222, 239, 261, 271, 309, 313; Anderson (1992a), 67–70. Cf. Anderson (1995), 2–3; Tyack (1976).
2. Cf. Miller, P. (1989); Davey (1987); Landes and Salmon (1972).
3. Lenman and Stocks (1972), 23; Anderson (1995), 68–72, 296, 298–9; Myers (1972), 73–4; Corr (1989), 294–5.
4. Hurt (1979), 23, 59–60; Harget (1980), 175–6; Cruickshank (1963), 17–18.
5. Mitch (1992), 117–19; Stephens (1987), 58, 75, 90, 204, 264; Ball (1983), 209; Murphy (1972), 28–35; Anderson (1995), 86, 89, 98; Hurt (1979), 63–80; Simon, B. (1960), 360–5; Jones, D. K. (1977), 13–27; Harget (1980).
6. Stephens (1987), 181–2.
7. Myers (1972), 73–4, 88; Withrington (1972), 122; Withrington (1997), 36–7, 58; Anderson (1995), 53, 68–72, 298–9; Corr (1989), 294–5; Cruickshank (1963), 37, 93, 117.
8. Green, A. (1990), 300–1; Simon, B. (1960), 354–7; Anderson (1995), 68–9.
9. Marcham (1970), 23–7; Withrington (1972), 107; Bain (1978); Lenman and Stocks (1972); Hurt (1979), 68–9, 76; Sutherland (1971), 27; Anderson (1995), 68–9; Anderson (1983), 103–4; Corr (1989), 294–5.
10. Cf. Stannard (1990), 121; and see pp. 15–16.

11.  Gardner (1984); Laqueur (1976).
12.  West (1965), Chs 9, 10 and p. 154 (quot. 'cancer cells'); West (1975), Ch. 8;
     Stephens (1987), 50; Hurt (1971), 147ff.; Johnson (1977). Cf. West (1970).
13.  Anderson (1983a), 534; Anderson (1995), 76–7.
14.  Cf. Stephens (1987), 196; Gardner (1984), Ch. 3.
15.  Stephens (1987), 25; Laqueur (1976), 192–3; Anderson (1995), 77–8;
     Marsden, W. E. (1992), 117–18.
16.  Laqueur (1976), 192; Stephens (1987), 49, 255; Houston (1985), 115, 117,
     235; Withrington (1988), 174–7; Anderson (1983a), 525–6; Mitch (1992),
     Ch. 5. Cf. Gardner (1984), 50.
17.  West (1975), 72 (quot.); West (1970), 75–7.
18.  Anderson (1983a); Withrington (1988), 175–8. Cf. Mason, D. M. (1985);
     Anderson (1985a).
19.  West (1975), 96–106; West (1965), 144–50; Scotland (1969), ii. 19.
20.  Stephens (1987), 153, 155; Anderson (1995), 136; McCann (1969), 24–5;
     Sutherland (1971), 19; Murphy (1972), 37–8.
21.  Corr (1989), 294; Hurt (1971a); McCann (1969); Gardner (1984), Ch. 5;
     Mitch (1992), 147–9; Kiesling (1983).
22.  Withrington (1997), 53–4; Anderson (1995), 97.
23.  *Hansard*, 3rd ser., cxxxviii, col. 1811. E.g. Public Record Office, HO 129/
     495. Cf. Stephens (1987), 60.
24.  McCann (1969), 32–3; Sutherland (1971), 26; Stephens (1987), 58, 90, 99,
     180–2, 194–5, 204, 234–5, 267–8; Corr (1989), 292, 294; Anderson (1995),
     89.
25.  National Society, *Schools for the Poor in England and Wales in the Years 1866
     and 1867* [n.d.], 34–5.
26.  See, e.g., Stephens (1987), 182–3; *Minutes Committee of Council on Education,
     1848–50*, 7; *Reps. Committee of Council on Education, 1866–7*, 21 and *1868–9*,
     230.
27.  *Second Rep. R.C. on Employment of Children . . . in Agriculture*, PP 1868–9, xiii
     (a), 39.
28.  Withrington (1997), 53, 59–60.
29.  Stephens (1987), 90, 180–1, 204; *Minutes Committee of Council on Education,
     1855–6*, 417 (quot.).
30.  Musgrave (1968), 40.
31.  Mitch (1992), 127–32. Cf. Harget (1980), 203.
32.  *Reps R.G., England and Wales*, PP 1873, xx; PP 1886, xvii; *Reps R.G., Scot-
     land*, PP 1884, xx, PP 1889, xxvi; Stephens (1987), 323, 341, 343; Ander-
     son (1995), 306–7. Cf. Stephens (1975a), 12; and see pp. 33–5.
33.  Quot. Stephens (1987), 89.
34.  Stephens (1987), 323; *Reps. R.G., Scotland*, PP 1884, xx; PP 1889, xxvi; and
     see pp. 37–9.
35.  Cf. Hurt (1979), 59; Anderson (1995), 108, 137, 140; *Minutes Committee of
     Council on Education, 1840–1*, 176–7; Stephens (1980), 239.
36.  Stephens (1987), see index under 'schools: glove, lace, plait'.
37.  *Second Rep. R.C. on Employment of Children . . . in Agriculture*, PP 1868–9,
     xiii (a), 132.

38. *Rep. R.C. on Popular Education*, PP 1861, xxi (pt II), 249.
39. E.g. Stephens (1987), 151.
40. Ball (1983), 208; Hurt (1979), Ch. 2; Scotland (1969), ii. 16–18; Anderson (1995), 128, 133–4, 137, 139; Stephens (1987), 122–4, 126–9, and sections on 'Attitudes to Education'.
41. *Rep. Commissioner on Population in Mining Areas*, PP 1850, xxiii, 59–64.
42. Hodgson (1867); Stephens (1987), 69–70, 99–100, 161, 184, 205, 263, 267–8; Ball (1983), 208; Sutherland (1973), Ch. 5.
43. Stephens (1987), 116–18, 120–1, 168–70, 178; Hurt (1979), 26. Cf. Hair (1982), 46–54.
44. Mitch (1992), 162–7; Roxburgh (1971), 171. Cf. Anderson (1995), 137–9; Anderson (1985a), 524, 528, 531.
45. *Rep. Committee of Council on Education, 1866–7*, 47–8; Heward (1992), 146; Stephens (1987), 89, 92, 259; Roxburgh (1971), 171; *Rep. Select Committee on Education of Destitute Children*, PP 1861, vii, 101 (Carpenter). Cf. Anderson (1995), 137–9.
46. Robson (1931), 82, 173; Mitch (1992), 162, 171; Stephens (1987), 75, 121.
47. Stephens (1987), 318–19; Anderson (1995), 133, 135–9.
48. West (1965), 134–5.
49. Mitch (1992), 209; Stephens (1987), 322–3; Vincent (1989), 96–7. Cf. Campbell, J. (1983), 33.
50. Mitch (1992), 188, 209–11. Cf. Mitch (1986).
51. Anderson (1985b), 463; Anderson (1995), 234; Mitch (1992), 188.
52. *Rep. Committee of Council on Education, 1872–3*, 71–4; Davies, J. A. (1973), 39.
53. Hurt (1979), 71, 82, 155–61. Cf. Seaborne (1992), 172.
54. Cf. Seaborne (1992), 172, 174–6; West (1965), 150.
55. Hurt (1971), 224; Sutherland (1971), 29–30; Murphy (1972), 76–8; Armytage (1965), 150–6; West (1975), 189–93; Sharp (1995), 24; Cruickshank (1963), 48–51, 55–8, 61–4, 67, 70–1.
56. This paragraph and the next draw on Murphy (1972), 68–70; Lawson and Silver (1973), 319–21; Hurt (1979), Ch. 4; Sturt (1967), 308–11; Cruickshank (1963), Ch. 3; Simon, B. (1965), 158–62; Gosden (1966), Ch. 7.
57. Murphy (1972), 78–9; Gordon, Aldrich and Dean (1991), 9–10.
58. Jones, D. K. (1977), 72–4, 81; Sutherland (1971), 32–3; Webb, S. (1904); Armytage (1965), 145–7; Cruickshank (1963), 38–9; Lawson and Silver (1973), 318–23, 330–1, 378–9.
59. For background to the 1902 Act, see Daglish (1996); Eaglesham (1956); Cruickshank (1963). For technical instruction committees, see pp. 102, 134.
60. Platten (1975), 297–300; Green, A. (1990), 306; Lawson and Silver (1973), Ch. 10; Sharp (1995), 24–5; Cruickshank (1963), 85–9 and Ch. 5.
61. Lenman and Stocks (1972), 103; Scotland (1969), ii. 4, 46; Anderson (1995), 223–5, 308.
62. Anderson (1983), 103–12; Anderson (1995), 299.
63. Scotland (1960), ii. 5, 13–17. Cf. Lenman and Stocks (1972), 98–9; Anderson (1983), 111–12; Anderson (1995), 203–4, 224, 231, 271, 298.
64. Anderson (1995), 296–7, 299; MacKinnon (1972).

65. Vincent (1989), Ch. 4 and 270–1.
66. See Daglish (1996), 444, 446; Hurt (1979), Chs 5 and 6; Anderson (1995), 191–206 and works cited. For disabled children, see Hurt (1985), 61–2, works cited; Hurt (1988).

## 6  Secondary and Higher Education from the 1860s to 1914

1. Gosden (1966), Ch. 4.
2. Marsden, W. E. (1987), Ch. 4.
3. Roach (1991), 4, 21, 31–2, 34, 41, 69, 70, 80–1, 144–5; Balls (1967), 208–9, 212–13; Balls (1968), 226; Allsobrook (1986), 241, 252.
4. Roach (1991), 157–65, 168–9, 188–9, 247; Simon, B. (1965), 180; Bryant (1986), 163–7, 419; and for the preparatory schools, Leinster-Mackay (1976); Leinster-Mackay (1984).
5. Mack (1941), 106–7; Roach (1991), 243; Ogilvie (1957), 180, 183, 189.
6. Honey (1977), Ch. 5; Roach (1971), 4, 141–3, 216–18; Anderson (1992), 50–3; Roach (1986), 233, 264–9; Rubinstein (1986), 191–2; Rubinstein (1993), 15–19; Wilkinson (1964), 21–2, 25, 31–2, 115–16; Bamford (1967), 63, 209–17, 229; Mack (1941), 108–9, 121–2 (quot.); Mangan (1981), 8–9; Mangan (1983a), 22–3 and Ch. 2; Simon and Bradley (1975), various essays.
7. Kazamias (1966), 70, 97–8, 144; Sharp (1968); Roach (1991), Chs 9, 10; and see pp. 133–6.
8. Roach (1991), 80–1, 83, 245–6, 249–50, and Chs 8–10; Simon, B. (1965), 185.
9. Seaborne (1992), 142, 156–7, 169; Archer (1921), 291–4; Jones, G. E. (1982), 3–10; Evans, L. W. (1974), 15–20; Evans, W. G. (1982).
10. Simon, B. (1965), 239–42; Bamford (1967), 259–62; Kazamias (1966), 138–9; Marsden, W. E. (1982a), 55; Allsobrook (1986), 264–5; Sherington (1981), 13. For the complex political and administrative background of educational change in this period, see especially Daglish (1996).
11. Anderson (1992), 18–19. Cf. Bryant (1986), 306–7, 442.
12. Kazamias (1966), 130–5, 138–42; Jenkins (1979), 7–8; Bryant (1986), 442; Daglish (1996), 217–18, 226.
13. Jones, G. E. (1982), 442; Roach (1991), 95–6; Sherington (1981), 12; Bryant (1986), 442.
14. Sanderson (1987), 23; Bamford (1967), 263–4; Kazamias (1966), 46–7, 170–81; Sherington (1981), 7; Daglish (1996), 217–18, 226; Bryant (1986), 305, 438.
15. Reeder (1987), 243–4; Kazamias (1966), 204–5; Daglish (1996), 226, 445.
16. Mangan (1983), 313, 320; Baron (1954–5), 234; Simon and Bradley (1975), 16–17; Roach (1991), 243–4; Honey (1987), 157.
17. Roach (1971), viii, 140–1. Cf. Perkin (1989), 87–8.
18. Gordon, Aldrich and Dean (1991), 21; Kazamias (1966), Ch. 6 and 205–9; Kamm (1965), 230; Sanderson (1988a); Sanderson (1994), Chs 1, 2; Argles (1964), 39, 59; Bryant (1985), 683–4; Bryant (1986), 396, 406–9; Lawson and Silver (1973), 384; and see pp. 135–6, 138–9.

19.  Quot. Withrington (1997), 69. The following paragraphs draw on Scotland
     (1969), ii. 38–9, 57–8, 61–4, and Ch. 5; Anderson (1983), Ch. 5 and 202–3,
     206–7, 217, 219, 223, 226–32, 238; Anderson (1985), 186–7, 193–4;
     Anderson (1995), 188, 206–7, 228, 238, 246–54, 262, 297; Paterson
     (1983); Withrington (1997), 70.
20.  Anderson (1985), 179, 192, 195–201.
21.  Scotland (1969), ii. 62–3; Anderson (1983), 243.
22.  Anderson (1983), 23, 243; Anderson (1985), 202; Anderson (1995), 257–60,
     297; Lenman and Stocks (1972), 104.
23.  Corr (1989), 299; Anderson (1983), 243, 247–9; Anderson (1985), 193;
     Anderson (1995), 244, 262.
24.  Anderson (1985), 201; Anderson (1991), 234. Cf. Osborne (1966), 25.
25.  Evans, W. G. (1990), 199–200, 207; Pedersen (1987), 35–6; Bryant (1979),
     101, 108; Pedersen (1979), 77–9; Kamm (1965), 233; Dyhouse (1981), 3,
     13, 50.
26.  Kamm (1965), 216–18, 236; Bryant (1979), 109, 115; Roach (1991), 237–41;
     Dyhouse (1976); Dyhouse (1981), 162–9.
27.  Roach (1971), Ch. 5; Pedersen (1987), 85–90, 195–6; Bryant (1979), Ch. 2.
28.  Roach (1971), 135.
29.  Bryant (1979), 91–3, 103–4, 106; Pedersen (1987), ii–v, 3, 11, 15–19, 26–7,
     55–6; Pedersen (1979), 62, 71ff.; Dyhouse (1981), 57–8, 64–6, 172; Roach
     (1971), 111–12; Bryant (1985), 24.
30.  Fletcher (1980), 5–6, 151, 171–2, 190, 203 and *passim*; Roach (1991), 207,
     211–12; Bryant (1986), 235; Bryant (1979), 101; Kamm (1965), 214.
31.  Pedersen (1987), 62.
32.  Kamm (1965), 233.
33.  Avery (1991), 132–3, 144–5; Dyhouse (1981), 53–5; Bryant (1986), 340–3,
     357–8.
34.  Pedersen (1987), vi–vii, 2, 84–7, 318–21. Cf. Dyhouse (1981), 2, 58, 170–5;
     Pedersen (1979), 71–2; Bryant (1986), 354–6; Bryant (1979), 118–19, 123;
     Roach (1991), 228, 231–2; Digby (1982), 3–6; Dyhouse (1976), 34, 41–3;
     Jenkins (1979), 13–14, 171, 174.
35.  Bryant (1979), 64–7, 72, 102–3; Pedersen (1987), Ch. 8; Roach (1991),
     224–6; Kamm (1965), 214–25; Dyhouse (1981), 75.
36.  Roach (1991), 233–4; Bryant (1979), 35–6, 80–1, 117; Pedersen (1979), 65,
     71ff.; Pedersen (1987), Ch. 10; Bryant (1986), 311.
37.  Moore (1992), 12, 29, 31–2; Anderson (1983), 135, 254, 276; Anderson
     (1995), 209; Scotland (1969), ii. 80–1.
38.  Anderson (1995), 246; Anderson (1983), 135, 256.
39.  Corr (1993); Anderson (1983), 179–81, 185, 187; Anderson (1985), 194–5;
     Anderson (1995), 245–6; Anderson (1985c), 84.
40.  Anderson (1995), 234–5; Moore (1992), 30–1.
41.  Perkin (1983), 214–15; Anderson (1992), 9, 12.
42.  Green, V. H. H. (1969), 73–4; Sanderson (1975), 142–3; Slee (1988), 83–4;
     Anderson (1992), 15–16.
43.  Lowe (1983), 44–7; Anderson (1992), 22–3; Anderson (1991), 232;
     Sanderson (1975), 32, 242.

44. Sanderson (1972), Chs 3, 4.
45. Jones, D. R. (1988), 92–3 and *passim*; Lowe (1983), 46; Armytage (1955), Ch. 10; Sanderson (1975), 243; Ringer (1978), 189; and see pp. 136–7.
46. Davie (1961), 77–8; Anderson (1992), 31–2; Sanderson (1975), 32, 186; Jones, D. R. (1988), 172; Finn (1983), 187–8. Cf. Wright (1979).
47. Sanderson (1975), 11–12; Perkin (1983), 211, 214; Rothblatt (1983), 132–3; Lowe (1983), 37; Jones, G. E. (1988), 39, 86.
48. Anderson (1992), 9, 20, 47–8; Jones, D. R. (1988), 40–1, 71–81, 185; Sanderson (1975), 83.
49. Bryant (1979), 84–9; Kamm (1965), 250–67; Anderson (1983), 254–7, 273–7; Lowe (1983), 46; Dyhouse (1995), 12–13. British figures embrace: England 18 per cent; Scotland 24 per cent; Wales 35 per cent.
50. Howarth and Curtoys (1987); Sutherland (1987); Dyhouse (1995), 13–27; and see p. 109.
51. Pedersen (1987), Ch. 10; Anderson (1992), 57; Dyhouse (1981), 69–70; Anderson (1991), 245.
52. Lowe (1983), 49–51; Anderson (1991), 237–8.
53. Roach (1971), 64, 73, 140–1; Scotland, ii. 65–70.
54. Armytage (1955), 255–6; Jones, D. R. (1988), 41–2, 78–80, 95–6, 100–1, 181; Green, V. H. H. (1969), 113–14; Perkin (1983), 211–12; Rothblatt (1983), 136–8, 140; Williams, J. G. (1993), 172–6, 180, 199.
55. Perkin (1983), 213–15; Ringer (1979), 236–7, 239, 243–4; Anderson (1992), 53–4; Lowe (1987), 176; Simon, B. (1960), 298–9; Simon, B. (1965), 111–12; Sherington (1981), 8; Anderson (1991), 238–9.
56. Scotland (1969), ii. 152–4; Anderson (1991), 232–5; Anderson (1992), 32–4. For Welsh resistance, see Gosden (1966), 102, 113–15; Cruickshank (1963), 88.
57. Deduced from Anderson (1991), 234–5 and Williams, J. G. (1993), 202–4.
58. Sanderson (1975), 13–14, 18; Ringer (1979), 236; Rubinstein (1986), 191–2.
59. Lowe (1983), 46; Sanderson (1987), 42.
60. Perkin (1983), 218; Anderson (1991), 225, 228, 233, 237, 243–4; Anderson (1992), 33, 54–5; Sanderson (1975), 18–20 (quot.).
61. Sanderson (1975), 16–17; Lowe (1987), 168–9; Simon (1965), 86–92, 303–11.
62. Anderson (1991), 25–6, 38–9; Anderson (1995), 237; Roach (1991), 243; Müller, Ringer and Simon (1987), *passim*; Simon, B. (1960), 336–7; Perkin (1969), 302; Lowe (1983), 37, 56.
63. Simon, B. (1987), 93–4, 104–7; Reeder (1987), 145–7; Marsden, W. E. (1987), 118 (quot.).
64. Marsden, W. E. (1987), Ch. 5.
65. Anderson (1995), 238 (quot.).
66. Albisetti (1987), 210–11; Steedman (1987); Ringer (1979), 232–3; Reeder (1987), 140; Anderson (1995), 238; Lowe (1987), 172; and see pp. 102–5.
67. Lowe (1987), 173–4; Anderson (1992), 19–22, 37.
68. Jones, D. R. (1988), 168.
69. Ringer (1987), 241–2; Müller, Ringer and Simon (1987), 7.
70. Anderson (1991), 238; Jones, D. R. (1988), 154; Lowe (1987), 171.
71. Schriewer and Harney (1987), 204–5: and see pp. 102–5, 108.

72.  Albisetti (1987), 212–13.
73.  Anderson (1992), 12, 39; Anderson (1995), 238.
74.  Cf. Edgerton (1996), 23 and works cited.
75.  Anderson (1992), 54–5; Lowe (1983), 47; Sanderson (1972c), 253; and see pp. 136, 139.
76.  Schriewer and Harney (1987), 203–4.

## 7  Science, Technology, Education and the Economy from the 1850s to 1914

1.  See, e.g., on the one hand: Elbaum and Lazonick (1986); Wiener (1981); Barnett (1985); Landes (1972); Dintenfass (1992); and works by Aldcroft, Crafts and Roderick and M. D. Stephens (cited in the Bibliography); and, on the other: Pollard (1989); Edgerton (1996); Collins and Robbins (1990); and works by Floud and McCloskey (cited in the Bibliography). Further references may be found in the following notes.
2.  Elbaum and Lazonick (1986), various essays; Aldcroft (1964), 118, 133; Aldcroft (1966); Aldcroft (1991), 111–13; 118; Kennedy (1974), 434, 438, 440; Kennedy (1987); Crafts (1979); Lazonick (1983), 229–30; Barnett (1985).
3.  Allen, G. C. (1979), 37–8 (quot.); Wiener (1981), *passim*; Barnett (1972), 24–43; and see Raven (1989), 180; Rubinstein (1993), 16–17, 20, 22 and works cited; Edgerton (1996), works cited.
4.  Ward (1967), 52 (quot.); Wiener (1981).
5.  See especially Roderick and Stephens (1972, 1978, 1981, 1982); Cardwell (1972), Ch. 6; Wrigley (1986).
6.  Roderick and Stephens (1972), 29–30, 32–5, 38, 41; Roderick and Stephens (1978), 37, 40 (quots); Shrosbree (1988), 52; Lawson and Silver (1973), 336, 345; Honey (1977), 137; Pollard (1989), 170; Jenkins (1979), 2–3, 6, 13–14, 30–7, 171, 174, 176. Cf. Vlaeminke (1990); and see pp. 102–3.
7.  Roderick and Stephens (1972), 30; Roderick and Stephens (1981), introd., 8–9; Jones, M. J. (1997); Roderick and Stephens (1976), 52–7, 65n.
8.  Anderson (1983), 144–8, Ch. 6; Anderson (1985), 183–4, 194; Anderson (1995), 266–7 (quot.), 282–3.
9.  Green, A. (1995), 124, 131–3; Sanderson (1994), 12–14; Landes (1972), 346–8; Roderick and Stephens (1982), 19–22; Pollard (1989), 152–4, 196; Aldcroft (1964), 120; Roderick and Stephens (1978), 107; Spring (1990), 246–9 and works cited; Donovan (1993); Sanderson (1972), 24.
10.  See, e.g., Landes (1972), 344; Wrigley (1986); and references in Fox and Guagnini (1985), 147n.
11.  See, e.g., Collins and Robbins (1990), various essays; Edgerton (1996).
12.  Rubinstein (1990), 78–9; James, H. (1990), 91–106, 122–3; Raven (1989), 183–6; Pollard (1994), 76; Perkin (1989), 365–6: Guagnini (1993), 23–4; Erickson (1959), 12, 20, 230–2; Kaelble (1979–80), 407; Ringer (1967), 123, 133; Fox and Guagnini (1985).

13. Berghoff (1990), 150. For other critics of Wiener, see especially Robbins (1990), 6–9, 29–37; Rubinstein (1990); Edgerton (1996), 7–8, 21 and works cited.
14. Honey (1977), 297; Rubinstein (1990), 112.
15. Coleman (1973), 105; Pollard (1994), 74; Rubinstein (1993), 112ff.; Berghoff (1990); Berghoff (1991).
16. Rubinstein (1993), 112, 119–20, 123, 127–8 and works cited; Ward (1967), 49–50; Berghoff (1991), 233–4; Sanderson (1988a), 41–2.
17. Rubinstein (1993), 121 (quot.); Berghoff (1990), 153.
18. Cassis (1985), 212–15; Rubinstein (1993), 124–5, 167; Coleman (1973), 111, 113; Berghoff (1990), 153.
19. Rubinstein (1993), 139; Berghoff (1990), 166 (quot.).
20. Anderson (1995), 206, 283; and see Ch. 6 above.
21. E.g. Aldcroft (1964), 119.
22. Lundgreen (1984), 60; Edgerton (1996), 8.
23. Lequin (1978), 314–19; Fox and Guagnini (1985); Fox and Guagnini (1993), introd. 4; Zeldin (1967), 61.
24. Pollard (1989), 147–8 and cf. 164, 206; Lundgreen (1984), 65; Mitch (1990), 33 (quot.).
25. Lundgreen (1984), 64–7, 82; Berghoff and Möller (1994), 288; Pollard (1994), 76; Pollard (1989), 146–51 (quot. on the *Gymnasien*), 155; Kaelble (1979–80), 407; Fox and Guagnini (1993), introd. 3; Hennock (1990), 301–7; Russell (1983), 248, 250–1.
26. Roach (1986), 120–34 (quot.); Roach (1991), 174; Bryant (1969), 273; Pollard (1989), 170–1.
27. Roach (1991), Ch. 10 and works cited.
28. Jones, G. E. (1982), 3–11; Davies, W. (1989), 21, 104–7, 110–11; Jenkins (1979), 5, 7, 11; Vlaeminke (1990), 63–9. Cf. Pollard (1989), 168; and see pp. 102–5.
29. Anderson (1983), 224–5; Balfour (1903), 220; Anderson (1983), 194, 224–8; Anderson (1985), 194; and see pp. 107–8.
30. Sanderson (1994), 20–4, 27–9, 35–6; Bailey (1990), 99–104.
31. Argles (1964), 18–19; Bishop (1971), 152–6; Cardwell (1972), 86–90; Russell (1983), 236; Hennock (1990), 305; MacDonagh (1974–5), 608–11.
32. Hennock (1990), 305–7; Russell (1983), 247; Cotgrove (1958), 60–7; Pollard (1989), 179–80; Sanderson (1988a), 40; Cardwell (1972), 159–60; and see p. 102.
33. Guagnini (1993), 36–7.
34. Hennock (1990), 316–29; Guagnini (1991), 71, 80–85; Sanderson (1972), 106–18; Cardwell (1972), 197–8; Anderson (1995), 268–78; Anderson (1983), 77.
35. Hennock (1990), 312–13; Sanderson (1972), 10, 11, 103–6; Stephens (1975), 251, 275; Jones, P. (1988), Ch. 4; and see pp. 115–16, 122.
36. Sanderson (1972), 119.
37. Sanderson (1988), 99; Stephens (1975), 247–9; Roderick and Stephens (1978), 97, 120, 135–6; Sanderson (1972), Ch. 2 and 107–9; Sanderson (1972c), 244, 249–51, 258; Pollard (1994), 76–7; Jenkins (1979), 2, 12;

Roderick and Stephens (1981a), 192; Royle (1987), 372; Pollard (1989), 183, 193. Cf. Edgerton (1996), 19–20.
38. Robertson (1984), 39–40; Sanderson (1972), Ch. 6; Campbell, R. H. (1980); Anderson (1983), Chs 3 and 7; Pollard (1989), 185; Marsden, B. (1992), 319–46; Guagnini (1993), 16; Wilson (1992), 118–19, 124–5.
39. Sanderson (1972), Ch. 5; Pollard (1989), 187–8.
40. Pollard (1989), 155–6, 181–2, 207, 209–10. Cf. Floud (1982), 158–9; Cardwell (1972), 166.
41. Edgerton (1996), 20.
42. Pollard (1989), 181–2, 196–7 (quot. German scientists); Sanderson (1972), 22–3; Sanderson (1972c), 260 (quot. London University).
43. Roderick and Stephens (1978), 171.
44. Nicholas (1985), 88 and works cited; Russell (1983), 242. Cf. Pollard (1989), 189–92, 209.
45. Morse (1980), 15–16; Guagnini (1993); Nicholas (1985); Pollard (1989), 197; Roderick and Stephens (1978), 107.
46. Floud (1982), 161.
47. Floud (1982), 164–6 (quot.); Sanderson (1993), 4. Cf. Nicholas (1985).
48. Green, A. (1995), 137; Pollard (1989), 200; Inkster (1983), 43.
49. Quot. Betts (1984), 48. Cf. Vincent (1989), 118–19.
50. Robertson (1974), 222.
51. Floud (1982), 165.
52. Pollard (1989), 139, 143, 147, 206; Lundgreen (1984), 65–6.
53. Mitch (1990), 33: Lundgreen (1975), 79; Tortella and Sandberg (1990), 16–18, 20–1; Tortella (1990), various essays; Lundgreen (1975), 72; Matthews, Feinstein and Odling-Smee (1982), 105–13; Pollard (1989), 136–8 and works cited; Edgerton (1996), 8.
54. Pollard (1989), 139, 141–2; Mitch (1990), 38–9; Vincent (1989), 117–24.
55. Konig (1993) and various other essays in Fox and Guagnini (1993); Pollard (1989), 157–62 (quot.).
56. Pollard (1989), 135; Mitch (1990), 32; Vincent (1989), 114–15.
57. Sanderson (1988a), 38, 40–2.
58. McCloskey (1974), 277; Nicholas (1988), 580; Payne (1978), 208; Saul (1969); Edgerton (1996), 3; Coleman and Macleod (1986), 599, 610–11; Payne (1974), 56; Pollard (1994), 78–9, 89; Byres (1967), 253, 289–90; Robbins (1990), 8; Wengenroth (1995); Habakkuk (1962), 215–16.
59. Coleman and Macleod (1986), 595; Sandberg (1981), 119; McCloskey (1970); Brown, K. D. (1989); McCloskey (1974a); Nicholas (1984); Payne (1990), 26–7, 30–1 and works cited. Decisions by individuals might well have been sound without being advantageous to the economy.
60. Rubinstein (1990), 73; Rubinstein (1993), 24, 39–40; Lee, C. H. (1984), 139, 143–8, 153–4; Pollard (1985), 512–13; Inkster (1983), 43, 45; Floud (1994), 22–3; Lee, C. H. (1986), 12, 14.
61. McCloskey (1970), 459. Cf. McCloskey (1979); McCloskey and Sandberg (1981).
62. Rubinstein (1993), 25. Cf. Nicholas (1986), 89.

63.  Coleman and Macleod (1986), 599–602; Aldcroft (1991), 112; Pollard (1994), 88–9; Payne (1974), 57–8; Robbins (1990), 6–7; Phillips (1989), 411–12.
64.  Pollard (1989), 213.
65.  Cf. Inkster (1983), 43.
66.  Cf., e.g., Edgerton (1996); Rubinstein (1993), Ch. 1; Matthews, Feinstein and Odling-Smee (1982), 31–2, 499. But see Sanderson (1988a).

## 8   The Growth of a Literate Culture

1.  Cf. Murdoch and Sher (1988), 127–8; Vincent (1989), especially Chs 1, 2, 5, 7.
2.  See especially Webb, R. K. (1955); Altick (1957); Hollis (1970); and bibliographies in Boyce, Curran and Wingate (1978); Neuburg (1977); Brown, L. (1985).
3.  Aspinall (1949); Altick (1957), 48, 51; Cranfield (1962), 65, 85–7; Read (1961), 59, 62; Chitnis (1976), 33.
4.  Black (1993), 68–71, 77–8; Cranfield (1962), 124, 137–8; Read (1961), 69–73, 205. Cf. Brown, L. (1985), 55–61, 70, 274.
5.  Cranfield (1962), 271–2; Maxted (1990), 115, 116; Shepard (1973), 115, 118; Mason, J. (1978), 288–92; Brown, L. (1985), Chs 3, 9; Lee, A. J. (1974); Lee, A. J. (1976), Ch. 5, and 210–12; Lee, A. J. (1978); Boyce (1978).
6.  Mason, J. (1978); Altick (1957), 46–8; Murdoch and Sher (1988), 133–4.
7.  Dixon (1986), 133–48; Altick (1957), 362.
8.  Houston (1993), 373, 381–3; McDougall (1990); Rees (1988), xxx, xlvii, xlix; Murdoch and Sher (1988), 131–7; Feather (1985), 41–2; Kaufman (1967), 6, 24, 25, 30, 38ff. and Apps. a, B; Knott (1972), 227; Mowat (1980), 8; Kelly (1992), 54, 85–6; Chitnis (1976), 19.
9.  Jones, A. (1993), 159–60; Brown, L. (1985), 4, 273–4 and Ch. 6; Lee, A. J. (1976), 37–8; Williams, R. (1965), 197–8, 220; Perkin (1957), 431.
10.  Altick (1957), Ch. 5; Mountjoy (1978), 268; Billington (1986), 113–23; Webb, R. K. (1969), 206.
11.  Chitnis (1976), 195–210; and see pp. 62–3.
12.  Stephens (1980a), Ch. 2; Morris, R. J. (1983).
13.  Perkin (1957), 425–6, 429; Mitch (1992), 70–9; Williams, R. (1965), 195–7.
14.  Aspinall (1949), Ch. 1; Mitch (1992), 44, 47.
15.  Mitch (1992), 48–9, 60; Stephens (1987), 20–1; Altick (1957), 306–9, 312–17, 331–59; Plant (1965), Chs 13–16; Brown, L. (1985), 4, 8–14.
16.  See Kelly (1992), Chs 7–15 for details.
17.  Mitch (1992), 48, 50; Vincent (1989), 32–52; James, L. (1976), 25–7.
18.  Webb, R. K. (1955), 31–2; Vincent (1989), Ch. 6.
19.  Vincent (1989), 131, 208; Webb, R. K. (1955), 28–31; Vicinus (1974), Ch. 1; Vicinus (1975), 8–9; Feather (1985), 40–1; Altick (1957), Ch. 12.
20.  Herd (1952), 234–8; Berridge (1978), 247, 249, 252; Mason, Tony (1976), 168; Lee, A. J. (1976), 38, 40.

21. Berridge (1978), 247, 249; Vincent (1989), Ch. 6 and 241–58, 270–4; Mitch (1992), 50–2, 60–1; Williams, R. (1978).
22. Jones, A. (1993), 159–60; Perkin (1957), 431–2.
23. Public Record Office, HO 42.
24. Koss (1983), 50; Hollis (1970), 8 and Chs 6, 7.
25. Watson (1989); Radcliffe (1986); Carter (1975–6).
26. Webb, R. K. (1955), Chs 4–7; Simon, B. (1960), Chs 4, 5: Vicinus (1975), Chs 2, 3; Kelly (1992), Ch. 9; Harrop (1984), 196, 199, 201.
27. Perkin (1957), 426; Shepard (1973), 66; Jones, A. (1993), 155–6; Read (1961), 95–7; Fraser, W. H. (1988), 283–6.
28. Vincent (1989), 246–7.
29. Hopkin (1978), 294–8, 305; Read (1961), 97–8; Vincent (1989), 241–58; Simon, B. (1965), 47; Curran (1978), 67–8; Williams, R. (1978), 49.
30. Webb, R. K. (1955), 37.
31. Altick (1957), 321–2, 327–30, 339–40; Hollis (1970); Read (1961), 66–8; Aspinall (1949), Chs 2–16; Curran (1978), 61–4.
32. Smith (1983).
33. Rees (1988), lxii; James, L. (1976), 29–32; Webb, R. K. (1955), 25–8; Rees (1990), 8. Vicinus (1975), 9; Neuburg (1977), 250–6.
34. Altick (1957), 35–8; Scott (1969); Lee, A. J. (1976), 39–40; Billington (1986), 126, 132; Kelly (1992), 151–3.
35. Lee, A. J. (1976), 43; Webb, R. K. (1955), 66–73, 85–90, 114–22, 125–7, 139–41, 144; Altick (1957), 269–73.
36. Hollis (1970), 3, 10–25, 295–304; Curran (1978), 53–60; Lee, A. J. (1976), Ch. 3; Wickwar (1928).
37. Vincent (1989), 152, 160; Altick (1957), 271; Neuburg (1977), 259–64.
38. Kelly (1992), 168–70; Hollis (1970), 137. Lack of space prevents detailed treatment of public libraries: see Kelly (1992), 176–7, 213–14 and works cited.
39. Webb, R. K. (1955), 63–81, 158–61; Neuburg (1977), Ch. 4; Harrop (1984), 201; Harrison (1961), 49–54; Anderson (1995), 159; Lee, A. J. (1976), 37; Altick (1957), 269–77, 280–3; Knott (1972), 248; Vincent (1981), Ch. 7; Kelly (1992), 173–7.
40. Vincent (1989), 210–27; Herd (1952), Ch. 12; Mitch (1992), 76.
41. Stone (1969), 119; Laqueur (1976b), 270.
42. Houston (1983), 285. Possibly the same applied to remote Welsh-speaking areas, but Welsh written literature was more extensive than that in Gaelic.
43. Stephens (1987), 13–14, 266; Stephens (1983), 6; Stephens (1990), 567–8; Houston (1985), 193–6; Vincent (1989), 50.
44. Vicinus (1975), 1, 6 and Ch. 5; Vincent (1989), 276; Webb (1955), 114.
45. Vincent (1989), 270, 273–5; Vincent (1981), 152, 160; and see p. 90.
46. Jones, A. (1993), 160.
47. Vincent (1989), 271, 274; Tholfsen (1976), 314–16; Laqueur (1976b), 270; Hollis (1970), 301–3.

# BIBLIOGRAPHY

*This is confined to secondary works cited in the notes by author (or editor) and date. Some titles are not given in full. Primary sources are cited in full or abbreviated form in the notes: Parliamentary Papers (PP) are distinguished by session and volume number.*

## Abbreviations Used

| | |
|---|---|
| *AS* | *Annals of Science* |
| *BH* | *Business History* |
| *BHR* | *Business History Review* |
| *BJES* | *British Journal of Educational Studies* |
| *BJHS* | *British Journal for the History of Science* |
| *BJS* | *British Journal of Sociology* |
| *EcHR* | *Economic History Review* |
| *EEH* | *Explorations in Economic History* |
| *HE* | *History of Education* |
| *HEQ* | *History of Education Quarterly* |
| *HJ* | *Historical Journal* |
| *HR* | *Historical Research* |
| *HU* | *History of Universities* |
| *HW* | *History Workshop* |
| *JBS* | *Journal of British Studies* |
| *JCH* | *Journal of Contemporary History* |
| *JEAH* | *Journal of Educational Administration and History* |
| *JEEH* | *Journal of European Economic History* |
| *JEH* | *Journal of Economic History* |
| *JSH* | *Journal of Social History* |
| *P&P* | *Past and Present* |
| *PH* | *Paedagogica Historica* |
| *SER* | *Scottish Educational Review* |
| *SES* | *Scottish Educational Studies* |
| *SESH* | *Scottish Economic and Social History* |
| *SH* | *Social History* |
| *SHR* | *Scottish Historical Review* |
| *SSS* | *Social Studies of Science* |
| *VCH* | *Victoria History of the Counties of England* |
| *WHR* | *Welsh Historical Review* |

Adamson, J. W. (1930), *English Education, 1789–1902.*
Albisetti, J. (1987), 'Systematisation: a Critique', in Müller, Ringer and Simon (eds) (1987).
Aldcroft, D. H. (1964), 'The Entrepreneur and the British Economy, 1870–1914', *EcHR* 17.
Aldcroft, D. H. (1966), 'Technical Progress and British Enterprise, 1875–1914', *BH* 8.
Aldcroft, D. H. (1991), 'Technical and Structural Factors in British Industrial Decline', in Mathias and Davis (eds) (1991).
Allen, E. A. (1982), 'Public School Élites in Early Victorian England', *JBS* 21.
Allen, G. C. (1979), *The British Disease.*
Allsobrook, D. I. (1986), *Schools for the Shires.*
Altick, R. D. (1957), *The English Common Reader.*
Anderson, C. A. and M. J. Bowman (eds) (1966), *Education and Economic Development.*
Anderson, R. D. (1983), *Education and Opportunity in Victorian Scotland.*
Anderson, R. D. (1983a), 'Education and the State in Nineteenth-Century Scotland', *EcHR* 36.
Anderson, R. D. (1985), 'Secondary Schools and Scottish Society in the Nineteenth Century', *P&P* 109.
Anderson, R. D. (1985a), 'School Attendance in Nineteenth-Century Scotland', *EcHR* 38.
Anderson, R. [D.] (1985b), 'Education and Society in Modern Scotland', *HEQ* 25.
Anderson, R. D. (1985c), 'In Search of the "Lad of Parts" ', *HW* 19.
Anderson, R. D. (1991), 'Universities and Élites in Modern Britain', *HU* 10.
Anderson, R. D. (1992), *Universities and Elites in Britain since 1800.*
Anderson, R. D. (1992a), 'The Scottish University Tradition', in Carter and Withrington (eds) (1992).
Anderson, R. D. (1995), *Education and the Scottish People, 1750–1918.*
Archer, R. L. (1921), *Secondary Education in the Nineteenth Century.*
Argles, M. (1964), *From South Kensington to Robbins: An Account of English Technical and Scientific Education Since 1851.*
Armytage, W. H. G. (1955), *Civic Universities.*
Armytage, W. H. G. (1965), *Four Hundred Years of English Education.*
Armytage, W. H. G. (1966), 'Education and Innovative Ferment in England, 1588–1805', in Anderson and Bowman (eds) (1966).
Ashton, T. S. (1948), *The Industrial Revolution, 1760–1830.*
Ashton, T. S. (1972), 'Some Statistics of the Industrial Revolution in Britain', in Musson (ed.) (1972).
Aspinall, A. (1949), *Politics and the Press, c. 1780–1850.*
Avery, G. (1991), *The Best Type of Girl.*
Babbage, C. (1835), *On the Economy of Machinery and Manufactures.*
Bailey, Bill (1990), 'Technical Education and Secondary Schools, 1905–1945', in Summerfield and Evans (eds) (1990).
Bain, W. H. (1978), ' "Attacking the citadel": James Moncrieff's Proposals to Reform Scottish Education, 1851–69', *SER* 10.

Balfour, G. (1903), *The Educational System of Great Britain and Ireland*.

Ball, N. (1963), *Her Majesty's Inspectorate, 1839–1849*.

Ball, N. (1983), *Educating the People ... 1840–1870*.

Balls, F. E. (1967), (1968), 'The Endowed Schools Act 1869 and the Development of the English Grammar Schools in the Nineteenth Century', *Durham Research Rev.* 5.

Bamford, T. W. (1967), *The Rise of the Public Schools*.

Barnett, C. (1972), *The Collapse of British Power*.

Barnett, C. (1985), 'Long-term Industrial Performance in the UK: the Role of Education and Research, 1850–1939', in D. Morris (ed.), *The Economic System in the UK* (1985).

Baron, G. (1954–5), 'The Origins and Early History of the Headmasters' Conference', *Education Review* 7.

Benson, J. (1970), 'The Motives of 19th-Century Colliery Owners in Promoting Day Schools', *JEAH* 3.

Berg, M. and P. Hudson (1992), 'Rehabilitating the Industrial Revolution', *EcHR* 45.

Berghoff, H. (1990), 'Public Schools and the Decline of the British Economy, 1870–1914', *P&P* 129.

Berghoff, H. (1991), 'British Businessmen as Wealth-holders, 1870–1914', *BH* 33.

Berghoff, H. and R. Möller (1994), 'Tired Pioneers and Dynamic Newcomers? ... English and German Entrepreneurial History, 1870–1914', *EcHR* 47.

Berridge, V. (1978), 'Popular Sunday Papers and Mid-Victorian Society', in Boyce, Curran and Wingate (eds) (1978).

Betts, R. S. (1984), 'The Samuelson Commission of 1881–1884', *History of Education Soc. Bulletin* 34.

Billington, L. (1986), 'The Religious Periodical and Newspaper Press, 1770–1870', in Harris and Lee (eds) (1986).

Bishop, A. S. (1971), *The Rise of a Central Authority for English Education*.

Black, J. (1993), 'Politicisation and the Press in Hanoverian England', in Myers and Harris (eds) (1993).

Bondi, Sir H. (1990), 'The Sciences', in F. M. L. Thompson (ed.), *The University of London and the World of Learning, 1836–1986* (1990).

Boot, H. M. (1995), 'How Skilled were Lancashire Cotton Factory Workers in 1833?', *EcHR* 48.

Bowman, M. J. and C. A. Anderson (1963), 'Concerning the Role of Education in Development', in Geertz (ed.) (1963).

Boyce, G. (1978), 'The Fourth Estate', in Boyce, Curran and Wingate (eds) (1978).

Boyce, G., J. Curran and P. Wingate (eds) (1978), *Newspaper History from the 17th Century to the Present Day*.

Bradburn, N. M. and D. Berlew (1961), 'Need for Achievement and English Economic Growth', *Economic Development & Cultural Change* 10.

Bradshaw, J. (1983), 'Occupation and Literacy in the Erewash Valley Coalfield, 1760–1850', in Stephens (ed.) (1983).

Brown, G. C. (1981–3), 'The Sunday School Movement in Scotland', *Records Scottish Church History Soc.* 21.

Brown, K. D. (1989), 'Models in History: a Micro-Study of Late Nineteenth-Century British Entrepreneurship', *EcHR* 42.

Brown, L. (1985), *Victorian News and Newspapers.*

Bryant, M. (1969), 'Private Education from the Nineteenth Century', *VCH: Middlesex* 1.

Bryant, M. (1979), *The Unexpected Revolution: A Study in the History of the Education of Women and Girls in the Nineteenth Century.*

Bryant, M. (1985), 'Reflections on the Nature of the Education of Women and Girls', in Purvis (ed.) (1985).

Bryant, M. (1986), *The London Experience of Secondary Education.*

Burn, W. L. (1964), *The Age of Equipoise.*

Burns, T. and S. B. Saul (eds) (1967), *Social Theory and Economic Change.*

Burstyn, J. (1980), *Victorian Education and the Ideal of Womanhood.*

Byres, T. J. (1967), 'Entrepreneurship in the Scottish Heavy Industries, 1830–1900', in Payne (ed.) (1967).

Bythell, D. (1969), *The Handloom Weavers.*

Cameron, R. (1985), 'A New View of European Industrialization', *EcHR* 38.

Campbell, J. (1983), 'Occupation and Literacy in Bristol and Gloucestershire, 1755–1870', in Stephens (ed.) (1983).

Campbell, R. H. (1980), *The Rise and Fall of Scottish Industry, 1707–1931.*

Cardwell, D. S. L. (1972), *The Organisation of Science in England.*

Carter, I. R. (1975–6), 'The Mutual Improvement Movement in North-east Scotland in the Nineteenth Century', *Aberdeen University Rev.* 46.

Carter, J. J. and D. J. Withrington (eds) (1992), *Scottish Universities.*

Cassis, Y. (1985), 'Bankers in English Society in the Late Nineteenth Century', *EcHR* 38.

Checkland, S. G. (1964), *The Rise of Industrial Society in England, 1815–1885.*

Chitnis, A. C. (1976), *The Scottish Enlightenment.*

Chitnis, A. C. (1986), *The Scottish Enlightenment and Early Victorian English Society.*

Cipolla, C. (1969), *Literacy and Development in the West.*

Cipolla, C. (ed.) (1973), *The Fontana Economic History of Europe* 3.

Clark, E. A. G. (1969), The Early Ragged Schools and the Foundation of the Ragged School Union', *JEAH* 1.

Clark, E. A. G. (1977), 'The Superiority of the "Scotch System": Scottish Ragged Schools and their Influence', *SES* 9.

Clark, E. A. G. (1982), 'Sir Stafford Northcote's Omnibus: the Genesis of the Industrial Schools Act', *JEAH* 14.

Clark, E. A. G. (1982a), 'The Last of the Voluntaryists: the Ragged School Union in the School Board Era', *HE* 11.

Clark, E. A. G. (1988), 'The Diffusion of Educational Ideas: the Case of Ragged and Industrial Schools, 1841–57', *JEAH* 20.

Clegg, C. A. (1980), 'Craftsmen and the Origins of Science', *Science and Society* 43.

Coleman, D. C. (1973), 'Gentlemen and Players', *EcHR* 26.

Coleman, D. C. and C. Macleod (1986), 'Attitudes to New Techniques: British Businessmen, 1800–1950', *EcHR* 39.

Collins, B. and K. Robbins (eds) (1990), *British Culture and Economic Decline.*

Colls, R. (1976), ' "Oh happy English Children!" ': Coal, Class and Education in the North-East', *P&P* 73.

Corr, H. (1983), 'The Sexual Division of Labour in the Scottish Teaching Profession, 1872–1914', in Humes and Paterson (eds) (1983).

Corr, H. (1989), 'An Exploration into Scottish Education', in Fraser and Morris (eds) (1989).

Cotgrove, S. F. (1958), *Technical Education and Social Change*.

Crafts, N. F. R. (1977), 'Industrial Revolution in England and France', *EcHR* 30.

Crafts, N. F. R. (1978), 'Entrepreneurship and a Probabilistic View of the British Industrial Revolution', *EcHR* 31.

Crafts, N. F. R. (1979), 'Victorian Britain Did Fail', *EcHR* 32.

Crafts, N. F. R. (1981), 'The Eighteenth Century: a Survey', in Floud and McCloskey (eds) (1981) 1.

Crafts, N. F. R. (1985), *British Economic Growth during the Industrial Revolution*.

Cranfield, G. A. (1962), *The Development of the Provincial Newspaper, 1700–1780*.

Cruickshank, M. (1963), *Church and State in English Education: 1870 to the Present Day*.

Curran, J. (1978), 'The Press as an Agency of Social Control', in Boyce, Curran and Wingate (eds) (1978).

Daglish, N. D. (1996), *Educational Policy-Making in England and Wales... 1895–1911*.

Dale, R. *et al.* (eds) (1976), *Schooling and Capitalism*.

Davey, I. (1987), 'Capitalism, Patriarchy and the Origins of Mass Schooling', *History of Education Rev.* 16.

Davie, G. E. (1961), *The Democratic Intellect: Scotland and her Universities in the Nineteenth Century.*

Davies, J. A. (1973), *Education in a Welsh Rural County, 1870–1973*.

Davies, W. (1989), *The Curriculum and Organization of the County Intermediate School, 1880–1926*.

Deane, P. (1967), *The First Industrial Revolution*.

Deane, P. (1973), 'The Role of Capital in the Industrial Revolution', *EEH* 10.

Devine, T. M. and R. Mitchison (eds) (1988), *People and Society in Scotland, vol. I: 1760–1830*.

Dick, M. (1980), 'The Myth of the Working-Class Sunday School', *HE* 9.

Dickson, T. and T. Clark (1986), 'Social Concern and Social Control in Nineteenth-Century Scotland: Paisley, 1841–1843', *SHR* 65.

Digby, A. (1982), 'New Schools for the Middle-Class Girl', in Searby (ed.) (1982).

Digby, A. and P. Searby (1981), *Children, School and Society in Nineteenth-Century England*.

Dintenfass, M. (1992), *The Decline of Industrial Britain, 1870–1980*.

Dixon, D. (1986), 'Children and the Press, 1866–1914', in Harris and Lee (eds) (1986).

Donajgrodski, A. P. (1977), *Social Control in Nineteenth-Century Britain*.

Donovan, A. (1993), 'Education, Industry, and the American University', in Fox and Guagnini (eds) (1993).

Drake, F. (1970), 'The Poor Law Commissioners and Education', *JEAH* 3.

Drake, F. (1976), 'Pauper Education', in D. Fraser (ed.), *The New Poor Law in the Nineteenth Century* (1976).

Duffy, B. (1981), 'Debate: Coal, Class and Education in the North-East' *P&P* 90.

Durkacz, V. (1977), 'Gaelic Education in the Nineteenth Century', *SES* 9.

Dyhouse, C. (1976), 'Social Darwinistic Ideas and the Development of Women's Education in England, 1880–1920', *HE* 5.

Dyhouse, C. (1981), *Girls Growing Up in late Victorian and Edwardian England.*

Dyhouse, C. (1995), *No Distinction of Sex? Women in British Universities, 1870–1939.*

Eaglesham, E. [J. R.] (1956), *From School Board to Local Authority.*

Eaglesham, E. J. R. (1967), *Foundations of Twentieth-Century Education.*

Edgerton, D. (1996), *Science, Technology and the British Industrial 'Decline', 1870–1970.*

Elbaum, B. and W. Lazonick (eds) (1986), *The Decline of the British Economy.*

Emerson, R. C. (1980), 'The Philosophical Society of Ealing, 1837–47', *BJHS* 12.

Erickson, C. J. (1959), *British Industrialists: Steel and Hosiery, 1850–1950.*

Evans, L. W. (1971), *Education in Industrial Wales, 1700–1900.*

Evans, L. W. (1974), *Studies in Welsh Education.*

Evans, W. G. (1982), 'The Aberdare Report and Education in Wales, 1881', *WHR 11.*

Evans, W. G. (1990), 'The Welsh Intermediate and Technical Education Act, 1889', *HE* 19.

Eversley, D. E. C. (1964), 'Industry and Trade, 1500–1800', *VCH: Warwickshire* 7.

Feather, J. (1985), *The Provincial Book Trade in Eighteenth- Century England.*

Field, A. J. (1979), 'Occupational Structure, Dissent and Educational Commitment: Lancashire, 1841', *Research in Economic History* 4.

Finn, M. E. (1983), 'Social Efficiency, Progressivism and Secondary Education in Scotland, 1885–1905', in Humes and Paterson (eds) (1983).

Fleming, D. (1952), 'Latent Heat and the Invention of the Watt Engine', *Isis* 43.

Fletcher, S. (1980), *Feminists and Bureaucrats.*

Flinn, M. W. (1966), *Origins of the Industrial Revolution.*

Flinn, M. W. (1967), 'Social Theory and the Industrial Revolution', in Burns and Saul (eds) (1967).

Floud, R. (1982), 'Technical Education and Economic Performance: Britain, 1850–1914', *Albion* 14.

Floud, R. (1994), 'Britain, 1860–1914: a Survey', in Floud and McCloskey (eds) (1994).

Floud, R. and D. McCloskey (eds) (1981), *The Economic History of Britain since 1700*, 1st edn, 1 and 2.

Floud, R. and D. McCloskey (eds) (1994), *The Economic History of Britain since 1700*, 2nd edn, 2.

Foreman, H. (1977), 'Baptists and the Charity School Movement', *Baptist, Quarterly* 27.

Foster, J. (1974), *Class Struggle and the Industrial Revolution.*

Fox, R. and A. Guagnini (1985), 'Britain in Perspective: the European Context of Industrial Training and Innovation, 1880–1914', *History and Technology* 2.

Fox, R. and A. Guagnini (eds) (1993), *Education, Technology and Industrial, Performance in Europe, 1880–1939.*

Fraser, D. (ed.) (1980), *A History of Modern Leeds.*

Fraser, W. H. (1988), 'Patterns of Protest', in Devine and Mitichison (eds) (1988).

Fraser, W. H. and R. J. Morris (eds) (1989), *People and Society in Scotland, vol. II: 1830–1914*.

Frith, S. (1977), 'Socialization and Rational Schooling: Elementary Education in Leeds before 1870', in McCann (ed.) (1977).

Fussell, G. E. (1969), 'Science and Practice in Eighteenth-Century British Agriculture', *Agricultural History Rev.* 43.

Gardner, P. (1984), *The Lost Elementary Schools of Victorian England*.

Garner, A. D. and E. W. Jenkins (1984), 'The English Mechanics' Institutes: the Case of Leeds, 1824–42', *HE* 13.

Gaski, J. (1982), 'The Cause of the Industrial Revolution', *JEEH* 11.

Geertz, C. (ed.) (1963) *Old Societies and New States*.

Gillispie, C. C. (1957), *The Discovery of the Leblanc Process*.

Gillispie, C. C. (1972), 'The Natural History of Industry', in Musson (ed.) (1972).

Goldstrom, J. M. (1972), *Education: Elementary Education, 1780–1900*.

Goldstrom, J. M. (1977), 'The Content of Education and the Socialization of the Working-Class Child, 1830–1860', in McCann (ed.) (1977).

Goodenow, R. K. and W. E. Marsden (eds) (1992), *The City and Education in Four Nations*.

Gordon, P., R. Aldrich and D. Dean (1991), *Education and Policy in England in the Twentieth Century*.

Gosden, P. H. J. H. (1966), *The Development of Educational Administration in England and Wales*.

Gosden, P. H. J. H. and A. J. Taylor (eds) (1975), *Studies in the History of a University, 1874–1974*.

Gospel, H. F. (ed.) (1991), *Industrial Training and Technological Innovation*.

Graff, H. J. (1995), *Labyrinths of Literacy*.

Grayson, J. (1983), 'Literacy, Schooling and Industrialization: Warwickshire, 1760–1850', in Stephens (ed.) (1983).

Green, A. (1990), *Education and State Formation*.

Green, A. (1995), 'Technical Education and State Formation in Nineteenth-Century England and France', *HE* 24.

Green, V. H. H. (1969), *The Universities*.

Guagnini, A. (1991), 'The Fashioning of Higher Technical Education in Britain: the Case of Manchester, 1851–1914', in Gospel (ed.) (1991).

Guagnini, A. (1993), 'Worlds Apart: Academic Instruction and Professional Qualifications in the Training of Mechanical Engineers in England, 1850–1914', in Fox and Guagnini (eds) (1993).

Habakkuk, H. J. (1962), *American and British Technology in the Nineteenth Century*.

Hagen, E. E. (1962), *On the Theory of Social Change*.

Hagen, E. E. (1967), 'British Personality and the Industrial Revolution', in Burns and Saul (eds) (1967).

Hair, P. E. H. (1982), 'Children in Society, 1850–1980', in T. Barker and H. Drake (eds), *Population and Society in Britain, 1850–1980* (1982).

Hall, A. R. (1974), 'What Did the Industrial Revolution in Britain Owe to Science?' in N. McKendrick (ed.), *Historical Perspectives* (1974).

Hankins, T. L. (1985), *Scotland and the Enlightenment*.

Hans, N. (1951), *New Trends in Education in the Eighteenth Century.*

Hardie, D. W. F. (1972), 'The Macintoshes and the Origins of the Chemical Industry', in Musson (ed.) (1972).

Harget, L. (1980), 'The Welsh Education Alliance and the 1870 Elementary Education Act', *WHR* 10.

Harris, J. R. (1970), 'Technological Divergences and Industrial Development in Britain and France before 1800', *5th International Conference of Economic History* 7 (Moscow, 1970).

Harris, M. and A. Lee (eds) (1986), *The Press in English Society from the Sixteenth to Nineteenth Centuries.*

Harrison, J. F. C. (1961), *Learning and Living, 1790–1960.*

Harrop, S. A. (1983), 'Literacy and Educational Attitudes as Factors in the Industrialization of North-East Cheshire, 1760–1830', in Stephens (ed.), (1983).

Harrop, S. A. (1984), 'Adult Education and Literacy . . . in the Eighteenth and Nineteenth Centuries', *HE* 13.

Hartwell, R. M. (1967), *Causes of the Industrial Revolution in England.*

Hartwell, R. M. (1971), *The Industrial Revolution and Economic Growth.*

Hawke, G. (1993), 'Reinterpretations of the Industrial Revolution', in O'Brien and Quinault (eds) (1993)

Heesom, A. J. (1981), 'Debate: Coal, Class and Education in the North-East', *P&P* 90.

Hennock, E. P. (1990), 'Technological Education in England, 1850–1926: the Uses of a German Model', *HE* 19.

Herd, H. (1952), *The March of Journalism.*

Heward, C. M. (1992), 'Compulsion, Work and Family: a Case Study from Nineteenth-Century Birmingham', in Goodenow and Marsden (eds) (1992).

Higginson, J. H. (1974), 'Dame Schools', *BJES* 22.

Hill, F. (1836), *National Education: Its Present State and Future Prospects,* 1.

Hodgson, W. B. (1867), 'Exaggerated Estimates of Reading and Writing as Means of Education', repr. in Graff (1995).

Hollis, P. (1970), *The Pauper Press.*

Honey, J. R. de S. (1977), *Tom Brown's Universe: The Development of the Victorian Public School.*

Honey, J. [R. de S.] (1987), 'The Sinews of Society: the Public Schools as a "System" ', in Müller, Ringer and Simon (eds) (1987).

Hopkin D. (1978), 'The Socialist Press in Britain, 1890–1910', in Boyce, Curran and Wingate (eds) (1978).

Houston, R. A. (1982), 'The Literacy Myth? Illiteracy in Scotland, 1630–1760', *P&P* 96.

Houston, R. A. (1983), 'Literacy and Society in the West, 1500–1850', *SH* 8.

Houston, R. A. (1985), *Scottish Literacy and the Scottish Identity: Illiteracy and Society in Scotland and Northern England, 1600–1800.*

Houston, R. A. (1993), 'Literacy, Education and the Culture of Print in Enlightenment Edinburgh', *History* 78.

Howarth, J. and M. Curtoys (1987), 'The Political Economy of Women's Higher Education in Late Nineteenth and Early Twentieth Century Britain', *HR* 60.

Humes, W. M. and H. M. Paterson (eds) (1983), *Scottish Culture and Scottish Education, 1800–1980.*

Humphries, S. (1979), '"Hurrah for England": Schooling and the Working Class in Bristol, 1870–1914', *Southern History* 1.

Hurt, J. [S.] (1971), *Education in Evolution: Church, State, Society and Popular Education, 1800–1870.*

Hurt, J. S. (1971a), 'Professor West on Early Nineteenth-Century Education', *EcHR* 24.

Hurt, J. S. (1975), *Education and the Working Classes from the Eighteenth to the Twentieth Century.*

Hurt, J. S. (1979), *Elementary Schooling and the Working Classes, 1860–1918.*

Hurt, J. [S.] (ed.) (1981), *Childhood, Youth and Education in the late Nineteenth Century.*

Hurt, J. S. (1988), *Outside the Mainstream: A History of Special Education.*

Inkster, I. (1975), 'Science and the Mechanics' Institutes, 1820–1850', *AS* 32.

Inkster, I. (1976), 'The Social Context of an Educational Movement': a Revisionist Approach to the English Mechanics' Institutes, 1820–1850', *Oxford Rev. of Education* 2.

Inkster, I. (1983), 'Aspects of the History of Science and Culture in Britain, 1780–1850', in Inkster and Morrell (eds) (1983).

Inkster, I. (1983a), 'Technology as the Cause of the Industrial Revolution', *JEEH* 12.

Inkster, I. (ed.) (1985), *The Steam Intellect Societies.*

Inkster, I. (1991), *Science and Technology in History.*

Inkster, I. and J. Morrell (eds) (1983), *Metropolis and Province.*

James, H. (1990), 'The German Experience and the Myth of British Cultural Exceptionalism', in Collins and Robbins (eds) (1990).

James, L. (1976), *Print and the People, 1819–1851.*

Jarausch, K. H. (ed.) (1983), *The Transformation of Higher Learning, 1860–1930.*

Jenkins, E. W. (1979), *From Armstrong to Nuffield.*

Jewkes, J., D. Sawers and R. Stillman (1958), *The Sources of Invention.*

Johnson, R. (1970), 'Educational Policy and Social Control in Early Victorian England', *P&P* 49.

Johnson, R. (1976), 'Notes on the Schooling of the English Working Class, 1780–1850', in Dale *et al.* (eds) (1976).

Johnson, R. (1977), 'Educating the Educators: "Experts" and the State, 1833–9', in Donajgrodski (ed.) (1977).

Jones, A. (1993), 'Constructing the Readership in 19th-Century Wales', in Myers and Harris (eds) (1993).

Jones, D. K. (1977), *The Making of the Education System, 1851–81.*

Jones, D. R. (1988), *The Origins of Civic Universities.*

Jones, G. E. (1982), *Controls and Conflicts in Welsh Secondary Education, 1889–1994.*

Jones, G. E. (1997), *The Education of a Nation.*

Jones, G. S. (1978), 'Class Expression Versus Social Control', *HW* 4.

Jones, M. G. (1964), *The Charity School Movement* (repr. of 1938 edn).

Jones, M. J. (1997), 'The Agricultural Depression, Collegiate Finance, and Provision for Education at Oxford, 1871–1913', *EcHR* 50.

Jones, P. (ed.) (1988), *Philosophy and Science in the Scottish Enlightenment.*

Kaelble, H. (1979–80), 'Long-term Changes in the Recruitment of the Business Élite: Germany Compared with the U.S., Great Britain and France since the Industrial Revolution', *JSH* 13.

Kaestle, C. F. (1976), ' "Between the Scylla of Brute Ignorance and the Charybdis of a Literary Education": Élite Attitudes to Mass Schooling: England and America', in Stone (ed.) (1976).

Kamm, J. (1965), *Hope Deferred: Girls' Education in English History.*

Kaufman, P. (1967), 'The Community Library: a Chapter in English Social History', *Trans. American Phil. Soc.* n.s. 57 (7).

Kazamias, A. M. (1966), *Politics, Society and Secondary Education in England.*

Kelly, T. (1957), *George Birkbeck.*

Kelly, T. (1992), *A History of Adult Education in Great Britain.*

Kennedy W. P. (1974), 'Foreign Investment: Trade and Growth in the United Kingdom, 1870–1913', *EEH* 11.

Kennedy, W. P. (1987), *Industrial Structure, Capital Markets and the Origins of British Economic Decline.*

Kiesling, H. J. (1983), 'Nineteenth-Century Education According to West', *EcHR* 36.

Knott, J. (1972), 'Circulating Libraries in Newcastle in the 18th and 19th Centuries', *Library History* 2.

Konig, W. (1993), 'Technical Education and Industrial Performance in Germany', in Fox and Guagnini (eds) (1993).

Koss, S. (1983), *The Rise and Fall of the Political Press in Britain, vol. 1: The Nineteenth Century.*

Kronick, D. A. (1962), *A History of Scientific and Technical Periodicals.*

Landes, D. S. (1972), *The Unbound Prometheus.*

Landes, D. S. (1993), 'The Fable of the Dead Horse; or the Industrial Revolution Revisited', in Mokyr (ed.) (1993).

Landes, W. M. and L. C. Salmon (1972), 'Compulsory Schooling Legislation: an Economic Analysis of Law and Social Change in the Nineteenth Century', *JEH* 32.

Langford, J. A. (1868), *A Century of Birmingham Life...1741–1841*, 2 vols.

Laqueur, T. [W.] (1974), 'Debate: Literacy and Social Mobility in the Industrial Revolution in England', *P&P* 64.

Laqueur, T. W. (1976), 'Working-Class Demand and the Growth of English Elementary Education, 1750–1850', in Stone (ed.) (1976).

Laqueur, T. W. (1976a), *Religion and Respectability: Sunday Schools and Working-Class Culture, 1780–1850.*

Laqueur, T. [W.] (1976b), 'The Cultural Origins of Popular Literacy in England, 1500–1850', *Oxford Rev. of Education* 2.

Laqueur, T. W. (1979), review in *SH* 4.

Laurent, J. (1984), 'Science, Society and Politics in Late Nineteenth-Century England', *SSS* 14.

Lawson, J. and H. Silver (1973), *A Social History of Education in England.*

Lazonick, W. (1983), 'Industrial Organization and Technological Change', *BHR* 57.

Lee, A. [J.] (1974), 'The Radical Press', in A. J. A. Morris (ed.) (1974).

Lee, A. J. (1976), *The Origins of the Popular Press in England, 1855–1914*.

Lee, A. [J.] (1978), 'The Structure, Ownership and Control of the Press, 1855–1914', in Boyce, Curran and Wingate (eds) (1978).

Lee, C. H. (1984), 'The Service Sector, Regional Specialization and Economic Growth in the Victorian Economy', *Jnl. Historical Geography* 10.

Lee, C. H. (1986), *The British Economy since 1700*.

Leinster-Mackay, D. P. (1976), 'The Evolution of "t'other Schools"', *HE* 5.

Leinster-Mackay, D. P. (1976a), 'Dame Schools: a Need for Review', *BJES* 24.

Leinster-Mackay, D. [P.] (1984), *The Rise of the English Prep School*.

Lenman, B. and J. Stocks (1972), 'The Beginnings of State Education in Scotland, 1872–1885', *SES* 4.

Lequin, Y. (1978), 'Labour in the French Economy Since the Revolution', in Mathias and Postan (eds) (1978).

Levine, D. (1979), 'Education and Family Life in Early Industrial England', *Jnl Family History* 4.

Levine, D. (1980–1), 'Illiteracy and Family Life during the First Industrial Revolution', *JSH* 14.

Lilley, S. (1973), 'Technological Progress and the Industrial, Revolution, 1700–1914', in Cipolla (ed.) (1973).

Lowe, R. (1983), 'The Expansion of Higher Education in England', in Jarausch (ed.) (1983).

Lowe, R. (1987), 'Structural Change in English Higher Education, 1870–1920', in Müller, Ringer and Simon (eds) (1987).

Lundgreen, P. (1975), 'Industrialization and the Educational Formation of Manpower in Germany', *JSH* 9.

Lundgreen, P. (1984), 'Education for the Science-based State? The Case for 19th-Century Germany', *HE* 13.

McCann, W. P. (1966), 'Samuel Wilderspin and the Early Infant Schools', *BJES* 14.

McCann, W. P. (1969), 'Elementary Education in England and Wales on the Eve of the 1870 Education Act', *JEAH* 2.

McCann, [W.] P. (ed.) (1977), *Popular Education and Socialization in the Nineteenth Century*.

McClelland, D. C. (1961), *The Achieving Society*.

McCloskey, D. [N.] (1970), 'Did Victorian Britain Fail?', *EcHR* 23.

McCloskey, D. [N.] (1974), 'Victorian Growth: a Rejoinder', *EcHR* 27.

McCloskey, D. [N.] (1974a), *Economic Maturity and Entrepreneurial Decline: British Iron and Steel, 1870–1913*.

McCloskey, D. [N.] (1979), 'No It Did Not: a Reply to Crafts', *EcHR* 32.

McCloskey, D. N. (ed.) (1981), *Enterprise and Trade in Victorian Britain*.

McCloskey, D. N. and L. G. Sandberg (1981), 'From Damnation to Redemption: Judgments on the Late Victorian Entrepreneur', in McCloskey (ed.) (1981).

McCloy, S. T. (1952), *French Inventions of the Eighteenth Century*.

McCrory, P. (1981), 'Poor Law Education and the Urban Pauper Child . . . 1840–1896', in Hurt (ed.) (1981).

MacDonagh, O. (1974–5), 'Government, Industry and Science in Nineteenth-Century Britain', *Historical Studies* 16.

McDougall, W. (1990), 'Scottish Books for America in the Mid-18th Century', in Myers and Harris (eds) (1990).

Mack, E. C. (1938), *Public Schools and British Opinion, 1780–1860*.

Mack, E. C. (1941), *Public Schools and British Opinion since 1860*.

MacKinnon (1972), 'Education and Social Control in Nineteenth-Century Scotland: Paisley, 1841–1843', *SES* 4.

McLachlan, H. (1931), *English Education under the Test Acts*.

MacLeod, C. (1988), *Inventing the Industrial Revolution*.

MacLeod, C. (1992), 'Strategies of Innovation: the Diffusion of Technology in Nineteenth-Century British Industry', *EcHR* 45.

MacLeod, C. (1995), 'The Springs of Invention and British Industrialisation', *Refresh* 20.

Mangan, J. A. (1981), *Athleticism in the Victorian and Edwardian Public School*.

Mangan, J. A. (1983), 'Grammar Schools and the Games Ethic in the Victorian and Edwardian Eras', *Albion* 15.

Mangan, J. A. (1983a), *The Games Ethic and Imperialism*.

Mantoux, P. (1928), *The Industrial Revolution in the Eighteenth Century*.

Marcham, A. J. (1970), 'The "Myth" of Benthamism, the Second Reform Act, and the Extension of Popular Education', *JEAH* 4.

Marsden, B. (1992), 'Engineering Science in Glasgow', *BJHS* 25.

Marsden, W. E. (1982), 'Diffusion and Regional Variation in Elementary Education in England and Wales, 1800–1870', *HE* 11.

Marsden, W. E. (1982a), 'Schools for the Urban Middle Class', in Searby (ed.) (1982).

Marsden, W. E. (1987), *Unequal Educational Provision in England and Wales*.

Marsden, W. E. (1992), 'Social Stratification and Nineteenth-Century English Urban Education', in Goodenow and Marsden (eds) (1992).

Mason, D. M. (1985), 'School Attendance in Nineteenth-Century Scotland', *EcHR* 38.

Mason, J. (1954), 'Scottish Charity Schools in the 18th Century', *SHR* 33.

Mason, J. (1978), 'Monthly and Quarterly Reviews, 1865–1914', in Boyce, Curran and Wingate (eds) (1978).

Mason, Tony (1976), 'Sporting News, 1860–1914', in Harris and Lee (eds) (1976).

Mathias, P. (1969), *The First Industrial Nation*.

Mathias, P. (ed.) (1972), *Science and Society, 1600–1900*.

Mathias, P. (1991), 'Resources and Technology', in Mathias and Davis (eds) (1991).

Mathias, P. and J. A. Davis (eds) (1991), *Innovation and Technology in Europe*.

Mathias, P. and M. M. Postan (eds) (1978), *The Cambridge Economic History of Europe* 7 (1).

Matthews, R. C. O., C. H. Feinstein and J. C. Odling-Smee (1982), *British Economic Growth, 1856–1973*.

Maxted, I. (1990), 'Single Sheets from a County Town', in Myers and Harris (eds) (1990).

Miller, P. (1989), 'Historiography of Compulsory Schooling', *HE* 18.

Miller, P. J. (1973), 'Factories, Monitorial Schools and Jeremy Bentham', *JEAH* 5

Milward, A. S. and S. B. Saul (1979), *The Economic Development of Continental Europe, 1780–1870*.

Minchinton, W. E. [1957], 'The Merchants in England in the Eighteenth Century', in B. Supple (ed.), *The Entrepreneur* [1957].

Mitch, D. F. (1986), 'The Impact of Subsidies to Elementary Schooling on Enrolment Rates in Nineteenth-Century England', *EcHR* 39.

Mitch, D. [F.] (1990), 'Education and Economic Growth . . . : from Human Capital to Human Capabilities', in Tortella (ed.) (1990).

Mitch, D. F. (1992), *The Rise of Popular Literacy in Victorian England*.

Mitch, D. (1993), 'The Role of Human Capital in the First Industrial Revolution', in Mokyr (ed.) (1993).

Mokyr J. (ed.) (1993), *The British Industrial Revolution*.

Mokyr, J. (1993a), 'The New Economic History and the Industrial Revolution', in Mokyr (ed.) (1993).

Moore, L. (1992), 'Education for the Women's Sphere', in E. Breitenbach and E. Gordon (eds), *Out of Bounds: Women in Scottish Society* (1992).

Morrell, J. B. (1995), 'Bourgeois Science Schools and Industrial Innovation in Britain, 1780–1850', *JEEH* 24.

Morris, A. J. A. (ed.) (1974), *Edwardian Radicalism, 1900–1914*.

Morris, R. J. (1980), 'Middle-class Culture, 1700–1914', in Fraser (ed.) (1980).

Morris, R. J. (1983), 'Voluntary Societies and British Urban Élites, 1780–1850', *HJ* 26.

Morse, C. (1980), *Skill and the English Working Class, 1870–1914*.

Mountjoy, P. R. (1978), 'The Working-class Press and Working-Class Conservatism', in Boyce, Curran and Wingate (eds) (1978).

Mowat, I. R. M. (1980), 'Literacy, Libraries and Literature in 18th and 19th Century Easter Ross', *Library History* 2.

Müller, D. K., F. Ringer and B. Simon (eds) (1987), *The Rise of the Modern Educational System*.

Murdoch, A. and R. B. Sher (1988), 'Literacy and Learned Culture', in Devine and Mitchison (eds) (1988).

Murphy, J. (1972), *The Education Act, 1870*.

Musgrave, P. W. (1968), *Society and Education in England since 1800*.

Musson, A. E. (ed.) (1972), *Science, Technology and Economic Growth in the Eighteenth Century*.

Musson, A. E. (1978), *The Growth of British Industry*.

Musson, A. E. and E. Robinson (1960), 'Science and Industry in the Late Eighteenth Century', *EcHR* 13.

Musson, A. E. and E. Robinson (1969), *Science and Technology in the Industrial Revolution*.

Myers, J. D. (1972), 'Scottish Nationalism and the Antecedents of the 1872 Act', *SES* 4.

Myers, [J.] D. (1983), 'Scottish Schoolmasters in the Nineteenth Century', in Humes and Paterson (eds) (1983).

Myers, R. and M. Harris (eds) (1990), *Spreading the Word: The Distribution Networks of Print, 1550–1850*.

Myers, R. and M. Harris (eds) (1993), *Serials and their Readers, 1620–1914*. ·

Neuburg, V. E. (1977), *Popular Literature: A History and Guide . . . .*

Nicholas, S. J. (1984), 'The Overseas Marketing Performance of British Industry, 1870–1914', *EcHR* 37.

Nicholas, S. J. (1985), 'Technical Education and the Decline of Britain, 1870–1914', in Inkster (ed.) (1985).

Nicholas, S. [J.] (1988), 'British Economic Performance and Total Factor Productivity Growth, 1870–1940', *EcHR* 38.

Nicholas, S. [J.] (1990), 'Literacy and the Industrial Revolution', in Tortella (ed.) (1990).

Nicholas, S. J. and J. M. Nicholas (1992), 'Male Literacy, "Deskilling" and the Industrial Revolution', *Jnl Interdisciplinary History* 23.

Nunez, C. E. (1990), 'Literacy and Economic Growth in Spain, 1860–1977', in Tortella (ed.) (1990).

O'Brien, P. (1991), 'The Mainsprings of Technological Progress in Western Europe, 1750–1850', in Mathias and Davis (eds) (1991).

O'Brien, P. and R. Quinault (eds) (1993), *The Industrial Revolution and British Society.*

O'Day, R. (1982), *Education and Society, 1500–1800.*

Ogilvie, V. (1957), *The English Public School.*

Osborne, G. S. (1966), *Scottish and English Schools.*

Paterson, H. M. (1983), 'Incubus and Ideology: the Development of Secondary Schooling in Scotland, 1900–1939', in Humes and Paterson (eds) (1983).

Payne, P. L. (ed.) (1967), *Studies in Scottish Business History.*

Payne, P. L. (1974), *British Entrepreneurship in the Nineteenth Century.*

Payne, P. L. (1978), 'Industrial Entrepreneurship and Management in Great Britain', in Mathias and Postan (eds) (1978).

Payne, P. L. (1990), 'Entrepreneurship and British Economic Decline', in Collins and Robbins (eds) (1990).

Paz, D. G. (1980), *The Politics of Working-Class Education in Britain, 1830–50.*

Paz, D. G. (1981), 'Working-Class Education as Social Control in England 1860–1918', *HEQ* 21.

Pedersen, J. S. (1979), 'The Reform of Women's Secondary and Higher Education', *HEQ* 19.

Pedersen, J. S. (1987), *The Reform of Girls' Secondary and Higher Education in Victorian England.*

Perkin, H. J. (1957), 'The Origins of the Popular Press', *History Today* July 1957.

Perkin H. J. (1961), 'Middle-Class Education and Employment in the Nineteenth Century', *EcHR* 14.

Perkin, H. [J.] (1968), 'The Social Causes of the British Industrial Revolution', *Trans. Royal Historical Soc.* 5th ser. 18.

Perkin, H. [J.] (1969), *The Origins of Modern English Society, 1780–1880.*

Perkin, H. [J.] (1983) 'The Pattern of Social Transformation in England', in Jarausch (ed.) (1983).

Perkin, H. [J.] (1989), *The Rise of Professional Society in England since 1880.*

Phillips, W. H. (1989), 'The Economic Performance of Late Victorian Britain', *JEEH* 18.

Plant, M. (1965), *The English Book Trade*.

Platten, S. G. (1975), 'The Conflict over the Control of Elementary Education, 1870–1902', *BJES* 23.

Pollard, S. (1963), 'Factory Discipline in the Industrial Revolution', *EcHR* 16.

Pollard, S. (1965), *The Genesis of Modern Management*.

Pollard, S. (1978), 'Labour in Great Britain', in Mathias and Postan (eds) (1978).

Pollard, S. (1985), 'Capital Exports, 1870–1914', *ECHR* 38.

Pollard, S. (1989), *Britain's Prime and Britain's Decline*.

Pollard, S. (1994), 'Entrepreneurship, 1870–1914', in Floud and McCloskey (eds) (1994).

Pratt, D. H. (1978), *English Quakers and the First Industrial Revolution*.

Pritchard, F. G. (1948), *Methodist Secondary Education*.

Purvis, J. (1980), 'Working-class Women and Adult Education in Nineteenth-Century Britain', *HE* 9.

Purvis, J. (ed.) (1985), *The Education of Girls and Women*.

Purvis, J. (1989), *Hard Lessons: The Lives and Education of Working-Class Women in Nineteenth-Century England*.

Purvis, J. (1991), *A History of Women's Education in England*.

Radcliffe, C. J. (1986), 'Mutual Improvement Societies in the West Riding of Yorkshire, 1855–1900', *JEAH* 18.

Ralston, A. G. (1988), 'The Development of Reformatory and Industrial Schools in Scotland, 1832–1872', *SESH* 8.

Raven, J. (1989), 'British History and the Enterprise Culture', *P&P* 123.

Read, D. (1961), *Press and People, 1790–1850*.

Reeder, D. A. (ed.) (1977), *Urban Education in the Nineteenth Century*.

Reeder, D. [A.] (1987), 'The Reconstruction of Secondary Education in England, 1869–1920', in Müller, Ringer and Simon (eds) (1987).

Reeder, D. A. (1992), 'History, Education and the City', in Goodenow and Marsden (eds) (1992).

Rees, E. (1988), *The Welsh Book Trade before 1820*.

Rees, E. (1990), 'Wales and the London Book Trade before 1820', in Myers and Harris (eds) (1990).

Rimmer, W. G. (1960), *Marshalls of Leeds, Flaxspinners, 1788–1886*.

Ringer, F. K. (1967), 'Higher Education in Germany in the Nineteenth Century', *JCH* 2.

Ringer, F. K. (1978), 'The Education of Élites in Modern Europe', *HEQ* 18.

Ringer, F. K. (1979), *Education and Society in Modern Europe*.

Roach, J. (1971), *Public Examinations in England, 1850–1900*.

Roach, J. (1986), *A History of Secondary Education in England, 1800–1870*.

Roach, J. (1991), *Secondary Education in England, 1870–1902*.

Robbins, K. (1990), 'British Culture versus British Industry', in Collins and Robbins (eds) (1990).

Robertson, P. L. (1974), 'Technical Education in the British Shipbuilding and Marine Engineering Industries, 1863–1914', *EcHR* 27.

Robertson, P. [L.] (1984), 'Scottish Universities and Scottish Industry, 1860–1914', *SESH* 4.

Robson, A. H. (1931), *The Education of Children Engaged in Industry in England, 1833–76*.

Roderick, G. W. and M. D. Stephens (1972), *Scientific and Technical Education in Nineteenth-Century England.*

Roderick, G. W. and M. D. Stephens (1976), 'Scientific Studies at Oxford and Cambridge, 1850–1914', *BJES* 24.

Roderick, G. W. and M. D. Stephens (1978), *Education and Industry in the Nineteenth Century.*

Roderick, G. [W.] and M. [D.] Stephens (eds) (1981), *Where Did We Go Wrong? Industrial Performance, Education and the Economy in Victorian Britain.*

Roderick, G. [W.] and M.[D.] Stephens (1981a), 'The Universities', in Roderick and Stephens (eds) (1981).

Roderick, G.[W.] and M.[D.] Stephens (1982), *The British Malaise.*

Roehl, R. (1976), 'French Industrialization', *EEH* 13.

Rosen, B, (1984), 'Education and Social Control of the Lower Classes in England in the Second Half of the Eighteenth Century', *PH* 14.

Rostow, W. W. (1973), 'The Beginning of Modern Growth in Europe', *JEH* 33,

Rostow, W. W. (1975), *How It All Began: Origins of the Modern Economy.*

Rostow, W. W. (1978), 'No Random Walk', *EcHR* 31.

Rothblatt, S. (1983), 'The Diversification of Higher Education in England', in Jarausch (ed.) (1983).

Roxburgh, J. M. (1971), *The School Board of Glasgow, 1873–1919.*

Royle, E. (1971), 'Mechanics' Institutes and the Working Classes, 1840–1860', *HJ* 14.

Royle, E. (1987), *Modern Britain: A Social History, 1750–1985*

Rubinstein, W. D. (1986), 'Education and the Social Origins of British Élites, 1880–1970', *P&P* 112.

Rubinstein, W. D. (1990), 'Cultural Explanations for Britain's Economic Decline', in Collins and Robbins (eds) (1990).

Rubinstein, W. D. (1993), *Capitalism, Culture and Decline in Britain, 1750–1990.*

Russell, C. A. (1983), *Science and Social Change, 1700–1900.*

Samuel, R. (1977), 'Workshop of the World', *HW* 3.

Sandberg, L. G. (1981), 'The Entrepreneur and Technological Change', in Floud and McCloskey (eds) (1981).

Sandberg, L. G. (1990), 'Education and Economic Growth', in Tortella (ed.) (1990).

Sanderson, J. M. (1962), 'The Grammar School and the Education of the Poor, 1786–1840', *BJES* 11.

Sanderson, [J.] M. (1967), 'Education and the Factory in Industrial Lancashire, 1780–1840', *EcHR* 20.

Sanderson, [J.] M. (1968), 'Social Change and Elementary Education in Industrial Lancashire, 1780–1840', *Northern History* 3.

Sanderson, [J.] M. (1972), *The Universities and British Industry, 1850–1970.*

Sanderson, [J.] M. (1972a), 'The National and British School Societies in Lancashire, 1803–1839', in T. G. Cook (ed.), *Local Studies in the History of Education* (1972).

Sanderson, [J.] M. (1972b), 'Literacy and Social Mobility in the Industrial Revolution in England', *P&P* 56.

Sanderson, [J.] M. (1972c), 'The University of London and Industrial Progress, 1880–1914', *JCH* 7.

Sanderson, [J.] M. (1974), 'Rejoinder', *P&P* 64.

Sanderson, [J.] M. (1975), *The Universities in the Nineteenth Century.*

Sanderson, [J.] M. (1983), *Education, Economic Change and Society in England, 1780–1870.*

Sanderson, [J.] M. (1987), *Educational Opportunity and Social Change in England.*

Sanderson, [J.] M. (1988), 'The English Civic Universities and the "Industrial Spirit", 1870–1914', *HR* 61.

Sanderson [J.] M. (1988a), 'Education and Economic Decline, 1890–1980s', *Oxford Rev. of Economic Policy* 4.

Sanderson, [J.] M. (1993), 'Education and the Economy, 1870–1939', *Refresh* 17.

Sanderson [J.] M. (1994), *The Missing Stratum: Technical School Education in England, 1900–1990.*

Sargant, W. L. (1867), 'On the Progress of Elementary Education', *Jnl Statistical Soc. of London* 30.

Saul, S. B. (1969), *The Myth of the Great Depression.*

Schofield, R. E. (1956), 'Membership of the Lunar Society of Birmingham', *AS* 12.

Schofield, R. E. (1963), *The Lunar Society of Birmingham.*

Schofield, R. E. (1967) 'The Lunar Society and the Industrial Revolution', *University of Birmingham Historical Jnl* 11.

Schofield, R. E. (1972), 'The Industrial Orientation of Science in the Lunar Society of Birmingham', in Musson (ed.) (1972).

Schofield, R. S. (1973), 'Dimensions of Illiteracy, 1750–1850', *EEH* 10.

Schriewer, J. and K. Harney (1987), 'On "Systems" of Education and their Comparability', in Müller, Ringer and Simon (eds) (1987).

Scotland, A. (1969), *The History of Scottish Education*, 2 vols.

Scott, P. (1969), ' "Zion's Trumpet": Evangelical Enterprise and Rivalry, 1833–35', *Victorian Studies* 13.

Seaborne, M. (1992), *Schools in Wales, 1500–1900.*

Searby, P. (ed.) (1982), *Educating the Victorian Middle Class.*

Sell, A. P. F. (1992), 'Philosophy in the Eighteenth-Century Dissenting Academies of England and Wales', *HU* 11.

Shapin, S. (1972), 'The Pottery Philosophical Society, 1819–35', *Science Studies* 2.

Shapin, S. and B. Barnes (1977), 'Science, Nature and Control: Interpreting Mechanics' Institutes', *SSS* 7.

Sharp, P. R. (1968), 'The Entry of County Councils into Educational Administration, 1889', *JEAH* 1.

Sharp, P. [R] (1995), *School Governing Bodies in the English Education System.*

Shepard, L. (1973), *The History of Street Literature.*

Sherington, G. (1981), *English Education, Social Change and War, 1911–20.*

Shrosbree (1988), *Public Schools and Private Education: The Clarendon Commission, 1861–4, and the Public Schools Acts.*

Silver, H. (1965), *The Concept of Popular Education.*

Silver, H. (1975), *English Education and the Radicals, 1780–1850.*

Silver, H. (1977), 'Ideology and the Factory Child', in McCann (ed.) (1977).

Simon, B. (1960), *Studies in the History of Education, 1780–1870.*

Simon, B. (1965), *Education and the Labour Movement, 1870–1920.*

Simon, B. (1987), 'Systematisation and Segmentation in Education', in Müller, Ringer and Simon (eds) (1987).

Simon, B. and I. Bradley (eds) (1975), *The Victorian Public School.*

Simon, J. (1968), 'Was there a Charity School Movement?', in B. Simon (ed.), *Education in Leicestershire, 1640–1940* (1968).

Slee, P. (1988), 'The Oxford Idea of a Liberal Education, 1800–1860', *HU* 7.

Smith, J. V. (1983), 'Manners, Morals and Mentalities', in Humes and Paterson (eds) (1983).

Smout, T. C. (1969), *A History of the Scottish People, 1560–1830.*

Smout, T. C. (1970), 'Problems of Modernisation: Non-Economic Factors in Eighteenth-Century Scotland', in *5th International Conference of Economic History* 7 (Moscow, 1970).

Spring, J. E. (1990), *The American School, 1642–1990*

Stannard, K. P. (1990), 'Ideology, Education and Social Structure: Elementary Schools in Mid-Victorian England', *HE* 19.

Steedman, H. (1987), 'Defining Institutions: the Endowed Grammar Schools and the Systematisation of English Education', in Müller, Ringer and Simon (eds) (1987).

Stephens, M. D. and G. W. Roderick (1972), 'Science, the Working Classes and Mechanics' Institutes', *AS* 28.

Stephens, W. B. (1964), 'Social Life before 1815', *VCH: Warwickshire* 7.

Stephens, W. B. (1973), *Regional Variations in Education during the Industrial Revolution, 1780–1870.*

Stephens, W. B. (1973a), 'Early Victorian Coventry: Education in an Industrial Community, 1830–1851', in A. Everitt (ed.), *Perspectives in English Urban History* (1973).

Stephens, W. B. (1975), 'The Curriculum', in Gosden and Taylor (eds) (1975).

Stephens, W. B. (1975a), 'An Anatomy of Illiteracy in Mid- Victorian Devon', in J. Porter (ed.), *Education and Labour in the South West* (1975).

Stephens, W. B. (1977), 'Illiteracy and Schooling in the Provincial Towns, 1640–1870', in Reeder (ed.) (1977).

Stephens, W. B. (1980), 'Education and Literacy, 1770–1870', in D. Fraser (ed.) (1980).

Stephens, W. B. (1980a), *Adult Education and Society in an Industrial Town: Warrington, 1800–1900.*

Stephens, W. B. (ed.) (1983), *Studies in the History of Literacy: England and North America.*

Stephens, W. B. (1987), *Education, Literacy and Society, 1830–70.*

Stephens, W. B. (1990), 'Literacy in England, Scotland, and Wales, 1500–1900', *HEQ* 30.

Stewart, W. A. C. and [W.] P. McCann (1967), *The Educational Innovators, 1750–1850.*

Stone, L. (1969), 'Literacy and Education in England, 1640–1900', *P&P* 42.

Stone, L. (ed.) (1976), *Schooling and Society.*

Sturt, M. (1967), *The Education of the People*.

Summerfield, P. and E. J. Evans (eds) (1990), *Technical Education and the State since 1850*.

Supple, B. (ed.) (1963), *The Experience of Economic Growth*.

Sutherland, G. (1971), *Elementary Education in the Nineteenth Century*.

Sutherland, G. (1973), *Policy-making in Elementary Education, 1870–1895*.

Sutherland, G. (1987), 'The Movement for the Higher Education of Women', in P. J. Waller (ed.), *Politics and Social Change in Modern Britain* (1987).

Sylvester, D. W. (1974), *Robert Lowe and Education*.

Taylor, F. S. (1957), *A History of Industrial Chemistry*.

Theobald, M. R. (1988), 'The Accomplished Woman and the Propriety of Intellect', *HE* 17.

Tholfsen, T. R. (1976), *Working Class Radicalism in Mid-Victorian England*.

Thompson, E. P. (1968), *The Making of the English Working Class*.

Thompson, F. M. L. (1981), 'Social Control in Victorian Britain', *EcHR* 34.

Tompson, R. S. (1970), 'The Leeds Grammar School Case of 1805', *JEAH* 3.

Tompson, R. S. (1971), *Classics or Charity? The Dilemma of the 18th-Century Grammar School*.

Tompson, R. S. (1971a), 'The English Grammar School Curriculum in the 18th Century: a Reappraisal', *BJES* 19.

Tortella, G. (ed.) (1990), *Education and Economic Development since the Industrial Revolution*.

Tortella, G. (1994), 'Patterns of Economic Retardation and Recovery in Southwest Europe in the Nineteenth and Twentieth Centuries', *EcHR* 47.

Tortella, G. and L. Sandberg (1990), 'A Summary Report', in Tortella (ed.) (1990).

Tranter, N. L. (1981), 'The Labour Supply, 1780–1860', in Floud and McCloskey (eds) (1981), 1.

Tunzelman, G. A. von (1981), 'Technical Progress during the Industrial Revolution', in Floud and McCloskey (eds) (1981), 1.

Turner, D. A. (1970), '1870: the State and the Infant School System', *BJES* 18.

Turner, G. L. E. (1989), 'Experimental Science in Early Nineteenth-Century Oxford', *HU* 8.

Tyack, D. (1976), 'Ways of Seeing: an Essay on the History of Compulsory Schooling', *Harvard Educational Rev.* 46.

Vicinus, M. (1974), *The Industrial Muse: A Study of Nineteenth-Century British Working-Class Literature*.

Vicinus, M. (1975), *Broadsides of the Industrial North*.

Vincent, D. (1981), *Knowledge and Freedom: A Study of Nineteenth-Century Working-Class Autobiography*.

Vincent, D. (1989), *Literacy and Popular Culture: England, 1750–1914*.

Vlaeminke, N. (1990), 'The Subordination of Technical Education in Secondary Schools, 1870–1914', in Summerfield and Evans (eds) (1990).

Ward, D. (1967), 'Public Schools and British Industry', *JCH* 2.

Watson, M. I. (1989), 'Mutual Improvement Societies in Nineteenth-Century Lancashire', *JEAH* 21.

Webb, R. K. (1954), 'Literacy among the Working Classes in Nineteenth-Century Scotland', *SHR*.

Webb, R. K. (1955), *The British Working Class Reader, 1790–1848*

Webb, R. K. (1969), 'The Victorian Reading Public', in *Pelican Guide to English Literature* 6.

Webb, S. (1904), *London Education*.

Weinberger, B. (1981), 'Children of the Perishing and Dangerous Classes: Industrial and Reformatory Schools and the Elementary Education System', in Hurt (ed.) (1981).

Wengenroth, U. (1995), *The German and British Steel Industry, 1865–1895*.

West, E. G. (1965), *Education and the State*.

West, E. G. (1970), 'Resource Allocation and Growth in Early Nineteenth-Century British Education', *EcHR* 23.

West, E. G. (1975), *Education and the Industrial Revoluation*.

West, E. G. (1978), 'Literacy and the Industrial Revolution', *EcHR* 31.

Wickwar, W. H. (1928), *The Struggle for the Freedom of the Press, 1819–1832*.

Wiener, M. J. (1981), *English Culture and the Decline of the Industrial Spirit, 1850–1980*.

Wilkinson, W. (1964), *The Prefects*.

Williams, G. (1961), 'Welsh Circulating Schools', *Church Qtly Rev.* 162.

Williams, J. G. (1993), *The University Movement in Wales*.

Williams, R. (1965), *The Long Revolution*.

Williams, R. (1978), 'The Press and Popular Culture', in Boyce, Curran and Wingate (eds) (1978).

Wilson, D. B. (1992), 'Scottish Influences in British Natural Philosophy', in Carter and Withrington (eds) (1992).

Withers, C. (1982), 'Education and Anglicisation: the Policy of the SSPCK towards the Education of the Highlander, 1709–1825', *Scottish Studies* 26.

Withrington, D. J. (1962), The SPCK and Highland Schools in the Mid-Eighteenth Century', *SHR* 41.

Withrington, D. J. (1972), 'Towards a National System, 1867–72', *SES* 4.

Withrington, D. J. (1983), ' "Scotland a Half-Educated Nation" in 1834', in Humes and Patterson (eds) (1983).

Withrington, D. J. (1988), 'Schooling, Literacy and Society', in Devine and Mitchison (eds) (1988).

Withrington, D. J. (1993), 'Scotland: a National Educational System and Ideals of Citizenship', *PH* 29.

Withrington, D. J. (1997), *Going to School*.

Wood, P. (1988), 'Science and the Aberdeen Enlightenment', in Jones, P. (ed.) (1988).

Wood, P. (1994), 'Science, the Universities and the Public Sphere in Eighteenth-Century Scotland', *HU* 13.

Wright, C. J. (1979), 'Academics and their Aims: English and Scottish Approaches to University Education in the Nineteenth Century', *HE* 8.

Wrigley, J. (1986), 'Technical Education and Industry in the Nineteenth Century', in Elbaum and Lazonick (eds) (1986).

Zeldin, T. (1967), 'Higher Education in France, 1848–1940', *JCH* 2.

# INDEX